STUDIES IN THE HISTORY
OF CHRISTIAN MISSIONS

R. E. Frykenberg
Brian Stanley
General Editors

David
with best wishes
from
Tim Yates

18 July 2015
O J Remin

STUDIES IN THE HISTORY OF CHRISTIAN MISSIONS

Alvyn Austin
China's Millions: The China Inland Mission and Late Qing Society, 1832-1905

Chad M. Bauman
Christian Identity and Dalit Religion in Hindu India, 1868-1947

Michael Bergunder
The South Indian Pentecostal Movement in the Twentieth Century

Judith M. Brown and Robert Eric Frykenberg, *Editors*
Christians, Cultural Interactions, and India's Religious Traditions

Robert Eric Frykenberg
*Christians and Missionaries in India:
Cross-Cultural Communication Since 1500*

Susan Billington Harper
*In the Shadow of the Mahatma: Bishop V. S. Azariah
and the Travails of Christianity in British India*

Patrick Harries and David Maxwell, *Editors*
The Spiritual in the Secular: Missionaries and Knowledge about Africa

D. Dennis Hudson
Protestant Origins in India: Tamil Evangelical Christians, 1706-1835

Ogbu U. Kalu, *Editor,* and Alaine M. Low, *Associate Editor*
*Interpreting Contemporary Christianity:
Global Processes and Local Identities*

Donald M. Lewis, *Editor*
*Christianity Reborn: The Global Expansion of Evangelicalism
in the Twentieth Century*

Jessie G. Lutz
Opening China: Karl F. A. Gützlaff and Sino-Western Relations, 1827-1852

Jon Miller
*Missionary Zeal and Institutional Control: Organizational Contradictions
in the Basel Mission on the Gold Coast, 1828-1917*

Andrew Porter, *Editor*
The Imperial Horizons of British Protestant Missions, 1880-1914

Dana L. Robert, *Editor*
Converting Colonialism: Visions and Realities in Mission History, 1709-1914

Wilbert R. Shenk, *Editor*
North American Foreign Missions, 1810-1914: Theology, Theory, and Policy

Brian Stanley
The World Missionary Conference: Edinburgh 1910

Brian Stanley, *Editor*
Christian Missions and the Enlightenment

Brian Stanley, *Editor*
Missions, Nationalism, and the End of Empire

John Stuart
*British Missionaries and the End of Empire:
East, Central, and Southern Africa, 1939-64*

T. Jack Thompson
*Light on Darkness? Missionary Photography of Africa
in the Nineteenth and Early Twentieth Centuries*

Kevin Ward and Brian Stanley, *Editors*
The Church Mission Society and World Christianity, 1799-1999

Timothy Yates
The Conversion of the Māori: Years of Religious and Social Change, 1814-1842

Richard Fox Young, *Editor*
*India and the Indianness of Christianity: Essays on Understanding—Historical,
Theological, and Bibliographical—in Honor of Robert Eric Frykenberg*

The Conversion of the Māori

Years of Religious and Social Change, 1814-1842

Timothy Yates

WILLIAM B. EERDMANS PUBLISHING COMPANY
GRAND RAPIDS, MICHIGAN / CAMBRIDGE, U.K.

© 2013 Timothy Yates
All rights reserved

Published 2013 by
Wm. B. Eerdmans Publishing Co.
2140 Oak Industrial Drive N.E., Grand Rapids, Michigan 49505 /
P.O. Box 163, Cambridge CB3 9PU U.K.

Printed in the United States of America

19 18 17 16 15 14 13   7 6 5 4 3 2 1

Library of Congress Cataloging-in-Publication Data

Yates, T. E. (Timothy Edward), 1935-
The conversion of the Maori: years of religious and social change, 1814-1842 /
Timothy Yates.
    pages   cm. — (Studies in the history of Christian missions)
Includes bibliographical references and index.
ISBN 978-0-8028-6945-6 (pbk.: alk. paper)
1. Missions — New Zealand. 2. Conversion — Christianity.
3. Maori (New Zealand people) 4. New Zealand — Church history —
19th century.   I. Title.

BV3665.Y38   2013
266.0089'99442 — dc23

2013001751

www.eerdmans.com

D.V.M.M.C

C.R.N.R

R.F.B

historians and inspirers of historians in grateful memory

Contents

	PREFACE	xi
	ACKNOWLEDGMENTS	xiii
	ABBREVIATIONS	xv
1.	Māori Society: Background to European Contact	1
2.	Samuel Marsden and the New Zealand Mission to 1814	10
3.	Māori and Missionaries: Early CMS Interaction, 1814-1823	18
4.	Methodist Beginnings and Destruction at Whangaroa, 1819-1827	33
5.	CMS in Kerikeri and Paihia, 1823-1830	40
6.	Methodist Mission Reestablished: Hokianga, 1827-1837	56
7.	Change, Scandal, and Expansion, 1830-1838	64
8.	The Marists in New Zealand, 1838-1842	80
9.	The Treaty of Waitangi, 1840	90
10.	Expansion of a Mission: Māori Initiatives and the CMS, 1834-1842	99
11.	Indigenous Agents: Teachers, Catechists, and Martyrs	108
12.	Conversion: An Analysis	116

CONTENTS

APPENDIX: Richard Quinn and A. T. Yarwood   129

SOURCES   134

INDEX   144

Preface

In an earlier publication, *Venn and Victorian Bishops Abroad*, which included a chapter on New Zealand after the arrival of G. A. Selwyn as bishop of New Zealand in 1842 and dealt with his relationship with Henry Venn of the CMS, I became aware of the large-scale movement of Māori into the Christian churches between Marsden's original visit of 1814 and the Selwyn period nearly thirty years later. I hoped to revisit this phenomenon of Polynesian missionary history, and in the 1990s I was given the opportunity to do so by the provision of a research grant from the Pew Charitable Trusts in the United States, then funding projects in missionary history. I became a research grantee in 1996.

Whether as missionary or colonial historians, writers now compose in the shadow of Edward Said and his *Orientalism;* he has shown the danger of such studies treating non-European peoples as "the Other" and, in company with Michel Foucault and Jacques Derrida, the parallel danger of using postcolonial narrative as a further form of oppression. I have to hope that what follows will demonstrate my respect for the Māori people, a respect that was certainly present in the "Apostle to New Zealand," Samuel Marsden, who combined great admiration with some realism about the society he encountered. The study may strike some as traditional in approach, being narrative history based on close attention to sources in archives, which, on the missionary side, are voluminous, while early Māori sources for this purpose are virtually nonexistent, of which I was warned by a lifelong student of the missions at the outset. It is sadly inevitable therefore that the weight of substantiation has come from the European archives of missionary societies, a sharp contrast from the work of another Pew grantee, J. D. Y. Peel, and his fine work *Religious Encounter and the Making of the Yoruba* (2000).

PREFACE

In an earlier study of conversion, the main theme of this book, A. C. Underwood regarded it as *articulus aut stantis aut cadentis ecclesiae* (the issue by which the church stands or falls).[1] I have to hope that this account of conversion of the Māori people to Christianity has addressed so crucial a topic in a form that is ecumenical (Anglican, Methodist, Marist Roman Catholic), missiological, and historically informed in a way that shows among other aspects that missionaries were as mixed a body as the missioned, comprised of both tribal heroes and offenders. The narrative attempts to chart the change in society and religion over nearly thirty years in detail, so that it is a developing history of the conversion process. What begins with anthropology and continues with detailed history ultimately leads to a consideration of conversion as viewed by writers like Raoul Allier and Robin Horton; and of specifically Māori conversion as handled not least by members of the New Zealand historical academy, a body that has earned my deep respect, to which the footnotes bear witness, not least through the great and indispensable achievement of the *Dictionary of New Zealand Biography* since 1990.

I accept that, for some, 1842 as a closing date may appear arbitrary. This was the date when G. A. Selwyn, after arrival in New Zealand, judged that conversion was complete. Selwyn's presence as a bishop can be held to symbolize the movement from mission to church, marking an identifiable period that was ending. The period after 1842, to 1870, is equally worthy of close study and would include the considerable falling away of Māori Christians, not least among those faithfully overseen by William Williams, first bishop of Waiapu. Many were disillusioned, one factor among others being what was perceived as Selwyn's identification with British troops during the Māori wars in 1863-64. This book concentrates on the pioneering phase for the missions and attempts to present the process of conversion of a whole people.

---

1. A. C. Underwood, *Conversion: Christian and Non-Christian: A Comparative and Psychological Study* (London: Allen and Unwin, 1925), p. 45.

Acknowledgments

During the 1990s the mission studies academic community was greatly indebted to the Pew Charitable Trusts, who offered research grants under the Research Enablement Program (REP) administered by Dr. G. H. Anderson from the Overseas Ministries Studies Center based in New Haven, Connecticut. I was awarded a grant by the Trusts' assessors, among whom was Professor Charles Forman. I was indebted to Professor Forman for wise advice on how to pursue the subject initially, and I benefited from the stimulus of the REP symposium set up by Dr. Anderson for successful applicants. Pew Charitable Trusts funding financed my first research visit to New Zealand and the Hocken Library in the University of Otago, where I received much help from the staff and advice from Professor Elizabeth Isichei, then head of religious studies in the university, who encouraged me to consult Janet Murray, a lifelong student of the issues. I owe gratitude to both of them, as also to the authorities and the then Warden of Selwyn College, Dr. Paul Richardson, who made accommodation available for me. On a later visit, the staff of the Alexander Turnbull Library in Wellington gave valued help and I received advice and encouragement from a fellow researcher in Dr. Philip Parkinson. The main work reflected in the text was on the very extensive missionary resources held in the CMS archive in the University of Birmingham, and I was given much assistance by Dr. Christine Penney and her staff in the Heslop Room of the university library. My work here was greatly eased by provision of accommodation and support by the Queen's College, Birmingham, and its then principal, Dr. Peter Fisher. Encouraged by Professor Forman, I visited the Marist archive in Rome with help from Dr. Willi Henkel, then Director of the Pontifical Library. Father Gaston Lessard, then archivist of the Marists, and Father Charles Girard, who made a generous gift of his multivolume work of Marist documents, assisted greatly, and my wife and I received much kindness and friendship on this visit. Methodist sources were largely pursued by way of microfiche and microfilm, of which the Yale Divinity School has large holdings: I must pay special thanks to Martha Smalley and Joan Duffy, ever ready with assistance and advice for those who work in the Day Missions Library at Yale. Professor John Barker and his colleague, Dr. Jennifer Wagelie, gave me the benefit of their advice from the Department of Anthropology of the University of British Columbia. Apart from the Pew Charitable Trusts, my greatest debt is to Dr. Allan Davidson of the University of Auckland, who read my manuscript in full and made many helpful suggestions for its improvement, while also arranging for me to use the library of St. John's College, Auckland, and to stay in the college. His extensive knowledge of the field and the friendship of himself and his wife have been invaluable. I am indebted to the rare book department of the Cambridge University Library and its imaging services, as also to John Laurie of the University of Auckland's equivalent service, for help with illustrations. Finally, I must pay tribute to Professors Robert Frykenberg and Brian Stanley for their willingness to include this study in their series Studies in the History of Christian Missions, as well as for participation in the Currents in World Christianity project, in which Professor Stanley and Professor Andrew Porter encouraged me to submit an early paper on the Māori missions. To the publishers, William Eerdmans, I am also greatly indebted, and to Lynne Firth for her secretarial help. None of those mentioned can be held responsible for errors or deficiencies in this work. The dedication is to those historians who have fired my enthusiasm for history at different stages: David Mansel-Carey, Dick Routh, and Ralph Bennett, director of studies at Samuel Marsden's alma mater of Magdalene College, Cambridge.

Abbreviations

AIM	Auckland Institute and Museum
AML	Auckland Museum Library
ATL	Alexander Turnbull Library, Wellington
BFBS	British and Foreign Bible Society
CMR	*Church Missionary Record*
CMS	Church Missionary Society
DNZB	*Dictionary of New Zealand Biography*
DUHO	Hocken Library, Dunedin
IRM	*International Review of Mission*
JPS	*Journal of the Polynesian Society*
JRH	*Journal of Religious History*
LMS	London Missionary Society
MMS	Methodist Missionary Society
MR	*Missionary Register*
NZJH	*New Zealand Journal of History*
TPNZI	*Transactions of the Proceedings of the New Zealand Institute*
WMMS	Wesleyan Methodist Missionary Society

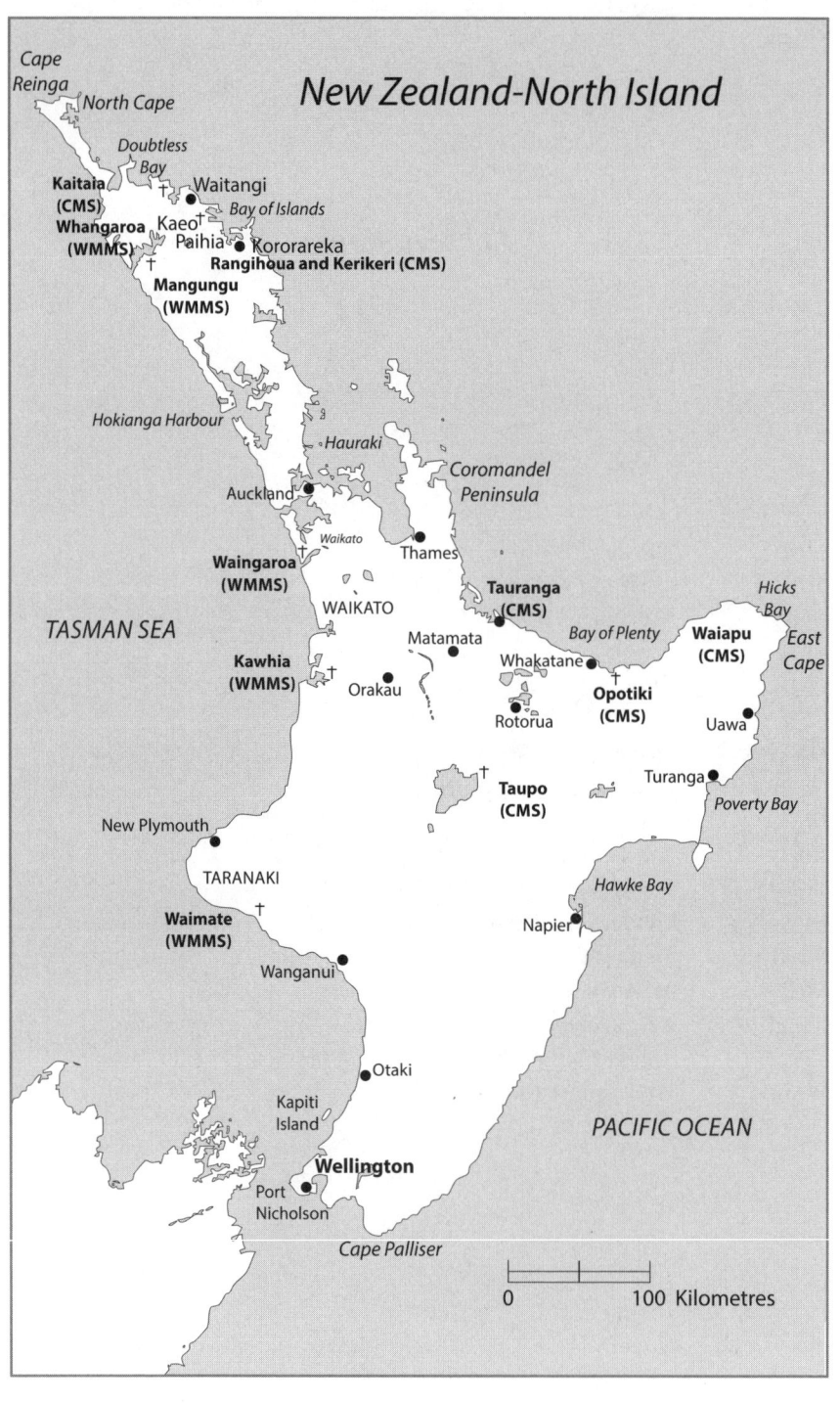

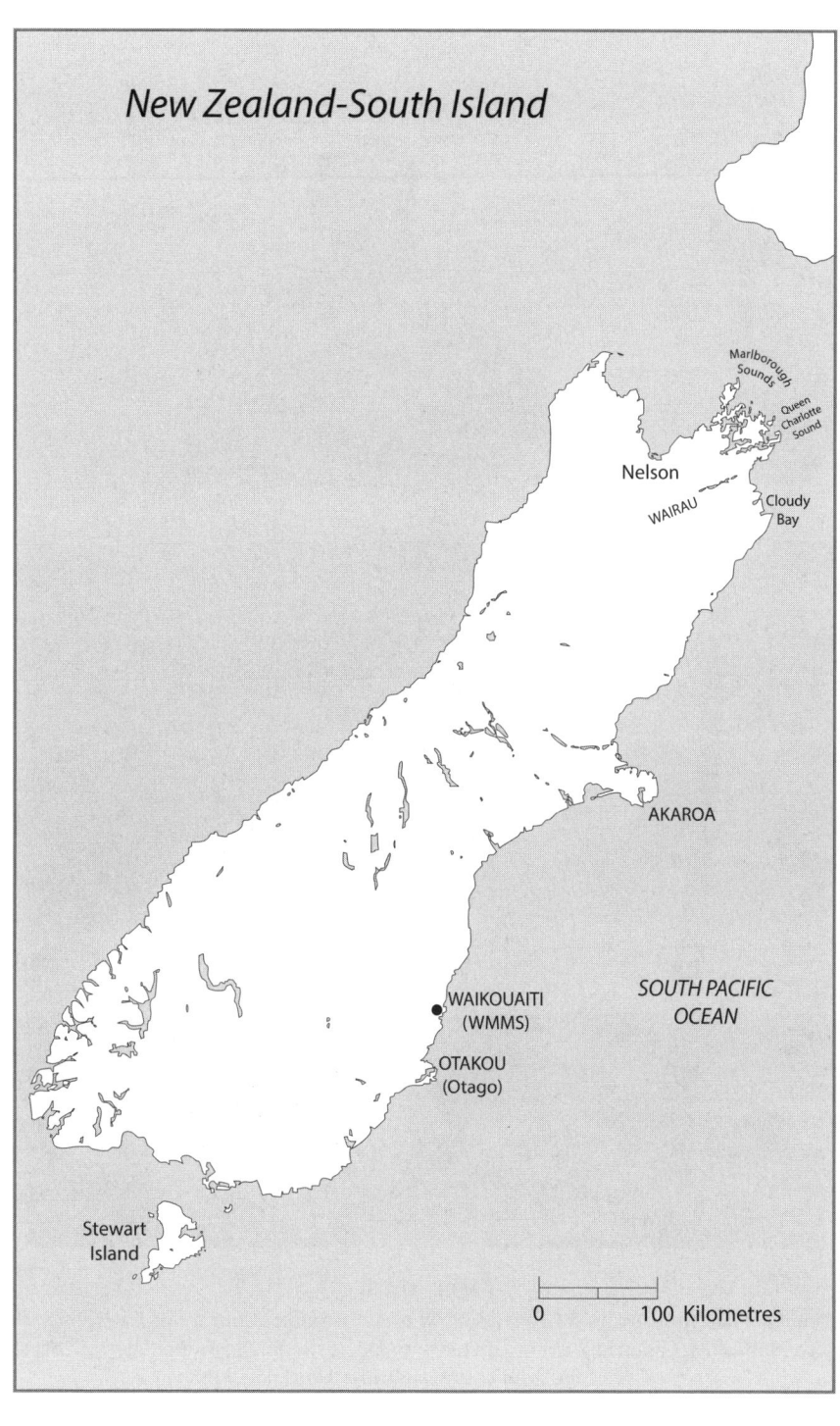

THE CONVERSION OF THE MĀORI

Māori chief.

Source: Plate from Richard Cruise, *Journal of Ten Months Residence in New Zealand* (London, 1823). Cambridge University Library C.37.55 (Rare). Reproduced by kind permission of the Syndics of Cambridge University Library

The Conversion of the Māori

Māori village.
Source: J. Polack, *New Zealand* (London, 1838), vol. I, p. 92. Cambridge University Library 0.21.9 (Rare). Reproduced by kind permission of the Syndics of Cambridge University Library

Māori cemetery at Hokianga.
Source: J. Polack, *New Zealand* (London, 1838), vol. I, p. 138. Cambridge University Library 0.21.9 (Rare). Reproduced by kind permission of the Syndics of Cambridge University Library

Samuel Marsden.
Source: Frontispiece from J. R. Elder, *Letters and Journals of Samuel Marsden* (p. 471). Cambridge University Library 455.c.93.73. Reproduced by kind permission of the Syndics of Cambridge University Library

The Conversion of the Māori

Hongi Hika, chief of the Nga Puhi.
Source: R. J. Barton, ed., *Earliest New Zealand* (Masterton, New Zealand, 1927), p. 155.
Reproduced by kind permission of Auckland University Library

Henry Williams.
Source: R. J. Barton, ed., *Earliest New Zealand* (Masterton, New Zealand, 1927), p. 261.
Reproduced by kind permission of Auckland University Library

The Conversion of the Māori

Patuone, Nga Puhi leader and peacemaker.
Source: R. J. Barton, ed., *Earliest New Zealand* (Masterton, New Zealand, 1927), p. 353.
Reproduced by kind permission of Auckland University Library

Te Rangihaeata, Ngati Toa leader.
Source: G. Clarke, *Notes on My Early Life in New Zealand* (Hobart, Australia, 1903), p. 81. Reproduced by kind permission of the Syndics of Cambridge University Library

Te Rauparaha, tribal leader of the Ngati Toa.
Source: P. Butler, ed., *The Life and Times of Te Rauparaha* (Martinborough, New Zealand, 1980), p. 77. Cambridge University Library RE.119.11 (Rare). Reproduced by kind permission of the Syndics of Cambridge University Library

CHAPTER 1

Māori Society: Background to European Contact

New Zealand–Aotearoa had developed apart from other landmasses for some fifty million years. In flora, fauna, and the natural world, this resulted in many indigenous species that were unknown elsewhere. Among them were flightless birds such as the *kiwi* and, most famously, the *moa,* untroubled by either four-footed or two-footed predators. *Moa* could stand as tall as ten feet high and proved an irresistible source of protein in both the North Island and the South Island under human occupation. They were to be hunted to extinction by the earliest settlers.

Polynesian people, to whom the Māori belong, were notable seafarers, who well deserve Sir Peter Buck's title *Vikings of the Sunrise.*[1] Their movements across the Pacific are still debated, but the consensus at present would point to Māori colonizers arriving from eastern Polynesia, perhaps from the Society or Cook Islands, and establishing themselves around A.D. 1200-1450, rather later than earlier assessment by anthropologists of around A.D. 850. Possible earlier landfalls without sustained occupancy may be indicated by the discovery of *kiore* (Polynesian rats) remains, apparently earlier than human dating.[2] Early settlers came by canoe, bringing with them the essentials for future survival, notably the *kumara* (sweet potato), which could survive the winters of the North Island, where they settled.[3] In Māori history, they came from "Hawaiki," a kind of mystical homeland to which, for example, Māori souls could return

---

1. P. H. Buck, *The Vikings of the Sunrise* (New York: F. A. Stokes, 1938).
2. M. King, *The Penguin History of New Zealand* (Auckland: Penguin Books, 2003), p. 48 n.
3. Keith Sinclair, ed., *The Oxford Illustrated History of New Zealand* (Auckland: Oxford University Press, 1990), p. 3.

after death; the first canoe was that of Kupe. Whether or not, as by tradition, he was followed later by "the Great Fleet," the canoes *(waka)* assumed great significance in Māori social organization, providing the basis for traditional genealogy. In the case of the traditional canoes of Tainui and Arawa, for instance, tribes claimed descent and shared a sense of common ancestry.[4]

Although Māori society was subject to change in the period 1200-1800, the basic outlines of the social context into which European missionaries entered can be established. Changes over these six hundred years were likely to be gradual compared to those that followed European contact. A comparison might be made between the pace of change in England in its agricultural years prior to the Industrial Revolution between 1200 and 1750 and the pace of change that followed, a reminder of what the introduction of new technologies can do to a society. For Māori, the metal nails with which Captain Cook traded after 1769 and the iron axes that soon followed, along with the catastrophic effects of the introduction of muskets, which wrought havoc in the North Island in the 1820s, show a civilization that had evolved to a high degree of sophistication through gentler change confronted with new and powerful catalysts. Nevertheless, as the economist R. H. Tawney wrote in his introduction to Sir Raymond Firth's *Economics of the New Zealand Māori*, "what are called primitive peoples are not . . . uncivilised . . . merely people with a different kind of civilisation"; he discerned in the society that Firth described "a widespread sense of personal dignity and collective satisfaction."[5]

Māori society, as Europeans discovered it, was characterized by fishing, agriculture, and some flax making. In addition to the basic social units of the canoes *(waka)*, there were the subordinate federations of the *iwi*, or tribes, comprised of subgroups and smaller and effective collectives called *hapu*. These last owned property collectively, as, for example, war canoes, which were *hapu* property.[6] They were a "strongly collective entity."[7] Below this social stratum was the *whanau*, effectively an extended family.[8] Various *whanau*

---

4. J. Metge, *The Māori of New Zealand* (London: Routledge, Kegan, Paul, 1967; rev. ed. 1976), pp. 129-31.

5. R. Firth, *Economics of the New Zealand Māori* (Wellington: R. E. Owen, 1928; 2nd ed. 1959), p. 11.

6. Firth, *Economics*, p. 351; A. Ballara, *Iwi: The Dynamics of Māori Tribal Organisation, c. 1769 to c. 1945* (Wellington: Victoria University Press, 1998), p. 219. *Hapu* is seen as the basic unit and descent group.

7. I. Goldman, *Ancient Polynesian Society* (Chicago: University of Chicago Press, 1970), p. 46.

8. J. Prytz-Johansen, *The Māori and His Religion* (Copenhagen: Munksgaard, 1954), pp. 15-16.

Māori Society

could combine into a *hapu*, and a number of these were incorporated into a tribe *(iwi)*. Village work would be organized by chiefs, and the terraced gardens, which Cook sighted in 1769 and Spöring drew from off the west coast of the North Island, bore testimony to the effectiveness of this system in the eighteenth century.[9] Chiefs fell into two categories: the *ariki*, who have been called "high chiefs,"[10] and the *rangatira*, a chiefly caste. It was a compliment to a missionary like Octavius Hadfield to be seen as a *rangatira*. Chiefs could look particularly fine in dog-skin cloaks with white albatross or other feathers decorating their heads. If disgraced, however, they could become *tutua* and so classed with slaves.[11] Other important community figures were the *tohunga*, often related to the chiefs, who were religious figures, called upon to provide appropriate incantations *(karakia)* at important moments like *kumara* planting or harvesting, while also acting as genealogists.[12] For the rest, they were commoners *(tangata ware)*.

Three central ideas in Māori society of supreme significance were *mana*, *tapu*, and *utu*. One writer, in considering the pursuit of *mana*, has drawn attention to the competitive nature of the society in which it was pursued.[13] *Mana* had to do with honor and personal sanctity and with the personal authority of the individual that both enhanced. A chief who lacked *mana* could be replaced. There were even cases on record where slaves, who showed sufficient personal authority, were accepted as chiefs on this basis. Once more it was a compliment paid by Māori to the missionary Henry Williams, that he possessed *mana* in their estimation. One important route to acquiring enhanced *mana* was through courage and ability in battle. Māori chiefs who will appear later in this text like Hongi Hika and Te Rauparaha were prime examples of generalship in war. Chiefs were surrounded by *tapu*, which had many wider implications and was well defined as "sanctity which demands reverential avoidance."[14] A chief's head was *tapu*, and to touch it a grave offense; even his hair was seen as part of his essential being, and had to be respected. Beaches where fishing nets were prepared were *tapu*; there were severe penal-

---

9. A. Salmond, *Two Worlds: First Meetings between Māori and Europeans, 1642-1771* (Auckland: Viking, 1991), p. 163 and illustration.

10. Firth, *Economics*, p. 106.

11. Goldman, *Ancient Polynesian Society*, p. 43.

12. P. H. Buck, *The Coming of the Māori*, 2nd ed. (Wellington: Whitcombe and Tombs, 1950), p. 476.

13. Ann Parsonson, "The Pursuit of Mana," in *The Oxford History of New Zealand*, ed. W. H. Oliver with B. R. Williams (Oxford and Wellington: Oxford University Press, 1981), p. 140.

14. Goldman, *Ancient Polynesian Society*, p. 11.

ties for infringement, and posts would be placed at *kumara* plantations to warn of potential infringement of *tapu*. A *tohunga* had the powers to remove *tapu* and, by certain procedures, to make a place or person *noa* (ordinary) again.

Utu, which missionaries met again and again, can be wrongly understood as "revenge." Properly it had to do with reciprocity; it can apply, for instance, to the making of gifts. Appropriate response to any gift was of great importance. Not to meet *utu* in this way could reduce the life force *(hau)* of the giver, which could even result in punishment by unseen spiritual forces.[15] Nevertheless, although this wider application is very important, *utu* all too frequently referred to personal or tribal slights, which the dishonored were under a strong obligation to set to rights. This meant that it was the root cause of much intertribal fighting, enslavement of enemies, and cannibalism. Here again there is room for misunderstanding. Missionary sources certainly give evidence that some Māori ate human flesh with relish, and there were cases where slaves, for example, were killed to enhance the food supply, aspects confirmed by twentieth-century study.[16] Nevertheless, the overwhelming reason for cannibalism was to wreak final vengeance on one's enemies and to acquire and nullify his life force. Cook had accepted the Māori explanation that they only ate those of their enemies "slain in battle" and did not eat them out of sheer savagery;[17] but the horror of the missionaries confronted by the preparation of ovens for such feasts, fresh as they were from the proprieties of late Georgian and early Victorian Britain, can be seen as amply justified.

When it came to religion, the missionaries were under the impression that there was no concept of the high god among Māori. There has been an extensive modern debate on the subject of "Io" and whether there was esoteric knowledge of a supreme god that was not available to ordinary Māori, because it was treated as closely guarded by the *tohunga* and taught only to chiefly initiates. The case against these speculations and Māori informants behind them going back to the 1850s is that they reflect the impact of Christian monotheism rather than precontact understandings. The only judgment possible to offer here is that, in the period under review, the primary sources do not give evidence of such belief.[18] By contrast, what is very evident is the

---

15. Firth, *Economics*, pp. 417-30; Metge, *Māori of New Zealand*, p. 15.

16. Firth, *Economics*, p. 148; P. Moon, *This Horrid Practice: The Myth and Reality of Traditional Māori Cannibalism* (Auckland: Penguin, NZ, 2008), pp. 88, 96-98.

17. Salmond, *Two Worlds*, p. 178.

18. In favor of "Io" see J. Irwin, *An Introduction to Māori Religion* (Adelaide: Australian Association of the Study of Religions, 1984), pp. 19, 33-34; E. Best, *The Māori*, 2 vols. (Wel-

widespread respect or dread of the *atua* (spirits), manifested too in the dread of lizards that were connected to them, and recognition by Māori of something of a pantheon of what have been called "departmental gods."[19] In Māori mythology, Rangi (the sky and a male figure) and Papa (the earth and a female figure) were forced apart (some would say by Io) for light to appear. Subsidiary or departmental gods presided over certain aspects of life, among which the missionaries probably most frequently encountered reference to Tane, god of knowledge and fecundity; Rongo, god of agriculture; Tu, the god of war; and Whiro, who is evil and seen in lizards.[20]

As in other societies, Māori marked the beginning and end of life with ritual. An infant was accorded the equivalent of baptism *(tohi)* when water was sprinkled over the child by means of a branch that had been dipped in it. Then followed elements of dedication; male children often to Rongo, the god of agriculture, and Tu, the god of war. This last was a dire sign to the missionaries of continuing strife, but probably for the participants it was an invocation to courage and bravery in battle, greatly prized and often badly needed in Māori life. The early Jewish trader Polack said this happened on the eighth day of the child's life, which might have reflected his view of Jewish circumcision, but the missionary Richard Taylor confirmed this timing and gave a full description of the ceremony.[21]

Māori appeared to have no rituals for puberty, which has puzzled anthropologists. Children were certainly encouraged toward independence and rarely rebuked, often to the despair of missionaries who looked for a more disciplined upbringing, not least in such matters as school truancy and ab-

---

lington: H. H. Tombs, 1924), pp. 65-66; and for a more cautious view see Buck, *Coming of the Māori*, pp. 443-535; Keith Sinclair, ed., *A History of New Zealand* (London: Penguin, 1959; rev. ed. 1969), p. 22. For a strong case against, see Jane Simpson, "Io as a Supreme Being: Intellectual Colonisation of the Māori?" *History of Religions* 37, no. 1 (August 1997): 50-85. I am indebted to Dr. Allan Davidson for drawing my attention to this important article. The missionary Richard Taylor, who was a serious student of all things Māori and normative for our period of the general understanding of missionaries, wrote on this: "properly speaking, (the Māori) had no knowledge of a Supreme Being." *Te Ika a Maui or New Zealand and Its Inhabitants* (London: Wertheim and Macintosh, 1855), p. 13; see also A. R. Tippett, *People Movements in South Polynesia: A Study in Church Growth* (Chicago: Moody Press, 1971), p. 44, for comparison to Tahiti, and appendix B, pp. 227ff., for "Io."

19. Karen Sinclair, "Maramatanga: Ideology and Social Process among the Māori of New Zealand" (D.Phil. thesis, Department of Anthropology, Brown University, June 1976), p. 48; Goldman, *Ancient Polynesian Society*, p. 559.

20. Buck, *Coming of the Māori*, pp. 454-60; Irwin, *Introduction to Māori Religion*, pp. 11-15; Karen Sinclair, "Maramatanga," p. 36.

21. J. S. Polack, *Manners and Customs of the New Zealanders*, 2 vols. (London: James Madden, 1840), pp. 49-50; Taylor, *Te Ika*, pp. 74-76; Buck, *Coming of the Māori*, pp. 352-53.

senteeism from domestic service. Whatever the omissions in midlife, there were elaborate provisions for the end of human existence, when the soul was transferred into *po,* the underworld. Death would be marked by a *tangi,* or wailing of grief, accompanied often by the slashing of bodies with sharp stones or obsidian, so that grieving widows and others would often be running with blood; these self-inflicted wounds were known as *haehae.* The corpse itself would be wrapped in mats and displayed in a sitting position, often on a platform.[22] Some time later, often a year or more, there would be a *hahunga,* a feast or wake, which marked the final deposition of the bones of the deceased in a cave or other resting place. In Māori understanding, the departed soul went to the underworld *(po)* by way of Te Reinga, a point at the tip of the North Island, over which rocky precipice the disembodied soul was thought to descend to the depths below. The farewell given by an orator at the *hahunga* was both a dismissal and an act of reassurance to the living against a lingering spirit.[23]

Again, in common with many such societies, there was a holism to Māori life that meant that everyday living and religion were closely intertwined; "religion was so interwoven with social and natural matters that the priests were absolutely necessary to the proper functioning of Māori society."[24] A *tohunga* or an *ariki* would make an offering of "first fruits" to the gods as a mark of respect, whether of *kumara* at the harvest, of fish caught, or of the first enemy killed in battle.[25] Ancestors and genealogy *(whakapapa),* as in African societies, assumed great importance, and ancestors were "often deified to become tribal family gods."[26] A number of missionaries witnessed what many regarded as acts of ventriloquism: the gods or *atua* were thought to whistle, when communed with by the *tohunga.* The scholarly civil servant Edward Shortland regarded it as ventriloquism when he experienced it, and Peter Buck wrote of a "squeaky, high voice," wondering if ventriloquism was used to enhance prestige. For the people, there was a general belief that the *tohunga* communed with the spirits *(wairua),* and these practices could have numinous effects even on Europeans like F. E. Maning, who recalled an experience of what seemed to him second sight in

22. On puberty see Goldman, *Ancient Polynesian Society,* p. 523; on *tangi,* Buck, *Coming of the Māori,* p. 463.

23. P. Buck, *Anthropology and Religion* (New Haven: Yale University Press, 1939), p. 57.

24. Buck, *Coming of the Māori,* p. 476.

25. Buck, *Anthropology and Religion,* pp. 24-25; E. Shortland, *Māori Religion and Mythology* (London: Longman, 1882), p. 34; Buck, *Coming of the Māori,* pp. 510, 520; Goldman, *Ancient Polynesian Society,* p. 510.

26. Karen Sinclair, "Maramatanga," p. 58; Buck, *Anthropology and Religion,* pp. 6-9.

Old New Zealand.[27] Magic arts *(makutu)* also existed and could be taught by apprenticeship.[28] The missionary Richard Taylor found what he took to be idols in caves in Wanganui, but this was an exceptional case. No missionary complained of the equivalent of fetishes, as many had done in Africa.[29]

A custom that caused missionaries much anxiety and considerable bemusement was "stripping," or *muru*. Whereas in some cases it had a kind of moral base and could be seen as suitable punishment resulting from, say, adultery,[30] on other occasions these raids seemed calculated to heighten a misfortune already experienced. So, a raiding party *(taua)* could result from illness in a home or death. It could result from a marriage. Fear of such a stripping caused the Methodists to evacuate their mission at Hokianga in 1827, and the rest of the missionaries lived in considerable fear through frequent threats of *muru* when Hongi, their protective chief, was in danger of dying from a musket wound in the same year, although the missionaries had no responsibility for his wound.[31] Again, Māori treatment of the sick troubled the missionaries with justice. They could be put out of the community, made *tapu*, and then left with too little to eat and drink to sustain life. Samuel Marsden, willing to accommodate to native custom, decided eventually to break the *tapu* of his friend and collaborator Ruatara, the first Māori chief to entertain missionaries, in order to feed and care for the sick man, though ultimately to no avail.[32]

Villages could be normal *(kainga)* or they could be fortified *(pa)*. The houses *(wharau)* were collectively owned property, belonging to the *whanau*, but such things as cooking utensils were owned by families.[33] Men never cooked and families ate apart, men being separate, but all classes worked together in the fields, chiefs alongside commoners, and work itself was considered honorable. The villages would contain *marae*, best understood as meeting spaces, where there could be communal gatherings *(hui)*; there might be a

---

27. E. Shortland, *Traditions and Superstitions of the New Zealanders* (London: Longman, 1854), pp. 65-77, 78; Buck, *Coming of the Māori*, p. 473; F. E. Maning, *Old New Zealand* (Auckland: Creighton and Scales, 1863; Leicester: University Press, 2001), pp. 159-61; E. Dieffenbach, *Travels in New Zealand*, 2 vols. (London: John Murray, 1843), p. 67.

28. Metge, *Māori of New Zealand*, p. 23.

29. R. Taylor, *The Past and Present of New Zealand* (London: William Macintosh, 1868), p. 16 n. 2.

30. Firth, *Economics*, pp. 135, 184.

31. King, *Penguin History*, pp. 137-38; N. Turner to secretaries of WMMS, 5 September 1825, MMS Microfilm/18.

32. *The Letters and Journals of Samuel Marsden, 1765-1838*, ed. J. R. Elder (Dunedin: Collins, Somerville, Wilkie, 1932), pp. 120-22. Ruatara died 3 March 1815 (p. 122).

33. Firth, *Economics*, p. 350.

meeting house *(whare runanga)*, some of which displayed fine carving.[34] There were carefully constructed latrines, set apart from the village. Tattooing *(moko)* was widely practiced, but the use of sharp implements on face, hips, and buttocks would be so painful that full tattooing could be slow. Men and women varied in the form of *moko* preferred. Implements of nephrite, New Zealand greenstone *(pounamu)*, were highly valued and were shaped into hand-held clubs *(patu)* carried by chiefs, although one governor, George Grey, found that such a prized weapon could be used as a gift toward peace.[35] Nose pressing *(hongi)* was the traditional greeting, behind which may have been the sharing of breath or vital essence *(hau ora)*.[36] The land itself, such a vital ingredient to their lives and well-being, subject to endless dispute after European contact, was seen as vested in the chief for his people but not owned by him. Boundary lines were carefully marked with boulders and posts.[37]

Enough has been written here to justify Tawney's comment that a difference in the understanding of civilization between Māori colonizers of New Zealand and their European successors is a better use of language than a confrontation between civilized and uncivilized peoples. Early European contact in the cases of observers like Governor King of Norfolk Island and Samuel Marsden at Parramatta saw very much to admire in the Māori they knew. Captain Cook's early judgment, sadly later revised, was of a people of "noble, open and benevolent disposition" who, even then, however, he recognized would not "put up with insults."[38] If Cook later regarded them as "vengeful, violent, treacherous," the German naturalist and explorer Dieffenbach, who left a scholarly examination of them in his *Travels in New Zealand* of 1843, wrote of them: "after the experience of some time I still continue to regard the New Zealanders as a very honest people, far more so than the lower classes of European colonists."[39]

Against the picture drawn by Firth and Tawney of a basically satisfied precontact society, however, must be set the portrait emerging from Paul Moon's work of 2008.[40] He emphasized the kind of perpetual fear induced by the threat of Māori raids on their communities, provoked by the killing, slav-

---

34. Metge, *Māori of New Zealand*, p. 9.
35. Firth, *Economics*, p. 415.
36. Irwin, *Introduction to Māori Religion*, p. 57.
37. Firth, *Economics* pp. 377, 390.
38. J. C. Beaglehole, ed., *Journal of Captain Cook* (Cambridge: Cambridge University Press, 1955-74), 2:653.
39. Dieffenbach, *Travels in New Zealand*, p. 105.
40. Moon, *This Horrid Practice*.

ery, and feasting on enemies that accompanied the many assaults, often based on revenge, sometimes for slights of many years' standing. For Moon "it was a nightmarish environment in which strains of paranoia hummed continually in the background and the reign of terror applied to those who spread it as well as those on the receiving end."[41] He wrote, "the turbulence of traditional Māori life, its almost institutionalised instability — such a far cry from the Noble Savage visions some Europeans imagined might apply in the region — was the perfect ingredient to help ferment the type of trauma that would contribute to, but by no means be solely responsible for, cannibalism taking place."[42] Polack, whom he quoted, had also noted the factor of fear in Māori culture: "from the earliest traditions these people have been in continual fear of one another. Every family has some tale of dreadful sufferings to relate, occasioned by acts of their neighbours. They are continually seeking opportunities for revenge; each tribe being observant of the politics of the surrounding villages. Children who care nothing for their parents when living, after their death, watch for years, when they may pounce, in an unguarded moment, on the enemy, who may have injured their parent."[43]

Precontact society can be portrayed neither as a kind of non-European utopia nor as a society without its own forms of civilization and social order. The admirable aspects that struck Governor King and Samuel Marsden existed alongside the savagery, revenge, and fear discerned by Polack. It was into this mixed scene of the people of the land *(tangata whenua)* that missionaries and colonists entered in the 1820s and received the Māori name of *pakeha*.

---

41. Moon, *This Horrid Practice*, p. 148.
42. Moon, *This Horrid Practice*, p. 162.
43. Polack, *Manners and Customs*, 2:47, quoted in Moon, *This Horrid Practice*, p. 173.

CHAPTER 2

Samuel Marsden and the New Zealand Mission to 1814

European contact with New Zealand had begun with the Dutch explorer Abel Tasman in 1642. Three of his sailors were killed and one mortally wounded in what became known as Mordenaars (Murderers') Bay.[1] Cook, with his distinguished observer Joseph Banks, arrived on the *Endeavour* in October 1769, narrowly missing a French ship under de Surville, which arrived in December. Cook was to return in his great voyages of 1772-75 and 1776-80, and Māori memories of his visits were recalled well into the nineteenth century, for example, to Polack in 1835.[2] Cook had learned to be wary of Māori, despite his initial admiration. The French captain Marion du Fresne must have shared his colleague Lt. Jean Roux's high opinion of New Zealanders, whom Roux called "a fine people, courageous, industrious and highly intelligent"; but whether or not because he broke *tapu*, as some have suggested, or because of treachery, du Fresne was killed in 1772, after entrusting himself to Māori on land.[3] Early contact between the two races has been well described by Anne Salmond in her two books *Two Worlds* (1991) and *Between Worlds* (1997).

As far as Christian mission was concerned, the decision of the British government to create a convict colony in New South Wales on Botany Bay in 1788 was to have major implications. William Wilberforce, leading example of

---

1. A. Salmond, *Two Worlds: First Meetings between Māori and Europeans, 1642-1771* (Auckland: Viking, 1991), p. 82.

2. Joseph Banks had been created a Fellow of the Royal Society in 1766; Salmond, *Two Worlds*, pp. 182, 184.

3. Salmond, *Two Worlds*, pp. 360, 381; A. Earle, *Narrative of a Residence in New Zealand*, ed. E. H. McCormick (Oxford: Oxford University Press, 1996), pp. 130-31 and editorial note, p. 131 n. 1.

evangelical philanthropy, secured a chaplain for the very first party of convicts by agreement with William Pitt. The choice fell on Richard Johnson (1775?-1827). Like Samuel Marsden, soon to follow him, Johnson was a Yorkshireman, educated like Marsden at Hull Grammar School and Magdalene College, Cambridge. Like Marsden, he had been supported toward ordination by the evangelical Elland Society, formed during his time as vicar of Huddersfield by the well-known evangelical preacher Henry Venn, and a source of finance to a number of comparatively poor young men of evangelical outlook who sought ordination in the Church of England.[4] It was to be Wilberforce again who asked the founder of the New Zealand mission to join Johnson in New South Wales in 1792.

Samuel Marsden (1765-1838) was the grandson of a yeoman farmer and son of a butcher in the hamlet of Farsley in Yorkshire; he was baptized in Calverley near Leeds. He became an apprentice blacksmith in his teens but showed enough intellectual promise and evangelical conviction to be supported toward Cambridge by the Elland Society in 1790. The historians of Magdalene College have shown how, at this time, it became a favored venue for Anglican evangelical students, through the presence among the dons of William Farish, later professor of chemistry, and Dr. Richard Hey of Leeds, who maintained contacts with Joseph Milner, the headmaster of Hull Grammar School. Men like Johnson, John Crowther (who was also assigned to New South Wales but turned back after shipwreck), Marsden, and the so-called "pious chaplains" of the East India Company, David Brown and Thomas Thomason, caused Ronald Hyam to write, "at no other point in more than five centuries had the college interacted so influentially with the main currents of national and indeed world history."[5] Marsden was at Cambridge during the notable incumbency of Charles Simeon at Holy Trinity Church, from whose circle men such as the early Anglican chaplain in India, Henry Martyn, emerged for missionary service. It has been suggested that the fines incurred by Marsden for late entry at night into the college resulted from extended periods at religious gatherings in

---

4. S. Piggin, in *Biographical Dictionary of Evangelicals*, ed. T. Larsen (Leicester: IVP, 2003), pp. 334-35. Piggin quotes Pitt to Wilberforce, 23 September 1786: "the colony for Botany Bay will be much indebted to you for your assistance in providing a chaplain . . . if you can find such a clergyman . . . we shall be very glad of it; but it must be soon." N. K. Macintosh, *Richard Johnson, Chaplain to the Colony of New South Wales: His Life and Times, 1755-1827* (Sydney: Library of Australian History, 1978).

5. R. Hyam, *Godliness, Hunting, and Quite Good Learning: A History of Magdalene College, 1792-1922* (Cambridge: Magdalene College, 1992), p. 9; cf. Eamon Duffy, *A History of Magdalene College, Cambridge, 1428-1988* (Cambridge: Magdalene College, 1994), pp. 185-93; J. Walsh "The Magdalene Evangelicals," *Church Quarterly Review* 159 (1958): 499-511.

Simeon's rooms.[6] Before he could complete a degree, Marsden was persuaded by Wilberforce, John Newton, and other leading evangelicals to accept appointment as an assistant chaplain to Johnson in 1792.[7]

For Marsden, the year 1793 was momentous. In January his appointment as a chaplain was confirmed. In March he was ordained deacon by the bishop of Bristol. He proposed marriage to Elizabeth ("Betsy") Fristan, daughter of a Hull family. His letter arrived at the London home of her uncle, the evangelical biblical scholar Thomas Scott, where she was staying, and in it he showed his best side: "I do not want to purchase my peace at the expense of your comfort." They were married at Holy Trinity Church, Hull, in April. In May Marsden was ordained a priest by the bishop of Exeter, and in July they sailed for Australia in the ship *William*. They arrived in New South Wales on 10 March 1794, three days after the birth of their first child, Anne, who was to marry into a missionary family, her father-in-law being Thomas Hassell, one of the pioneer LMS missionaries in the Pacific.[8] Marsden was given a grant of land in 1794 and, like Richard Johnson before him, set a high standard as an agriculturalist: his farm at Parramatta expanded to some six hundred acres and in time Australia was indebted to him for the introduction of Merino sheep.[9] With some reluctance he accepted appointment as a civil magistrate in 1796, though he expressed doubts to himself and to others about the incompatibility of a clergyman serving in the role. He earned a reputation for severity in dealing with the convict population, which has dogged him in Australia, as a "flogging magistrate," who was "an unrelenting castigator of blasphemy, Sabbath breaking and immorality."[10]

Marsden has attracted a variety of judgments from historians. For Harri-

---

6. A. T. Yarwood, *Samuel Marsden: The Great Survivor*, 2nd ed. (Melbourne: Melbourne University Press, 1996), pp. 14-55; see the quotation here from Thomas Thomason's journal: "Mr Marsden was (Simeon's) intimate friend." The same writer notes that Wilberforce gave £2,565 in one year to the Elland Society in 1782. Charles Simeon was also a subscriber (p. 9).

7. Yarwood, *Samuel Marsden*, p. 18.

8. Yarwood, *Samuel Marsden*, p. 20; for Marsden's letter of proposal, see *The Letters and Journals of Samuel Marsden, 1765-1838*, ed. J. R. Elder (Dunedin: Coulls, Somerville, Wilkie, 1932), p. 22, from the Hassall correspondence, Mitchell Library, Sydney.

9. Yarwood, *Samuel Marsden*, pp. 41-42; for the introduction of Merino sheep, a gift from George III, see S. Neill, "Marsden," in *Concise Dictionary of the Christian World Mission* (London: Lutterworth Press, 1971), p. 371; *Letters and Journals of Samuel Marsden*, p. 44.

10. Piggin, in *Biographical Dictionary*, pp. 407-8; for Marsden's doubts see *Letters and Journals of Samuel Marsden*, p. 36: "the duty of a civil magistrate and a clergyman may not appear compatible and I am not without my doubts about it" (17 September 1796).

son Wright in his deservedly influential study, Marsden was "a short, heavy, imposing humourless man . . . not a very amiable one. Vindictive, contradictory, stubborn, vain often intolerant. . . . yet he had something so magnificent about him that one cannot possibly dislike him." For Stephen Neill "his faults, which were many, are outweighed by his merits, which were great." To the French naval officer Laplace of *La Favourite,* a critic of the main missionary body, he was "the Las Casas of Polynesia" and greatly to be admired. To Gordon Parsonson, he was "much misunderstood in his generation and just as often misrepresented. In essence he was simple minded and honest, even to a fault. He was also open-handed, almost prodigal with his use of money . . . he often befriended convicts (and) . . . was extraordinarily generous towards those who disappointed him or even those who hated him. . . . if he had a serious fault, it was his predisposition to take offence."[11] What the missionary sources reveal is that, however ambiguous his reputation may have been in New South Wales, he was revered and admired by the missionaries of the second phase (1823-35), even if they took issue with some of his missionary opinions; and he was treated by something approaching veneration by the Māori, whom he had befriended and sought to understand on their own terms.

In the 1790s, Māori individuals were becoming more widely known outside New Zealand, partly through serving on ships, sealers and whalers, where they were often badly treated by captains, as was the case with Marsden's friend and ally Ruatara. In 1793 Governor King of Norfolk Island, who was well disposed toward Māori, had nevertheless arranged for two men to be kidnapped in the hope of learning the secrets of flax weaving. Tuki and Huru turned out to know nothing of this essentially female skill; but when Marsden visited King on Norfolk Island soon after, King described their "nobleness of character . . . the seed which would grow into the New Zealand mission had thus been sown."[12] Marsden was himself to provide hospitality for Māori on his farm at Parramatta. Meanwhile his missionary instincts had been harnessed by the LMS, whose first pioneers to the "South Seas" had sailed in the *Duff* in 1796.

---

11. H. M. Wright, *New Zealand, 1769-1840: Early Years of Western Contact* (Cambridge: Harvard University Press, 1959), p. 39; Neill, "Marsden," p. 371; G. S. Parsonson, *DNZB,* 1:373. Elder gives Laplace's judgment: "loin de moi l'intention de déprécier les travaux apostoliques des missionaires protestants . . . j'aurai cité principalement le révérend M. Marsden; par son zèle admirable à civiliser les aborigines . . . a merité d'être surnommé le las Casas de la Polynesie," from *Letters and Journals of Samuel Marsden,* p. 504. See in present volume, appendix on A. T. Yarwood and Richard Quinn.

12. *Letters and Journals of Samuel Marsden,* p. 28; A. Salmond, *Between Worlds: Early Exchanges between Māori and Europeans, 1772-1815* (Honolulu: University of Hawaii Press, 1997), pp. 208, 211-82.

When most of the party on Tahiti decided to take refuge in New South Wales, it was Marsden who provided hospitality in 1798. The society recognized him officially as a friend by appointing him their agent in 1804.[13] His experience of the LMS refugees gave Marsden firm ideas of what was needed in missionaries, which he expressed in 1800: "a missionary, were I to define his character, should be a pious good man . . . well acquainted with mankind (and) should possess some education . . . be easy of address and of an active mind. Some of the missionaries who have been to this colony are the opposite character (with) . . . lives and conduct and totally ignorant of mankind."[14]

Between 1800 and 1807 Marsden was unable to leave the colony. After Richard Johnson's departure in 1800, he was the only chaplain. He met, and was greatly impressed by, Te Pahi, who was in Port Jackson (Sydney) in 1805. He also met Ruatara (Marsden always writes the name "Duaterra") and confided in his diary of these Māori, "the more I examined into their natural character, the more I felt interested in their temporal and spiritual welfare." Eventually in 1807 Governor Bligh, famed and notorious as captain of the *Bounty* previously, gave Marsden permission to visit England, when he took the opportunity to put the case to the Church Missionary Society (then the Society for Africa and the East) for a mission to New Zealand, which he did on 4 April 1808. He struck some notes that were to recur in his missionary vision: the need for "the commerce and arts of civilisation" to be "planted first," which would then "open the way to the gospel by inculcating . . . moral habits." This pointed to the desirability of starting with "artisan settlers" such as a carpenter, a twine spinner, and the like, who would, through the practice of their skills, prepare the way, but this would not "prevent the settlers from simultaneously carrying out the functions of catechists in teaching the great doctrines of the gospel." Religious progress, however, in Marsden's view, was dependent on progress in "civilisation" and the countering of "vagrant habits" (perhaps a reflection on his experience among Australian aborigines, who presented special difficulties to missionaries of this kind).[15] The New Zea-

---

13. Piggin, in *Biographical Dictionary*, p. 408; Parsonson, *DNZB*, 1:271-72.

14. Salmond, *Between Worlds*, p. 258; for later views of Marsden by missionaries, see A. N. Brown Journal, 15-16 March 1836, 8 June 1837, 3 July 1839, C N/O 24/111-2; H. Bedgood, 12 November 1835, C N/O 22; C. Baker to secretaries, 6 September 1837; cf. 31 March 1837, C N/O 18; G. Clarke to secretaries, 31 March 1837, C N/O 30.

15. Yarwood, *Samuel Marsden*, p. 116; cf. P. Havard-Williams, ed., *Marsden and the New Zealand Mission: Sixteen Letters* (Dunedin: University of Otago Press and A. H. and A. W. Reed, 1961), Marsden to Pratt, 7 April 1808, where "civilization" was needed to "pave the way for the Introduction of the Gospel" and "that can only be accomplished among the Heathen by the Arts." This book has no pagination.

landers, he explained, were "very superior people in point of natural Endowments" and "a noble race of men ... capable of every mental improvement."[16]

Before returning to New Zealand, Marsden managed to recruit two such "godly mechanics" or artisan missionaries. He met William Hall from Leeds on 18 June 1808, "a very promising young man" who was a carpenter, and John King from Oxfordshire, who was a shoemaker but had knowledge of twine spinning and flax dressing. King had owed his Christian awakening and missionary calling to Daniel Wilson's visits as a preacher to his home church. Wilson, who was to go to India as bishop of Calcutta, was then vice-principal of St. Edmund's Hall, Oxford. To Marsden, King was a "quiet and noble man."[17] Marsden, Hall, and King boarded the *Ann* on 25 August 1809, where to Marsden's pleasure they found the Māori Ruatara onboard, last seen in Australia. The Ngapuhi chief, who came from the Bay of Islands, had enlisted as a merchant seaman, intending to reach London and, apparently, to see George III, a wish denied him by refusal of shore leave on arrival. On the *Ann*, through ill treatment and the beatings of other sailors, he was sick. Marsden's care for him in his weakness, in attendance and gifts of clothing, formed a bond between them. He became an enthusiast for a New Zealand mission, not least the benefits that would follow from the growing of wheat in his country, agricultural aims that were dear to Marsden's own heart. Marsden found him "dignified and noble" and "polite, engaging and courteous" with, however, "fire and animation in his eye."[18]

Arriving in Sydney in February 1810, Marsden was met by the news that Māori had set upon the brig *Boyd* at Whangaroa in December 1809 and had killed and eaten the crew, possibly in retaliation for abuses or individual ill treatment to Māori sailors that happened elsewhere in the Pacific, although the circumstances remain unclear in detail. Marsden was "devastated," both by the blow to his plans, now put indefinitely on hold, and further because at that stage Te Pahi, his friend from 1805, was held responsible for the outrage.[19]

---

16. Yarwood, *Samuel Marsden*; Marsden to CMS, 16 August 1813, in *MR* (1814), pp. 465-67.

17. Marsden to Pratt, 15 November 1809, from Rio de Janeiro, in Havard-Williams, *Marsden and the New Zealand Mission*, in the place cited.

18. *Letters and Journals of Samuel Marsden*, pp. 13, 14, 24; *DNZB*, 1:375-6; on King, see T. Higgins, *Soles and Souls: A Life of John King of Swerford, 1781-1854* (Swerford: Privately published, 2001), p. 11 (for Daniel Wilson and King).

19. Salmond, *Both Worlds*, pp. 386-92; "devastated," p. 417; Thomas Kendall absolved Te Pahi later but see J. Binney, *The Legacy of Guilt: A Life of Thomas Kendall* (Auckland: Oxford University Press, 1968), pp. 16-17, and her judicious note 10 for the confused background to this exoneration.

Hall and King had to be encouraged to make their way in the colony. Before long they were joined by a third missionary pioneer, Thomas Kendall, who had been recommended to the CMS by the evangelical preacher Basil Woodd in 1811. At that stage, Josiah Pratt of the CMS wrote, "the state of the affairs at New Zealand renders us doubtful whether we should send him: yet his heart seems so bent on going and he appears so well qualified in many respects for the purpose that I have some expectation that the Com. may embrace an early opportunity of sending him and his family."[20] Kendall and his wife Jane and five children arrived in Sydney on 10 October 1813.

Kendall came from Lincolnshire from a farming family. He had been a shopkeeper. By the mission he was treated as a schoolmaster, and Marsden used him at Parramatta to instruct young Māori men.[21] Marsden decided that the only way to visit New Zealand in the wake of the *Boyd* affair was to purchase his own vessel. In due course this ship, the *Active*, was used for Hall and Kendall to make an exploratory voyage to the Bay of Islands in March 1814. Marsden sent a letter to Ruatara, raising again the possibility of a mission and introducing Kendall as a teacher for the tribe's boys and girls and, by implication, Hall, to build houses for them.[22] The intending missionaries met Ruatara and two other chiefs, Korokoro and Hongi Hika, who agreed to accompany them back to Australia. Hongi, who was to become so central to the early mission, impressed Kendall as "a warrior but apparently . . . of a very mild disposition . . . little appearance of the Savage about him," while to Marsden later he seemed "a very fine character . . . unusually mild in his manners and very polite and well behaved at all times," while, in contrast, Korokoro was regarded as warlike.[23] Hongi was a many-sided human being, but they were to discover that first impressions were not definitive.

Finally, after an encouraging report by this party, Marsden obtained permission from the governor, Lachlan Macquarie, to visit New Zealand himself with a view to establishing the mission. The party consisted of thirty-five in all, including the Māori chiefs and the three missionary families; they sailed on 19 November 1814. In addition, they had onboard two convicts acting as servants, one Richard Stockwell, who accompanied the Kendalls, and one who was a blacksmith by trade, Walter Hall. Kendall's appointment as a justice of the peace was announced before they left, a distinction that, along with his status as a teacher, acted as an irritant in his relationship with the carpen-

---

20. Pratt to Marsden, 19 February 1811, in Binney, *Legacy of Guilt*, p. 10.
21. Salmond, *Between Worlds*, p. 428.
22. Thomas Kendall's journal quoted in Binney, *Legacy of Guilt*, p. 20.
23. Salmond, *Between Worlds*, pp. 438, 443.

ter, William Hall. Marsden had already described William Hall as "able but obstinate" in a letter of November 1809, while Hall had his disagreements with Marsden while in New South Wales: "I can do very well with Mr Marsden," Hall wrote, "if I never ask him for any money," a sign of tension roused by Hall's streak of independence. Now Hall noticed that Kendall, although, like Hall, still a layman at this stage, was asked to read prayers onboard. For the historian, a valuable additional passenger was John Liddiard Nicholas, who wrote an account of the voyage, *Narrative of a Voyage to New Zealand* (1817).[24] Apart from his comments on the variety of animals that accompanied the voyage, including goats, cats, dogs, sheep, and pigs — "a perfect resemblance to Noah's ark" — he recorded Ruatara's sudden dejection of spirit while onboard; people in Sydney had warned him of the potential for "fatal impact" through his introduction of the mission. A kind of "morose melancholy" took possession of him, so much so that Marsden offered to return to Sydney. They agreed, however, to proceed.

Nicholas noticed Hongi's skill as he reset the stock of a gun: "the most expert and finished mechanic could not possibly do it better." Nicholas played draughts with Ruatara, perhaps to distract him, while Hongi made a cartridge box of "much ingenuity."[25] They reached New Zealand on 17 December 1814 and, after a visit to the Cavalli Islands, came to the Bay of Islands on 22 December. Ruatara had chosen Rangihoua, with its steep slopes to the sea, as their setting, and three days later he made arrangements for a service of worship by constructing a pulpit for Marsden and acting as interpreter. "It being Christmas Day," Marsden wrote in his journal, "I preached from the second chapter of St Luke's gospel and the tenth verse 'Behold I bring you glad tidings of great joy.'"[26]

---

24. J. L. Nicholas, *Narrative of a Voyage to New Zealand, 1814 and 1815* (London: James Black, 1817), p. 38; Binney, *Legacy of Guilt*, pp. 24-25; Yarwood, *Samuel Marsden*, p. 167, 148-49, for Hall's complaints.

25. Nicholas, *Voyage,* pp. 25-27, 39-50.

26. Marsden's journal, Hocken Library, Dunedin DUHO-0030 MS176A, p. 89.

CHAPTER 3

Māori and Missionaries: Early CMS Interaction, 1814-1823

In a study about change, essentially from Māori religion and custom to Māori forms of Christianity, it is important to establish as far as possible a true picture of what the missionaries found in 1814 and after. Unlike a recent study of the Yoruba people of West Africa,[1] there is very little Māori writing to draw on, which makes the missionaries' reaction to and account of Māori religion and custom all the more valuable. While it is undoubtedly right to exercise what has been called "the hermeneutics of suspicion" over the missionary writing, remembering that much of it was intended to arouse the interest of societies and their supporters at the home base, it is also important to give due weight to contemporary descriptions, arising out of the immediate pressures and observations of the participants. For Marsden, as the pioneer observer, the Māori appeared "like a Superior Race of Men,"[2] "a noble race... capable of every mental improvement."[3] He was, however, clear-eyed about them: "cannibals they are and readily admit it... but they are very noble and actively kind and affectionate; and in many moral qualities, they would put normal Christians to the blush."[4] Marsden may have been a Calvinist in theology, holding a view of original sin and the fallenness of human

---

1. J. D. Y. Peel, *Religious Encounter and the Making of the Yoruba* (Bloomington: Indiana University Press, 2000).
2. Marsden to Pratt, 20 November 1811; cf. P. Havard-Williams, ed., *Marsden and the New Zealand Mission: Sixteen Letters* (Dunedin: University of Otago Press and A. H. and A. W. Reed, 1961), p. 41; cf. N. Gunson, *Messengers of Grace: Evangelical Missionaries in the South Seas, 1797-1860* (Melbourne: Oxford University Press, 1978), p. 111 ("suspicion").
3. Marsden to Macquarrie, 1 November 1813, in *MR* (1814), pp. 465-67.
4. *MR* (1818), p. 73.

beings that owed nothing to Rousseau's "noble savage," a theology that his experience in the convict colony may have served to reinforce, but he still recognized natural goodness in the Māori, as exemplified in the chief Patuone: "he has a fine open countenance, in which the greatest kindness and goodwill are expressed."[5]

In his role as sympathetic observer, Marsden wrote down all he could that "tended to throw any light on their Customs, Manners and Religion."[6] Elder, who wrote on him, reminded his readers that Marsden owed much of his understanding to a Māori source in Te Morenga, which gave his testimony "unique value."[7] Other Māori sources were also questioned, often at length. On Māori belief he wrote that "I have never met a New Zealander that did not consider (his) God as a vindictive Being . . . especially if guilty of any . . . omission of their sacred rites."[8] Māori, he decided, had "no idea of a God of mercy and love, willing to do them good: but believed that an angry being is always ready to kill and devour them, for the neglect of the smallest matter imaginable and, under such impressions, they frequently sicken, pine away and die."[9] Marsden met the phenomenon of "the whistling god." He discussed this with the priests *(tohunga)*, who claimed that all New Zealanders knew the whistling "to be true," though Marsden never heard it. Nevertheless, in his role as amateur anthropologist, he refused to close his mind to these and other claims, as he found the priests to be men of integrity in other matters and recognized that the belief they held was indeed widespread.[10]

He realized, and subsequent anthropology confirmed, that dead chiefs were accorded semidivine status: "when they die (they) deify them and offer up prayer to them."[11] This was the essential background to understanding Māori practice in relation to their enemies. In an extended section, which reflected both Te Morenga's and Hongi's accounts, Marsden recorded that "they eat the slain not so much for food or for mental gratification as to display publicly to their enemies their bitter revenge."[12] Like Marsden, French observers of 1824 realized that the bodies were "not thought of as food but as ac-

---

5. Marsden Journal of Second Voyage (September-November 1819), DUHO-0030-176A, p. 363 (hereafter Hocken 176A).
6. Marsden Journal, 9 November 1819, Hocken 176A, p. 407.
7. *The Letters and Journals of Samuel Marsden, 1765-1838,* ed. J. R. Elder (Dunedin: Collins, Somerville, Wilkie, 1932), p. 46.
8. Marsden Journal, February to December 1820, Hocken 176D, p. 460.
9. Marsden Journal, February to December 1820, Hocken 176D, p. 485.
10. Marsden Journal, February to December 1820, Hocken 176D, p. 480.
11. Marsden Journal, 28 September 1819, Hocken 176A, p. 323.
12. Marsden Journal, July 1819–September 1819, Hocken 176B, pp. 274-77.

cessory to the mysteries of religion."[13] Marsden's journal reinforces this impression through his description of the reverential attitudes of the victorious chiefs, who sit around with eyes averted, while the priests (here *arikis*) pray and pick pieces of flesh for their sacrifices: "they (the chiefs) are not permitted to look at these mysteries," in which the priests prepared baskets of flesh to offer to the gods as first partakers. His informants spared him nothing as they recounted the cannibalizing of a warrior chief, followed by his wife, all of which was to deny them any semblance of survival. Kendall told Marsden of the belief that the left eye of a chief could become a star, so ensuring immortality, but Hongi had seen to it that his adversary had no such future by swallowing it whole.[14]

Perhaps it was as well that some of these revelations lay in the future, but Marsden was under no illusions when he spent the night in a Māori camp at Whangaroa in 1814: "I viewed our situation with new sensations and feelings that I cannot express. Surrounded by cannibals, who had massacred and devoured our countrymen I wondered much at the mysteries of Providence . . . never did I behold the blessed advantages of civilisation in a more grateful light than now. I did not sleep much during the night; my mind was too seriously occupied by the present scene and the new and strange ideas."[15]

"Civilization" as a component of Christian mission was an important aspect of Marsden's understanding. As early as the work of the Methodist pioneer Thomas Coke and his directions for work among the Foulah people of West Africa in the 1790s, as also in the work initiated by Thomas Haweis through the LMS pioneers in the "South Seas," the missionary-minded had intended that European advances in the fields of agriculture and the "arts of civilization" should be extended to societies without them. "Nothing," wrote Marsden to Josiah Pratt, secretary of the CMS in London, "in my opinion can prepare the way for the introduction of the gospel but civilisation."[16] When he met with the CMS committee to persuade them to undertake a mission to New Zealand in 1808, he conceded that "although the New Zealanders (were) very superior people in part of mental endowments," they were not yet ready to hear the gospel. The "arts of civilization" should be planted first to open

---

13. A. Sharp, ed., *Duperrey's Visit to New Zealand in 1824* (Wellington: Alexander Turnbull Library, 1971), p. 91.

14. Marsden Journal, 1819, Hocken 176B, pp. 274-77, 254.

15. Marsden Journal, November 1814–March 1815, Hocken 176A, p. 82.

16. Marsden to Pratt in *Proceedings of the CMS 1806-9*, Appx. IV, p. 381; for Thomas Coke and his "selected mechanics," see G. G. Findlay and H. W. Holdsworth, *The History of the Wesleyan Methodist Missionary Society*, 5 vols. (London: Epworth Press, 1921-24), 4:76-77.

the way to the gospel by inculcating moral habits. A "first attempt should be made on a small scale by artisan settlers: a carpenter . . . a smith . . . a twine spinner," though these could simultaneously carry out the "function of catechists." First, the attention of the heathen had to be gained, vagrant habits corrected, and only then would religious progress be made.[17] No wonder Marsden viewed with such admiration the disciplined work of Hongi's people as observed in 1814, as they gathered a "very fine crop" of potatoes and appeared "very industrious": "they rose at the dawn of the day . . . busy making baskets of potatoes, others drawing flax and making nets."[18]

The early missionaries felt this emphasis on civilization, agriculture, flax making, and carpentry, even if catechizing was to be done in parallel with them, was too much, well before the arrival of Henry Williams in 1823. Marsden wrote in 1822 that "my heart has been set upon the civilisation and evangelism of the inhabitants of New Zealand for the last 16 years," and advances in agriculture were to be one means of weaning the Māori from their warlike tendencies,[19] but one after another of the settlers demurred. So Carlisle, a schoolmaster but not a CMS missionary, wrote in January 1820, "I am fully persuaded the attempts which are making such progress as some may suppose to civilize first . . . (and) . . . afterwards convert them (is) not the proper way. Nothing will effectively change their hearts and . . . outward conduct but the spirit of God (the gospel) will immediately convert."[20] True, the rope maker John Cowell saw the use of New Zealand hemp as something that would "bring poor heathen into a state of civilisation,"[21] but James Shepherd, engaged by Marsden primarily for his agricultural skills but proving an adept Māori linguist, wrote to Pratt: "I think the gospel will be the only means of civilising the heathen," and, while apologizing to Pratt for his dogmatism in "expressing [his] sentiments so freely," held that "Evangelisation goes before Civilisation."[22] Charles Gordon, like Shepherd an agriculturalist though not a CMS missionary, wrote to the CMS committee in July 1820 complaining of his treatment by Marsden as a "common labouring man," expected to work from 6 A.M. to 6 P.M. daily, but equally taking up Marsden's missionary strat-

---

17. A. T. Yarwood, *Samuel Marsden: The Great Survivor*, 2nd ed. (Melbourne: Melbourne University Press, 1996), p. 116.
18. Marsden Journal, 1814, Hocken 176A, p. 104.
19. Marsden to Kendall, 17 January 1822, Hocken MS M.1/71.
20. Carlisle to Pratt, 10 January 1820, CMS C N/O 27.
21. Cowell to Pratt, 13 August 1821, CMS C N/O 32/1-10; on Cowell see J. Binney, *The Legacy of Guilt: A Life of Thomas Kendall* (Auckland: Oxford University Press, 1968), pp. 116-17 and n. 76.
22. Shepherd to Pratt, 2 December 1822, C N/O 76.

egy: "Mr Marsden's plan is civilisation. I humbly contend that nothing will do the New Zealanders any good but preaching the gospel to them. While their hearts remain unchanged they will be savages still," though he added the Māori were "a people susceptible to tender impressions . . . very clever sensible people."[23] Kemp, the artisan missionary who had worked as a blacksmith, took the same view as Gordon: "I do not expect to see [them] far advanced in civilisation, until they receive the Gospel of Christ," a view he repeated to the CMS lay secretary Dandeson Coates: "when they have received the gospel . . . they will rise in everything else . . . (and) enjoy the blessings of civilisation (but) not before."[24]

Rangihoua had been chosen as the site for the mission through Marsden's relationship with Ruatara and because Marsden relied on his friend to provide adequate protection for the early settlement. It was a site of steep hills, with a Māori village of some 150-200 people on the summit.[25] Marsden had purchased 200 acres for the mission in exchange for twelve axe heads,[26] and the ground was made *tapu* and, in Māori eyes, placed under the *mana* of European gods and ancestors.[27] By the time of the purchase (13 February 1815), to Marsden's great distress, Ruatara was already very ill and weak. Marsden

---

23. Charles Gordon to CMS Committee, 19 July 1820, C N/O 42/2; cf. Butler to Pratt, 25 August 1823, where agricultural progress is needed alongside the spiritual.

24. Kemp to Pratt, 21 May 1824; to Coates, 31 December 1823, Hocken MS M.1/70. Coates, with John Beecham of the WMMS and William Ellis of the LMS, presented evidence on missionary work to the House of Commons, subsequently published as *Christianity the Means of Civilisation* (1837), though Ellis held that civilization followed conversion. Gunson, *Messengers of Grace*, p. 389 n. 2, regarded Marsden as the last exponent of a view whereby natural religion preceded revealed religion in mission, a theory advanced by Moravians whose weaknesses had been exposed by J. D. Lang. J. Garrett, *To Live among the Stars: Christian Origins in Oceania* (Suva and Geneva: WCC and Institute of Pacific Studies, University of the South Pacific, 1982, 1985), p. 68, shows shared ground between Marsden and Thomas Haweis, the LMS pioneer, on the use of "devout mechanics," but Haweis put preaching before civilization while Marsden held that the gospel followed "the arts." Yarwood shows that not all Moravians took the view above: Ignatius la Trobe held that "to evangelise is to civilize." Yarwood, *Samuel Marsden*, p. 167.

25. Binney, in *An Illustrated History of New Zealand, 1820-1920*, ed. J. Binney, J. Basset, and E. Olsen (London: Allen and Unwin, 1990), pp. 12-14; cf. R. A. Cruise, *Journal of Ten Months Residence in New Zealand* (London: Hurst, Rees, Orme, Brown, 1823), p. 40: "a high steep hill" with "very extensive native dwellings."

26. Marsden Journal, Hocken MS 176A, p. 162; *Letters and Journals of Samuel Marsden*, p. 123.

27. A. Salmond, *Between Worlds: Early Exchanges between Māori and Europeans, 1772-1815* (Honolulu: University of Hawaii Press, 1997), p. 505, who prefers exchange of *mana* to "purchase" as the understanding of what passed.

had ultimately defied the *tapu* put on the sick man to minister to his friend, but when the *Active* sailed he had to leave Thomas Kendall to support the chief. Ruatara died on 3 March, followed the day after by the suicide of his wife by hanging, which was a common but by no means universal custom among Māori widows. Hongi, the dead man's uncle, showed depth of emotion at his loss in tears and lament.[28] It was a serious setback for the mission. Rangihoua provided little possibility for agriculture, unlike the later purchase at Waimate, which made the mission heavily dependent on Māori for provisions by way of barter; it is no surprise that William Hall, who valued independence, made an attempt in 1816 to overturn Marsden's original choice of site, only to find that he was no longer guaranteed protection and was forced to return.[29] Marsden had judged, before he left on the *Active*, that "the settlement (is) assuming the pleasing appearance of civilisation . . . buildings erected and erecting . . . completing everything relating to the Establishment of the Mission."[30] Although initially one large building housed the missionary families in compartments, by the time Richard Cruise saw the settlement in 1822 there were "cottages . . . built in English style, of wood and as neat and comfortable as . . . the civilised world could admit of."[31] A school was constructed, which Kendall opened in 1816. He was joined in 1818 by another teacher, Francis Hall, who was followed by the new superintendent and clergyman John Butler in 1819. Until then the CMS missionary force was composed of John King, William Hall, and Thomas Kendall.

King, the twine spinner from Swerford in Oxfordshire, had been described by Marsden in 1809 as "a quiet, noble man" who was liked by a young Māori chief at Parramatta.[32] King, like Marsden, was observant of the Māori and recorded his findings. He wrote: "I cannot learn that they have any knowledge of a Supreme Being," but he confirmed the view that "after death, the chiefs become gods and the living pray to them."[33] He came across what we have called "departmental gods.": "the *Taniwa* or sea god was very angry and made a chief very sick and nearly drowned him. They also ascribe . . . thunder . . . to his anger."[34] A sick man told King that the *atua* were "eating him." These *atua*, as spiritual beings, were understood to "dispute and fight,

---

28. Salmond, *Between Worlds*, p. 507.
29. Binney, *Legacy of Guilt*, p. 33.
30. Marsden Journal, Hocken MS 176A, p. 152.
31. Cruise, *Journal*, p. 40.
32. Marsden to Josiah Pratt, 15 November 1809, in Havard-Williams, *Marsden and the New Zealand Mission*, in loc.
33. King to Pratt, 24 May 1823, CMS C N/O 55.
34. King to Pratt, 25 March 1825, CMS C N/O 55.

plant *kumara* and have abundance of provisions etc in the other world."
When a chief dies he becomes an *atua,* and at his death his soul goes to the
"Traingha" (King's version of Te Reinga) at the North Cape and sometimes
comes to speak to the relations left behind in their dreams. When they ask if
he has seen their departed friends, he replies in their dreams, "I have seen
them and they are all well." A ladder goes from "Traingha" to the depths, by
which the soul descends; but equally the *atua* come up it and he "looks towards the place where (the chief) has died to know if his relations have performed the customary ceremonies." If they have been neglected "the *atua*
[are] angry."[35] King had also observed the ceremony by which the corpse of
the chief was dressed, anointed with oil, and decorated with white feathers for
display, before eventual deposition in a cave when "all the crying and ceremonies are over."[36]

King discussed belief in witchcraft as the source of a chief's death and, in
an interesting sidelight from his days in rural England, found a parallel belief
in a "conjurer" or "cunning man," called in to summon up the likeness of a
thief or, here, "the likeness of the person who has bewitched their friends." After death, he is told that "the spirit hovers about the body and place of the deceased until the third day, when the Priest prays and directs the spirit to the
reinga (when) they are in a similar state as when in sleep or dreams in this
life." Widows will lament in a small house *(waretana)* as they make mats for
the corpse, a practice called *watu tangi,* knitting, crying. A widow should wait
for twelve months ("time sufficient to decay the flesh") before she accepts another husband or she is in danger of being "beat" and "plundered." The spirits
in Te Reinga also grow to maturity and die, but this second death is final.
Māori were much influenced by "dreams, imaginations and omens": in one
vivid case, great agitation resulted from parallel dreams by three members of
the same family, and appearance of their eldest brother to all three, which led
to the shooting of one of his wives on the grounds of adultery and her supposed male accomplice.

King's journal recorded the stress of these early years. His family, like others, was subject to sudden invasions. A Māori man, armed with a weapon,
leaped "over the fence" that protected the house, broke it, and "gave our children and Mrs King great fright — seeing and hearing so much about killing
and eating so often — a little alarms our children." He reverted to the same
incident: "my family received such a fright yesterday — the native was naked,
in such a formidable manner with the weapon in his hand . . . without the

---

35. King to Pratt, 1 December 1820, CMS C N/O 55.
36. King to Pratt, 1 December 1820, CMS C N/O 55.

least provocation."[37] It is little wonder that King later assessed the years 1814-23 to Governor Fitzroy as "a living martyrdom,"[38] although the French, on their visit in 1824, found that neither King nor William Hall had been "dismayed by a residence of nine years," all the more creditable to them in that Duperrey judged that results were minimal: whether the fault lay with "evangelical workers" or in the barrenness of the soil, "the word of God has not taken root" and, even if the mission was not a complete failure, it had "produced no harvest."[39] By 1824 King himself saw a glimmer of progress toward change in the Māori attitudes but not much to encourage him religiously: "formerly they were threatening our lives etc stealing and treating us with contempt and scorn — for the past year they have been peaceable and quiet and have not robbed us."[40] Nevertheless, Harrison Wright's judgment on these early years is surely all too accurate: "it is difficult to imagine a more depressing life than that spent by these four men in the years before 1823."[41]

William Hall, judging from his journals, was less observant of Māori practice than John King. Like King, however, he was active in catechizing the local Māori communities, and in August 1819 he made a discovery that pointed to the future. It was a Sunday and he was preaching in a village near Rangihoua when, to his evident surprise, a chief he had instructed entered into the teaching role and, Hall writes, "I found that he was a better preacher than I was."[42] Again and again in later years it was this transmission from Māori to Māori that was the main means by which the Christian faith was spread, but the comment spoke well for the European missionary and, as many Māori were natural orators of great skill, reflected the truth. Hall, like others, chafed at the amount of emphasis placed on "manual labour" when what he felt needed to be done was "instructing the natives in (the) gospel."[43] Hall's latent hostility to Kendall, present from the first voyage to New Zealand, boiled over in scathing criticism to Pratt in London in April 1822: "if you could have the faintest idea of the real character and conduct of Mr Kendall since he has come to New Zealand you would no more have ordained him then you would have ordained his

---

37. King Journals, Hocken MS 73, 23 July, 15 August, 21 September 1822; 16, 17 November 1823 (invasion); 5 August, 23 September 1824 (dreams).

38. R. Fitzroy, *Remarks on New Zealand as a Colony in 1846* (London: W. and H. White, 1846), p. 5.

39. Sharp, *Duperrey's Visit*, p. 76.

40. King Journals, Hocken MS 73 (October 1824).

41. H. M. Wright, *New Zealand, 1769-1840: Early Years of Western Contact* (Cambridge: Harvard University Press, 1959), p. 41.

42. William Hall Journal, 1 August 1819, Hocken MS M.1/6Y.

43. Hall to CMS secretaries, 28 December 1820, Hocken MS M.1/6 Y.

shoe black. . . . I could tell you . . . conduct that would make your hair lift up your hat." He went on to recount a quarrel between one of the Europeans and Kendall, which resulted in Kendall being threatened with two loaded pistols; Jane Kendall's unfaithfulness; and Kendall's scandalous life, now common knowledge to every European ship's crew, "from captain to cook."[44]

These years of 1814-23 were the years of Thomas Kendall's involvement in the mission. They have been covered admirably by Judith Binney in *The Legacy of Guilt*.[45] Of the early group, Kendall worked hardest to understand the Māori. He realized that there was a holism to Māori society: "language, idolatry, theology, mythology, tradition . . . are inseparably blended together," he wrote to the Reverend Thomas Hassall. This letter delved deeply into what Kendall understood as Māori metaphysics and the three states of existence that he discerned them to hold, of Peace, Presence, and Union.[46] But, as Judith Binney has written, "Kendall's descriptions are not clear . . . distorted by his reading — under the illusion that the Māori were descendants of the Egyptians — of late eighteenth century accounts of Egyptian religious beliefs, particularly from his 1797 edition of the *Encyclopaedia Britannica*."[47] Nevertheless, as the Frenchman Dumont d'Urville wrote after visiting the mission, Kendall was "the only missionary who has attempted any scientific research."[48] Kendall saw the importance of the mastery of the Māori language. In 1815 he had the first book printed in Sydney in the language, and in due course he published the first grammar. Kendall carried missionary identification, always a knife-edge issue for exceptional missionaries like the Jesuit de Nobili in India, to the point of personal shipwreck. Effectively, he "converted" to Māori custom and, in particular, to their sexual mores.[49] He admitted as much to Pratt in London; his "painful study" of "all their notions" had meant that he was "so possessed with the apparent sublimity of their ideas that I have been completely turned from a Christian to a heathen. All their carnal representations have a special signification . . . deeply rooted within superstitions."[50]

---

44. Hall to Pratt, 6 April 1822, Hocken MS M.1/6 Y.

45. For an imaginative reconstruction, see J. Corbalis, *Tapu: A Novel* (London: Sinclair and Stevenson, 1996).

46. Kendall to Hassall, 9 April 1823, Hocken MS M/1/71: cf. Kendall to Pratt, 27 July 1827, Hocken MS M/1/71.

47. J. Binney, in *DNZB*, 1:225.

48. Sharp, *Duperrey's Visit*, p. 36.

49. Cf. Gunson, *Messengers of Grace*, p. 213; Garrett, *Live among the Stars*, p. 65. Gunson comments that despite his "conversion" to Māori-dom, Kendall "still regarded himself as a missionary and Calvinist too."

50. Kendall to Pratt, 3 December 1822, Hocken MS M.1/71.

By 1820 Kendall's position had already been exacerbated by his wife's unfaithfulness with the convict they had brought with them to New Zealand, Richard Stockwell, a liaison beginning as early as 1816, when Kendall was absent from the mission compound and Jane sought consolation in his absence.[51] Marsden had shown considerable sympathy with him over this predicament[52] and earlier had expressed genuine admiration for him as "an admirable man for the work. His heart engaged in the cause . . . very mild in his manners, kind, tender, affectionate and well qualified to teach."[53]

Butler, who arrived in 1819 with Francis Hall, was ordained (as at this stage Kendall was not) and introduced by Marsden as the mission's superintendent. In this role he was tactless and overbearing, prompting Kendall to an outburst: "I would strongly recommend to the Revd. Mr Butler, in order to avoid future altercation, to drop the idea of any exclusive authority over missionaries."[54] Although the pursuit of the language was the primary motive and a real one, by 1820 Kendall had other reasons for deciding on a visit to England, made without either Marsden's authority or the Church Missionary Society's permission, in company with Hongi and Waikato. There is a poignancy in the note to his wife from his ship, onboard which he had a strong premonition of an early death: "I now thank you for all your office of kindness, which you have invariably performed towards my person . . . if I live to see you again I hope it will be the means of producing a reconciliation between us; particularly if there should be on your part no obstacle in the way."[55]

On this visit, recorded for posterity by the portrait by James Barry of Kendall, Hongi, and Waikato in 1820, the two chiefs met various social figures, royal dukes, and the king himself, George IV, who presented to Hongi a coat of chain mail and other presents, some of which Hongi was to exchange for muskets and powder on his return to New South Wales. The main motive for the journey was fulfilled through Kendall's consultations with Professor Samuel Lee of Cambridge, a polymath in language, who helped Kendall and his Māori informants toward the grammar and vocabulary that Kendall was to produce in 1820 and opened the way to the more rigorous approach to the language by the mission after 1823. Kendall also arranged an ordination by the bishop of Ely in March 1820, which would give him equivalent status to Butler on his return.

51. Garrett, *Live among the Stars,* p. 64; Binney, *Legacy of Guilt,* pp. 53-54.
52. Marsden to Pratt, 10 February 1820, Hocken MS 57/16; Yarwood, *Samuel Marsden,* p. 215.
53. Marsden to CMS, 15 March 1814, *MR* (February 1815), pp. 101-5.
54. Kendall to Butler and all missionary settlers, 16 February 1820, Hocken MS 71/1; Binney, *Legacy of Guilt,* p. 45.
55. Kendall to Jane Kendall, 27 May 1820, Hocken MS M.1/71.

Butler had made no secret of his disapproval of the visit to England. From the new station at Kerikeri, hard by Hongi's settlement and under his immediate patronage and protection, Butler wrote to Kendall: "I think your journey to England very ill timed . . . no object can justify you in leaving your family unprotected in a Heathen land. . . . I should have thought (that) you have suffered enough in your family . . . to permit you ever leaving them . . . by taking away Shunghee (Hongi) you take away all our protection,"[56] although in practice Rewa, chief in Hongi's absence, proved a firm and decisive friend to the mission. Matters were to become more aggravated on the vexed question of trading and muskets. Axe heads, fishhooks, and other articles steadily paled as currency as the Māori, Hongi not least, became aware of the strategic value of guns, which Hongi was to use with devastating effect in the "musket wars" farther south in the North Island against Māori adversaries in the 1820s, resulting in wholesale slaughter that ran into the thousands. Marsden had tried to prevent the trade, but there were times when the need for food on the mission made such exchange virtually necessary for life. In defending his actions to Marsden, Kendall wrote: "(the Māori) esteem fish hooks as equal in value to our copper, axes and hoes to our silver and muskets and powder to our gold. Nor can we dictate to them which of these they must receive in payment . . . they dictate to us . . . we are *subjects* of a heathen government."[57] The position was aggravated by personnel on visiting ships, who bought up Māori pork and had no scruples about trading in muskets and powder. At the end of his missionary career, however, Kendall conceded that he had been too complaisant to Māori demands: "I certainly have done very wrong as a missionary in being too easily prevailed upon by the New Zealanders to barter with them for muskets and powder," though he added to this, apropos of CMS rulings, "I have nevertheless a doubt (whether) . . . the society (was) well acquainted with the difficulties of our situation . . . in this respect."[58]

After his return from England, Kendall made his position increasingly untenable in the mission by taking a seventeen-year-old Māori girl, Tungaroa, daughter of a chief and *tohunga* from Rangihoua whom Kendall had taught in school, as his mistress.[59] Kendall's property was plundered in a *muru* that resulted from this girl, according to Francis Hall's account, having been "tabooed" by "Toue" (Towhe) for his wife. Kendall's property was invaded on

---

56. Butler to Kendall, 24 February 1820, Hocken MS 58.
57. Kendall to Marsden, 27 September 1821, Hocken MS M.1/71; cf. J. R. Elder, ed., *Marsden's Lieutenants* (Dunedin: A. H. Reed, 1934), p. 154.
58. Kendall to Pratt, 15 August 1823, Hocken MS M.1/71.
59. *DNZB*, 1:224-25.

5 February 1822, but by 29 March he had taken the girl from the mission to live in the Māori settlement, though by 4-6 April he appeared to regret his actions.[60] By 1823, James Kemp, living at Kerikeri as storekeeper, was able to write to Kendall: "dear (sir) I am glad to hear that you and Mrs Kendall are so comfortable in your cottage dear sir be assured of Mrs Kemps' and myself best wishes and prayers continually and as Peter was made so great a blessing to the Church of God after his fall so may you be able to follow him in the same spirit and preach the same Jesus to the poor New Zealanders."[61] By 1823, however, Marsden had decided that Kendall should leave the mission, partly on the grounds that he and Butler would never agree.

John Butler was assessed by Henry and Marianne Williams in that year with some acuteness. To Henry, he was "a singular looking man for a divine" but "very friendly," though "on several occasions we observed Mr Butler stifle his feelings and walk away from the committee table but return after a little . . . air." Marianne thought his manner "as kind as it was blunt."[62] Butler and Francis Hall, who both worked between 1819 and 1823, had their own perceptions of Māori life. Hall, who seems to have been an intelligent, gentle, and humane man and teacher, not strong physically but admired by Marsden, like him saw the Māori as "a very superior race"; but equally "very dirty and filthy . . . full of pride, superstition and lasciviousness." He was not the only European to be told by Māori that "they like the flesh of their own countrymen better than white man's flesh because it is not so salt." Hall regarded Marsden as "indefatigable" in trying to do the Māori good: "not one in ten thousand would put up with Mr Marsden's privations,"[63] he wrote, but he himself was "constantly vexed with their vile language, the crewd [sic] mockings and upbraidings of this libidinous people." Under continual provocation from Māori that included an attack on William Puckey's house in 1821, he asked whether the best course might not be to leave in the hope that such drastic action would improve the lot of those who stay. The school did not prosper, and Hongi had told him that he aimed "to fight and not to read," as Hall observed him assembling fifty fighting canoes and two thousand fighting men, armed with "perhaps a thousand muskets," in October 1821. His expression of general stress, in which he was by no means alone, elicited from Marsden an un-

---

60. Francis Hall Journal of 1822, C N/O 49/17.
61. Kemp to Kendall, 1 April 1823, Hocken MS M.1/71.
62. Williams Papers ATL Collections qms 2225-7, 5 August, 24 October; H. Williams to Pratt, 21 November 1823, "overbearing, boisterous, unguarded in his language," C N/O 101; cf. C. Fitzgerald, ed., *Letters from the Bay of Islands: The Story of Marianne Williams* (London: Sutton Publishing, 2004), pp. 56-57.
63. Francis Hall to Pratt, 8 November 1819, C N/O 49/1.

derstanding rejoinder: "I am very sorry to hear that you all are so uncomfortable in your situations. . . . I am not ignorant of the many causes which create your troubles. . . . I do not attach any blame to you nor ever did. If you wish to return to your mother country, I will pay your passage at any time. . . . New Zealand will fall in time. The Lord Jesus must be king amongst the heathen. Your work may be done and therefore you may with credit retire from the field."[64] Hall's journals record his increasing exasperation with Māori life, which led to his withdrawal. At Kemp's workshop, where the Māori were busy making musket balls, they piled "insult upon insult" on the missionaries. He saw Hongi's wife kill prisoners of war, and widows of fallen victors kill others by drowning. The missionaries were offered human flesh to eat as "better than pork" by Hongi himself, and heads of the defeated were displayed "because they know it is disgusting to us"; a girl of ten years of age was shot, wounded, and then killed by Hongi's children, who knocked her on the head with as little care as "the killing of a fowl or a goat." An old chief died and two wives, one being "the most beautiful woman I have ever seen in New Zealand," were shot, both to prevent them from marrying again and to bear him company in the next world. A party of Māori returning from stealing potatoes paused to mock a poor girl of eighteen who was dying of wounds from burning, though Hall had tried to dress her burns: he comments, "what a way to die." His relief at escaping from this environment on 5 December 1822 was very evident.[65]

Butler too observed these casual killings. Slaves, increasingly known as "cookeys" by both Europeans and English-speaking Māoris, were killed and eaten: "the chiefs think more of their dogs than the cookeys. A cookey in N(ew) Z(ealand) is . . . the most wretched and humble being alive." He found that Māori despised small people, cripples and cowards equally. Like Hall, he was offended by lack of cleanliness and the total lack of privacy accorded to the missionaries: "we have hundreds about us all the day and for their natural curiosity they throng the doors so that we are barely able to go out . . . their noise, singing, talking, laughing . . . lice and other filth is exceedingly disagreeable." While working in a clay pit with Māori laborers, "three strong lads," he told them that it was necessary for them to "learn the ways of Englishmen. How they love each other as Christians, how they plow, and sow, and reap, and mow and plant and build; how they clothe themselves, and

---

64. Marsden to Francis Hall (copy) in F. Hall to Pratt, 12 July 1823. F. Hall to Pratt, 26 November 1821 (libidinous); 16 October 1821 (Hongi); 12 July 1823, C N/O 49/1-9.

65. F. Hall Journals, 3 September 1821, 20 December 1821, 22 December 1821, 31 December 1821, 9 January 1822, 26 November 1822, 1 December 1822, C N/O 49/14-18.

wash themselves and keep themselves clean. All which tend to make them comfortable in this life: and by instruction of God's Holy word to (be) happy for ever after death." Puckey's twelve-year-old daughter had made damaging remarks about the chief while playing. This was used as a pretext to raid Puckey's house and the mission's stores of razors, axes, hoes, lamps, and teapots: "these are trying seasons; this is something of a missionary's life among . . . cannibals." Butler managed to redeem a Māori boy who had been given Butler's name by his father but had been enslaved: "I could not endure the thought of any child being a slave who was called after my name." The boy, not surprisingly, called Butler "ka pai, tangata pai," or very good, good man, and at the news of his freedom "the tears of joy stood in his eyes."[66]

The denouement came on Marsden's return in August-September 1823. He had intended to remove Kendall from the mission, having earlier suspended him on the grounds of fornication in June 1822. Kendall had agreed to return to New South Wales when Marsden sailed back in the *Brampton*. Marsden had safely delivered Henry and Marianne Williams with their family and the family of William Fairburn. Once again he had shown, in letters and his journal, his awareness of the pressures of life on the mission: "Mr Butler has toiled hard and suffered much anxiety in his way so has Mr Hall and so have you (Kendall) and for these things you have all merited commendation."[67] He noted in his journal the perils of isolation for the missionaries: "the present missionaries tho' some have erred greatly from the right way, yet all have had their trials and troubles: some allowance must be made for their particular situation their want of Christian society and public ordinances of religion."[68] Nevertheless, he wrote to Butler in 1823, "it is a most profound and disturbing thought that all these alarming evils have originated with the missionaries themselves and not the poor heathens whom they came to instruct. I see danger in your removal and danger in your remaining but the greatest, in my opinion, in the latter."[69] Butler was reported to have been drunk on a visit to a ship, a charge later disputed by other witnesses; but Marsden's first decision to remove Kendall was overtaken by the wreck of the *Brampton* soon after sailing and a change of mind on Kendall's part. This caused Marsden to change tack and to decide to remove Butler, an act of

66. J. Butler Journals, 9 December 1820 (privacy); 12-13 January 1820 (clay pit); 19 August 1820 (cookeys); 11 July 1821 (Puckey's daughter), Hocken MS 58.
67. Marsden to Kendall, 17 January 1822, Hocken MS 71; CMS had recommended Kendall's dismissal to Marsden in 1822 on general grounds; cf. Binney, *Legacy of Guilt*, pp. 88-89.
68. Marsden Journal, Hocken MS 176A, p. 597.
69. Marsden to Butler, 1 November 1823, Hocken MS 58.

doubtful justice, carried through with what Yarwood fairly calls "ruthless" effect.[70] Butler did eventually return to New Zealand for a further and seemingly effective ministry. Kendall, after sailing to Valparaiso and taking on a consulate chaplaincy in 1825, continued to work on the Māori language but drowned off New South Wales in 1832. Marsden had written to Kendall: "were you to ask me my opinion of you as a Christian and as a Man I should say as a Christian you possess many valuable qualifications for a missionary . . . as a Man I should say you were under the dominion of very strong angry passions . . . obstinately following your own opinions . . . regardless of future consequences . . . till you are involved in difficulties out of which you may not easily escape."[71] It is difficult not to agree with this judgment.

---

70. Yarwood, *Samuel Marsden*, p. 244. Affidavits given in favor of Butler against the charge of drunkenness by a seaman and by missionaries in 1823, Hocken MS 58. Cf. Binney, *Legacy of Guilt*, p. 121 and n. 15.

71. Marsden to Kendall, 28 December 1822, Hocken MS 71.

CHAPTER 4

Methodist Beginnings and Destruction at Whangaroa, 1819-1827

Samuel Leigh (1785-1852) was an ordained Methodist minister, originally intended for Canada until the threat of war in North America caused the Methodist authorities to redirect him to New South Wales. There he was active and successful in planting Methodist congregations.[1] He shared Samuel Marsden's evangelicalism and the two became friends. Unlike Marsden, Leigh was never strong physically, and it was toward the renewal of his health that Marsden first suggested a voyage to New Zealand. Leigh was well received in the Bay of Islands in 1819 by the CMS missionaries, and at some stage he must have decided that a Methodist mission to New Zealand should be attempted.[2] Two early glimpses of Leigh's relationship to Māori survive: first, he appears to have been at work in a *kumara* plantation, where a Māori was tending his own crop. The Māori was constructing a small, four-foot-high temple to the *atua,* by which he told Leigh he hoped to fend off the depredations of the caterpillar on his crop. He would put some potatoes into his temple for the *atua.* When Leigh asked about doing the same for his crop, he was told that as he was not a Māori his position was different. Leigh responded: "your temple is nothing good, there is but one God." After trying to convince the man that his practice was "empty and vain," he recorded that "we parted in friendship."[3] The second incident followed the killing of a young slave in 1819 for stealing sweet potatoes. Leigh saw the body laid out on a fire at Rangihoua, to be

---

1. *DNZB,* 1:239.
2. A comprehensive treatment of the early Methodist mission of the years 1819-27 in New Zealand can be found in J. M. R. Owens, *Prophets in the Wilderness: The Wesleyan Mission in New Zealand, 1819-1827* (Auckland: Oxford University Press, 1974).
3. MMS Microfilm 18/1819-25.

roasted and eaten. He exchanged the corpse for an axe, and John King recorded that "Mr Leigh and myself laid him in the grave," a burial "conducted in sight of a great many natives."[4]

As early as 1814, when Leigh was assigned to New South Wales, the MMS minutes showed that the executive at Hatton Gardens wanted a friendly but not subservient relationship with Marsden. Leigh's directions counseled a "friendly visit" to Marsden but the maintenance of independence.[5] From later correspondence it became clear that Marsden really wanted the field kept clear for the CMS in New Zealand. In an early display of the principle of comity in missionary work, he suggested to the Methodist leaders that the CMS should be assigned New Zealand, the LMS the South Sea Islands, and the MMS the Friendly Islands, but they did not agree.[6] Back in Australia, Leigh's health failed again and he was seriously ill, an illness that elicited a letter of sympathy from Thomas Kendall. In it he revealed his own temptations to loss of faith (a sign that Leigh had the confidence of the CMS party). Leigh was touched by the brotherly act when he "was at death's door."[7] A fresh voyage was planned, this time for England, and Leigh duly appeared in person at Hatton Gardens in June 1820 to argue the case for a Methodist mission to New Zealand and offer himself as a volunteer for this service or a mission to the Friendly Islands.[8] The committee greeted his New Zealand proposal with near incredulity; the society was facing a debt of £10,000 and was in no position to incur new expenditure. Leigh, who, despite his physical limitations, could show determination, responded by mounting a campaign in the north of England for support by way of goods in kind, ultimately a fateful decision if eminently successful initially. Goods for New Zealand flooded into headquarters from supporters in Lancashire and Yorkshire in response to Leigh's advocacy, filling the available warehouses; they were faithfully transported.[9]

---

4. John King's Journal, 4 June 1819, Hocken MS 73.

5. MMS Minutes Microfilm 1/193 (21 October 1814); cf. A. H. McLintock, *Crown Colony Government in New Zealand* (Wellington: R. E. Owen, 1958), p. 11, who holds that the significance of the directions to Leigh "cannot be overemphasized" because they brought New Zealand into relationship with London, "where the powerful missionary societies had their headquarters." See A. K. Davidson and P. J. Lineham, eds., *Transplanted Christianity*, 3rd ed. (Palmerston North: Massey University, 1995), pp. 31-33, for a published extract of Leigh's instructions of 17 January 1821.

6. MMS Microfilm 1/373 (Minutes of 23 January 1822).

7. Kendall to Leigh, 8 November 1819, MMS Microfilm 1/179.

8. MMS Microfilm 1/179 Minutes, 28 June 1820.

9. G. G. Findlay and H. W. Holdsworth, *The History of the Wesleyan Methodist Missionary Society*, 5 vols. (London: Epworth Press, 1921-24); 3:171, 172 and n. 1; Leigh's vigor over this campaign should qualify Garrett's judgment that in New Zealand he was "self-pitying,

Leigh's visit coincided with that of Hongi, Waikato, and Thomas Kendall, who were received at Hatton Gardens on 20 September 1820 and presented with gifts of axes and adzes with the "full approbation of the committee."[10] Leigh shared lodgings with Hongi and seemed to have made a friend of him by personal kindness. Hongi was later to assure Leigh of personal safety back in New Zealand: "Mr Leigh, I have grateful recollection of your kindness to me when I was in your country. I will not suffer a hand to touch you — Hongi has said it!"[11] Kendall and the chiefs attended the committee again on 6 December, when Kendall gave an estimate of 1,000 to 1,200 Māori in the area of the Bay of Islands and a grossly exaggerated idea of the total population of Māori in the North Island of millions, when 100,000 would have been a more accurate figure. More perceptively, he outlined the future of mission as among the rising generation, especially children.[12] The upshot was that through Leigh's general persuasion and efforts to raise support he was assigned to New Zealand as "General Superintendent of Missions to New Zealand and the Friendly Islands," while his wife was instructed to gain qualifications in midwifery. They arrived in the Bay of Islands on 22 February 1821[13] and were soon joined by a layman in James Stack.[14] To allay doubts the *Missionary Register* assured its readers that Leigh would begin his work "at such a distance from the Church Missionary Society as not at all to interfere with it."[15] Nathaniel Turner and William White were also assigned to the new mission.[16]

By the time Leigh reached New Zealand, the CMS had established a second station at Kerikeri; it was opened in 1819 and placed under Hongi's patronage. Leigh has left a description of it: "it resembles a neat little early village, with a good schoolhouse lately erected in the centre . . . geese, ducks and turkeys: and in the evening cows returning . . . the Mission families (get) . . . good milk and butter."[17] Relationships between the missionaries remained cordial. William White, like Leigh an ordained Methodist minister, wrote of the "candid affection" of the CMS to their Methodist friends soon

---

impractical and vacillating," when he was a sick man. J. Garrett, *To Live among the Stars: Christian Origins in Oceania* (Suva and Geneva: WCC and Institute of Pacific Studies, University of the South Pacific, 1982, 1985), p. 66.

10. MMS Microfilm 2/211 (Minutes of 20 September 1820).
11. Findlay and Holdsworth, *History,* 3:174.
12. MMS Microfilm 2/233 (Minutes of 6 December 1820).
13. MMS Microfilm 2/266 (Minutes of 14 March 1821).
14. Findlay and Holdsworth, *History,* 3:175.
15. *MR* (1821), p. 80.
16. MMS Microfilm 2/343.
17. *MR* (1821), p. 102.

after his arrival in May 1823.[18] The Leighs dined with Butler and the Halls at Kerikeri, and all expressed themselves sanguine about the prospects for the missions. Leigh reflected back on his first impressions: comparing them to what he now saw, he said "a change had taken place . . . in favour of the missions," and Butler recorded that Hall was "of the same mind." Butler himself agreed that there was "less thieving, insolence" and greater willingness on the part of the chiefs to pursue education for their children. Leigh, in accordance with much Methodist practice in England, attended Holy Communion with the Anglicans, but his friendship with Marsden did not lead him to agree with Marsden's suggestion for a site for the new mission. Instead he sought and obtained assistance from CMS personnel to establish "Wesleydale" at Whangaroa Bay, the site of the *Boyd* massacre of 1809. Butler, William Hall, and James Shepherd helped with finding the best site and building on it. Butler recorded again that Leigh and White had dined with him and Kemp at Kerikeri in "a spirit of love."[19]

The site at Kaeo, Whangaroa, was ostensibly under the protection of two Māori chiefs, Te Puhi and Te Ara, of the Ngati Uru tribe. The second of them had become known as "George" by Europeans. Like Hongi, they saw the mission as a means of attracting European trade. Between 1810 and 1815 there had been a slump in trade in Sydney, exacerbated for New Zealand by the *Boyd* incident in 1809, but ships were returning to the Bay of Islands in the 1820s.[20] The chiefs hoped for visiting ships but these did not materialize, adding to unresolved resentment against Europeans because their father, in the raid on the *Boyd*, had been killed by an accidental gunpowder explosion.[21] The chiefs' relationship with Hongi was also an uncertain factor. Despite these undercurrents, Leigh, James Stack, and Luke Wade, a sailor in sympathy with the mission, settled at Wesleydale, joined by William White, Nathaniel Turner, and John Hobbs, as the Methodist missionary force.

Of these Methodist pioneers, William White was to loom large in New Zealand Methodism.[22] Where Leigh came from Staffordshire, White origi-

---

18. White to MMS, 24 May 1823, MMS Microfilm 18.

19. Butler's Journal, Hocken MS 58, 25 January 1823; 31 March 1823 (Marsden); 19 May 1823 (help rendered); 22-23 May 1823 (second meal); 26, 28 May, 22 June 1823 (Wesleydale); M. B. Gittos, *Mana at Mangungu: A Biography of William White, 1794-1875* (Auckland: St. Alban's Print, 1982), pp. 1-10.

20. J. Binney, in *An Illustrated History of New Zealand, 1820-1920*, ed. J. Binney, J. Bassett, and E. Olsen (London: Allen and Unwin, 1990), pp. 13-14, 18. Professor Binney prefers the spelling Te Aara to the more usual Te Ara for the chief.

21. Marsden's Journal, Hocken MS 176A, p. 79.

22. *DNZB*, 1:589-90; Gittos, *Mana at Mangungu*.

nated in County Durham, where he had been both a carpenter and a lay preacher. He was a man of great energy and drive, but this went with an irritable and irascible temper, which could cause him to strike Māori laborers who displeased him. He and John Hobbs, the "artisan missionary," who came from Thanet in Kent, were, in White's words, "never likely to be comfortable together."[23] White managed to give offense to most of his missionary colleagues of both denominations at some stage, while still being able to charm Marianne Williams's relations in Southwell, when he paid a visit in Jane Austen–like surroundings.[24] In time he was to be accused of contravening his society's strict rules against trading (he became a successful timber trader) with justice and of unproven allegations of sexual irregularity with Māori women.[25] On first arrival, however, he threw himself into the work at Wesleydale, and by early July 1823 had the sickly Leigh housed in a wooden dwelling built under his supervision.[26]

James Stack was a very different man. Like Hobbs, he was an immigrant to New South Wales, where he had worked as a government surveyor. He had admired Leigh's ministry in the colony and sailed to New Zealand on his own initiative to offer his help. He provided a colleague who was well educated, businesslike, in time a good linguist, and described as "small, sensitive, intelligent."[27] Later he was to transfer to the CMS, but at this stage he was treated as a probationary Methodist missionary. Nathaniel Turner, like White an ordained minister, was a firm, loyal, devoted servant of the society, whether in New Zealand or Tonga. He, Leigh, and Stack were all soon able to preach in the language of the Māori, whom Turner referred to as "this noble race of beings"; but he was clear-eyed about the practice of infanticide and found Māori workmen *"Idle, Insolent, Dishonest."*[28] John Hobbs was a gifted man

---

23. White to MMS, 25 February 1831, in Gittos, *Mana at Mangungu*, p. 47.

24. Mary Williams to Marianne Williams, 26 June 1829, AML/MS/91/76 Folder 5; cf. same to same, 30 March 1827 (White's search for a wife).

25. Gittos, *Mana at Mangungu*, p. 16, and in *DNZB*, 1:389, "adultery . . . inconclusive." Garrett judged that White "succumbed to twin temptations" of adultery and moneymaking. Woon (a later Methodist missionary) seems to have regarded White guilty of the sexual charges and himself as "credulous" in the past. Woon Journal ATL Microfilm 244 for 3 January 1837.

26. Gittos, *Mana at Mangungu*, p. 8.

27. Findlay and Holdsworth, *History*, 3:175; T. M. I. Williment, *John Hobbs, 1800-1883: Wesleyan Missionary to the Ngapuhi Tribes of Northern New Zealand* (Wellington: Government Printer, 1985), p. 21.

28. Turner to MMS, 3 July 1823 (idle, etc., emphasis in original); 24 November 1824 (infanticide); they "squeeze the nose as soon as they are born" and kill the girls but never the boys; 1 January 1824 (noble race), MMS Microfilm/18.

with many skills. Son of a Kentish coach builder, he became fluent in the Māori language, was an effective preacher, and was practical with his hands but also a musician and hymnodist. He was critical of White but gave long and distinguished service to the society in both Tonga and New Zealand.[29]

When Marsden arrived at Wesleydale in August 1823, it was creditable that he expressed himself amazed at the progress achieved,[30] insofar as his advice had been disregarded both in London and in the Bay of Islands by the Methodists. He assessed Leigh's condition, who once again was very ill, and decided that his health required removal on the *Brampton* back to the colony; despite sharing in the shipwreck, Leigh did eventually return to Sydney, where he continued to minister for eight years. At Whangaroa, the mission built and dedicated two school chapels in 1824.[31] White and Turner discovered that blankets could serve as a form of barter with the Māori, the one currency desired other than muskets and powder: "blankets are the only articles by which we can purchase pork from the natives," White wrote to London.[32] In a fracas concerning the proposed gift of a dog, White seems to have so incensed Te Puhi that he flung his spear at the missionaries, wounding Turner,[33] one more sign of White's capacity to give offense. He left for New South Wales a few months later, leaving Turner in charge, but this departure turned into a trip to England in search of a wife, typically without reference to anyone in London or New Zealand. Meanwhile, Hobbs's journal showed his awareness that the abundance of material possessions in the station's keeping constituted a danger,[34] not least because Te Ara was sick in 1825 and likely to die, which could lead to a *muru* (stripping). As it turned out, Te Ara, who may have earlier planned *utu* for his father's death on the *Boyd*, left dying instructions to his people to be kind to the missionaries.[35] The danger from Hongi, however, remained.

In 1826 the missionaries recognized that their position was becoming increasingly difficult. They were dispirited by what Turner called "the dreadful depravity of the Māori,"[36] and Stack their "total indifference and deadness to

---

29. Gittos, *Mana at Mangungu*, p. 14, where Hobbs was "young, self-righteous and hyper-critical"; for Hobbs see *DNZB*, 1:195; Williment (as n. 27).
30. Findlay and Holdsworth, *History*, 3:182.
31. Findlay and Holdsworth, *History*, 3:185.
32. White to MMS, 5 January 1825, MMS Microfilm/18.
33. Gittos, *Mana at Mangungu*, pp. 25f., who believes that Turner never forgave White over this incident and his provocation of it.
34. Hobbs Journal, 10 September 1825, MMS Microfilm/18.
35. Gittos, *Mana at Mangungu*, p. 30.
36. Turner (2 October 1826), in Owens, *Prophets in the Wilderness*, p. 64.

spiritual things."[37] Although the two missions drew comfort from a deathbed conversion of Rangi, a CMS adherent, which drew forth comments from Hika, an MMS adherent, which pleased the missionaries,[38] the general mood by the end of the year was one of despair.[39] There were frequent consultations with the CMS personnel from 1825 onward as to the wisdom of continuing at Whangaroa, although Turner and Stack were reluctant to withdraw. Hongi's troops, which had made preliminary threats against the Ngati Uru in July 1825 and October 1826, now appeared in January 1827 to destroy Te Puhi's tribe. In the general assault the mission station was destroyed, and the goods stored in the outhouses were treated as bounty.[40]

Judith Binney noted that the station had accumulated £2,000 worth of goods, dating from the support Samuel Leigh had raised, but had failed in the eyes of the Māori to either attract trade or make the goods available. It was therefore "better to pluck the golden goose";[41] and, although Hongi stood by his promise to Leigh that missionaries' lives would be secure (they were warned to leave the station before it was destroyed), he appeared to be complicit in the plundering, sacking, and destruction during the general attack. A small and dejected party consisting of the Turners (and their five-week-old baby), John Hobbs, Luke Wade, and an English woman visitor and friend left the station in soaking rain for Kerikeri, escorted later in their journey by the friendly chief Patuone, whose appearance had impressed Samuel Marsden, and who later became their patron and protector when the mission was reestablished at Mangungu. Turner, in reporting the disaster to the MMS in London, emphasized their determination to continue.[42]

---

37. Stack, in Owens, *Prophets in the Wilderness*, p. 84.

38. Hobbs to secretaries, 21 March 1826, enclosing his journal of October 1825: Rangi's deathbed conversion had "filled our souls with holy courage," and Hika had commented: "the spirit of God came down from heaven into his heart and changed it and took away the fear of death"; MMS/18.

39. Owens, *Prophets in the Wilderness*, p. 84.

40. Findlay and Holdsworth, *History*, 3:193; for earlier plans to withdraw in 1825, see Turner to secretaries (20 March 1825), where it is the "unanimous opinion of all friends" at Kerikeri that their lives are in danger and they should withdraw; White to MMS in minutes of 5 October 1825, MMS Microfilm/1 and 18.

41. Binney, in *Illustrated History of New Zealand*, p. 17. Owens, *Prophets in the Wilderness*, p. 120, for Māori awareness of a mission "well endowed with goods."

42. Findlay and Holdsworth, *History*, 3:193-94; *MR* (1827), pp. 337-42, for a contemporary account; for Turner's account to MMS (6 June 1827), see Minutes, MMS Microfilm/2/ 423, 424.

CHAPTER 5

CMS in Kerikeri and Paihia, 1823-1830

When Marsden finally sailed for Sydney after the wreck of the *Brampton* in 1823, he left a mission inevitably demoralized by the disgrace of Kendall, the dismissal of Butler, and the departure of Francis Hall, the missionary who had applied some balm to the party's internal dissensions. Kemp at Kerikeri wrote of him: "we are sorry that he is going to leave us, we shall feel his loss very much."[1] As the comparatively sympathetic French observers had judged, the mission of these early years had very little to show for itself and "had produced no harvest."[2] The events at Whangaroa in relation to the Methodist station, up to and including the final debacle of 1827, brought the CMS mission to the very brink of withdrawal in the 1820s. Past and present seemed bleak, and the future extremely uncertain.

Henry Williams's replacement of John Butler as superintendent in 1823 did not immediately turn this tide, but in the long run it was undoubtedly a factor of great importance for the future of the CMS and Christianity in New Zealand. It was reinforced by the arrival of his brother William in 1826.[3] The Williams family, Welsh in origin, had moved to Nottingham, where the father had engaged in the flourishing lace-making industry. At the age of fourteen, Henry had enlisted in the Royal Navy. Although his family came from a Dissenting background, Henry's sister, Lydia, had married an Anglican Evangelical clergyman in E. G. Marsh, who had missionary interests and became an influence on his brother-in-law. During his naval service, Henry is thought to have had a

---

1. Kemp to Pratt, 3 November 1822, Hocken MS 70.
2. See above, chapter 3, note 39.
3. *DNZB*, 1:593-94 (Henry Williams); 1:597-99 (William Williams).

defining religious experience onboard the *Endymion* in the extreme circumstances of a storm allied to the threat of loss of the ship to its American prisoners of war; this experience contributed toward his missionary calling.[4] As a retired naval officer (lieutenant) on half pay, he supplemented his income by working as a drawing master in a Nottinghamshire school and remained a gifted draftsman and talented creator of sketches throughout his life. The Coldham family, with whom he became acquainted, like the Williamses, had sought their fortune in Nottingham from lace, leaving Yorkshire to do so. Both fathers were sufficiently successful as Nottingham burghers to become sheriffs of Nottingham, a recognition of their standing. Marianne Coldham became Henry's wife in 1818. E. G. Marsh saw to it that their thoughts were directed to the mission field by handing Henry a copy of the *Missionary Register* at his wedding reception. The couple offered to the CMS in 1819.[5]

As early as his initial dealings with the CMS, Henry Williams had emphasized that Marianne, too, was a missionary in her own right and did not simply go out as his wife. While assuring the CMS that he would follow their directions "as he did those of his Senior Officer when . . . in His Majesty's service," he added that "with regard to Mrs. Williams, I beg to say that she does not accompany me merely as a wife but as a fellow helper in the work."[6] They proved a remarkable and united missionary couple. Marianne already had to act as her dead mother's substitute for her younger sisters and a blind grandmother in her home, as also in supporting her father in his duties as Lord Mayor at civic functions.[7] By the time of their engagement, Henry's mother had lost her husband, his father; sold their business; and set up a school in the attractive Nottinghamshire minster town of Southwell, of which minster E. G. Marsh became a canon. It was in this school that Jane (née Nelson), future wife of William Williams, and Marianne's companion in mission in New Zealand, was a pupil teacher. William, Henry's younger brother, acquired medical training in Southwell before going to Hertford College, Oxford, for a degree in classics. He married Jane in 1825, a year he spent mostly at the CMS Training College at Islington.

---

4. H. Carleton, *The Life of Henry Williams, Archdeacon of Waimate*, 2 vols. (Auckland: Upton, 1877), 1:14. Carleton was Henry Williams's son-in-law.

5. *DNZB*, 1:593-94; C. Fitzgerald, ed., *Letters from the Bay of Islands: The Story of Marianne Williams* (London: Sutton Publishing, 2004), p. 4.

6. E. Stock, *The History of the Church Missionary Society: Its Environment, Its Men, and Its Work*, 4 vols. (London: CMS, 1899, 1916), 1:214; Fitzgerald, *Letters*, p. 6: this collection of Marianne Williams's letters provides invaluable insights into the CMS mission of the 1820s.

7. Fitzgerald, *Letters*, p. 3.

The combined talents of the Williams brothers and their two intelligent, able, and educated wives were to prove a powerful reinforcement to the CMS in New Zealand. The two men, both ordained, filled the places left by Kendall and Butler, Henry being ordained in 1822 and William in 1824.[8] Samuel Marsden, whom Henry and William first met at Hobart in February 1823, judged Henry to be "a man of superior character and better informed than any who have hitherto been employed in this mission" and hoped he would be able to remedy the evils of the past. Marianne he saw as "a woman of strong faith and sound piety (who) has no idea of fear and on these counts . . . well suited for the present situation," "happy and content at all times."[9] Marianne might later have questioned "at all times," but Marsden's basic assessment was to prove eminently sound.

There was little immediate change on their arrival in 1823; as Harrison Wright wrote: "new policies and new personnel . . . were at first no more effective than earlier missionaries had been."[10] Although Williams's emphases were important (and not less so because they were driven through by the disciplined application of an acknowledged leader), a missionary like Shepherd, as we have seen, had already disowned the heavy stress on "civilizing" from Marsden and had turned his proficiency in the Māori language toward translation of the New Testament, as well as recognizing the importance of ordered and disciplined community life.[11] Nevertheless, once Marsden had settled them in the beautiful surroundings of Paihia, under the friendly patronage of Te Koki, its chief, these were themes Henry Williams reverted to constantly. He wrote to Dandeson Coates in London, asking that the mission be "newly modelled": "it is our opinion that this people will be never civilised nor Christianised by the present mode of proceeding." Language and its mastery were the essential preliminary to effective missionary work: "communication is . . . (by) . . . only one channel . . . the language . . . it will require intensive ap-

---

8. *DNZB*, 1:593-94 (Henry Williams); 1:597-99 (William Williams); Fitzgerald, *Letters*, pp. xiii-xviii, 1-23.

9. *The Letters and Journals of Samuel Marsden, 1765-1838*, ed. J. R. Elder (Dunedin: Coulls, Somerville, Wilkie, 1932), pp. 384-85, 404.

10. H. M. Wright, *New Zealand, 1769-1840: Early Years of Western Contact* (Cambridge: Harvard University Press, 1959), p. 43; R. Fisher, "Henry Williams' Leadership of the CMS Mission in New Zealand," *NZJH* 9, no. 2 (October 1975): 142-53.

11. Shepherd to Pratt, 2 December 1822; cf. above, chapter 3, n. 22; on language and translation, Shepherd Journal, 29 August 1822 (writing a Māori account of creation, the Fall, and redemption); 26 October 1822 (translating Gospel of John); 14 September 1822 (the Māori Temarama "would be happy to live as we do [i.e. in order] . . . but with the different tribes being governed by so many chiefs it would be difficult to induce them to order and regularity"); C N/O 76/100.

plication for a considerable time," and this, not by individuals, but "of the body."[12] Especially after the arrival of his brother, but also before this, extensive blocks of time were set aside for language study (9 A.M. until noon daily)[13] by a general agreement at a mission meeting of 12 July 1826. His brother, with a mind trained to language study, made rapid progress, which Henry noted favorably, while he recognized the value of the younger William Puckey, brought up among Māori and enviably fluent, and the linguistic gifts of Shepherd, and later Hamlin, who acquired skill in the language.[14]

Meanwhile in the 1820s the CMS missionaries continued to have encounters with Māori at the religious level. Hongi had returned from England generally disenchanted and dismissive of the CMS, whose officers in London he felt to have treated him less well than he deserved. He made his displeasure felt in Kerikeri, where CMS missionaries were close at hand. He made no secret that he regarded their religion as unfit for warriors, although he would attend acts of worship from time to time. Shepherd confided his experiences of religious debates to his journal; one Māori had said: "The Grasshoppers and Caterpillars are their gods," and another that "they have no god and knowledge of no other gods than the Gods and the Caterpillars which destroy their food." He found that "they have no ideas of a Supreme Being. Their only knowledge of a God extends to the Worms and insects, destructive . . . of vegetables, which they say are gods because they are destructive. As . . . to a Being which is beneficent . . . they have no knowledge." He shot a bird regarded as sacred, but a Māori lad cooked it regardless of the *tapu*, saying, "I am not afraid to eat the God." The Māori's companion, in Shepherd's view, would have liked to share the cooked bird: "shame only prevented him from taking a share," from which both the strength and the weakness of Māori custom can be discerned in 1822. Another young Māori told him of the sacredness of the *kumara*, inviolate from theft, because a thief "is liable to go to the evil place," a reference to *po*, the underworld, rather than the hell of the missionaries. Cosmogony was a constant source of debate among the missionaries and their interlocutors: "I told them that there was one God who created the earth but they contradicted me by saying the Mawe [*sic*] did. I now told them that they

---

12. H. Williams to Coates, 15 May 1826, C N/O 93.

13. L. M. Rogers, *Te Wiremu: A Biography of Henry Williams* (Christchurch, NZ: Pegasus Press, 1973), p. 68.

14. H. Williams to Coates, 16 October 1826 (William Williams's progress); cf. Fitzgerald, *Letters*, pp. 108-10, and 104, "the study of the language occupies a large portion of time" (William Williams); R. Davis gave evidence of progress in translations of Gen. 1–3; Exod. 20; Matt. 5; John 1; the Lord's Prayer, and hymns: Davis to Coates, 17 September 1827, 3 November 1827, Hocken MS 66.

knew not God, their hearts being dark. They asked me if our hearts are light (enlightened) that we should know who did the Earth create." A sick man told Shepherd that his god "was eating him" and asked if "my God is not a God of wisdom; and if he could make him well." Shepherd replied that sin was the cause of sickness and that "God could heal both body and soul." A Māori whom Shepherd called Temarama, when asked about belief in God, replied that gods "are departed spirits" who return to the earth and converse with the living. When asked who had created the earth, this man said that his countrymen said it was caught like a fish; he added that his forefathers had "come from a distant place," according to the "account handed down to him by them," and that the "reason why they eat men is that some of the first who arrived here were killed and eaten."[15]

These entries over some nine months are an indication of a cultural debate with Māori in the vicinity, carried on by Shepherd, King, and Kemp. King, too, drew the conclusion that the Māori "had no knowledge of a supreme being; nor any idea of sinning against one or of punishment . . . or of any futer [sic] account to give on their present conduct . . . after death."[16] This dissonance with received Christian and evangelical orthodoxy caused him problems: "I find it difficult to give them any idea of Jehovah as all the gods they know of are the departed spirits of their friends or foes. They also believe that these spirits enter into lizards and all kinds of reptiles and insects." King learned Māori mythology from their carving: "at the bottom they were carving Mauwi, in the middle the serpent or lizard and Ina at the top." A Māori man, Warepoaka, interpreted the scene to him: "Mauwi . . . came out of the earth, he also planted the sea, the Ngarara or lizard came down from heaven to wander, idle and walk about this earth, to eat and devour mankind (this is the cause why they eat each other). . . . Ina . . . came down from heaven, to destroy the Ngarara . . . represented at the top of the image . . . of the lizard, ready to strike."[17] Kemp, in talking to chiefs in 1823, found determined opposition in the sphere of ideas: "their religion," they said to him, "was not like ours . . . we had not the same forefathers . . . because we did not eat human creatures as they did . . . there [their] God was not a god of love but he described him to be one of the most reached [wretched] beings that could possibly be. To this we replied that all mankind by nature was falling from God and so corrupted . . . that they had lost the knowledge of God and it was on

15. Shepherd Journal, 28 August 1821 (caterpillars); 4 March 1822 (supreme being); 27, 28 March 1822 (sacred bird, *kumara*); 2 April 1822 (creation); 1 June 1822 (sick man); 14 September 1822 (Temarama); C N/O 76/100.

16. King to Pratt, 9 November 1826, C N/O 55/11.

17. King Journal, 15 May 1823 (Jehovah), 31 July 1825 (carving), Hocken MS 73.

account of this that they did not believe we had one forefather. We tryed to convince them of this in any way that we could think of." The chiefs, however, said that "the natives would not attend to what we said. If we were in England the people might attend to us but they would not."[18] Plainly, getting a hearing for the missionary message continued to be a struggle.

In 1824 two new recruits joined the Kerikeri station in George Clarke, later to be Protector of Aborigines in the colonial period, and Richard Davis, missionary and agriculturalist who was to open up the Waimate as a successful farm. Clarke was to be a firm friend to the Māori, but his first impression was of their "cruel appearance" and fearsome reputation in March 1824. In company with Kemp he was invited to a demonstration of the power of the *atua*, the "whistling" god, by a Māori priest who was attending a sick chief: "if you come over just after sunset you will here [hear] him talking with us." Accompanied by Shepherd and the Puckeys, father and son, they kept this assignation and found slaves and chiefs laid out silently for fear of offending the god. The silence was insisted on for half an hour, at which point the priest began to pray, after which the sound of whistling was heard. They were asked if they had heard it and replied affirmatively. They were told it was the *atua* talking with the priest; and when they had the temerity to suggest that the priest himself had produced the sound, they were told that it was the god whistling at the back of the priest's head, "the absurdity of which we endeavoured to point out to them." At this, Hongi and the priest became very angry, warning that such talk could result in the god Taniwa, the god of water, overwhelming Kerikeri. In this religious confrontation, Hongi left Clarke in no doubt as to his view of missionary religion: "he said that the services of our God were [so] long and tedious that New Zealanders would not attend to them for they do not like that — rising and kneeling and sitting with which our services abound": he "would not approve of interfering with religion" and, although he wanted them to stay rather than leave New Zealand, on the following of religion they must "let them follow theirs without interfering with them." Clarke, to his credit, recognized that Hongi was "a superior character" who "in many things displays much taste," one sign of which was that, when his own daughter died, Hongi did not follow tradition by sacrificing slaves toward the next life, even though a mere three years before as many as fourteen had been sacrificed in similar circumstances. By 1825 Clarke admitted, "I do feel a strong affection for him for his kindness to us. I have never seen a native as friendly to Europeans, so gentle in his manners nor so affectionate to Europeans." Clarke recorded the story of Hongi's visit to Kemp's house, where a red jacket was hanging up that had be-

---

18. Kemp Journal, 21 December 1823, Hocken MS 70.

longed to his warrior son, now dead, the sight of which caused this Napoleon of the battlefield to be overwhelmed with grief. The loss was partly responsible for Hongi telling Clarke, with tears, that his departure on the campaign of December 1825 "should be the last time of his going," a promise to forgo battle not fully honored and leading to his fatal wounding in 1828.[19]

The year of the first Māori baptism in the station, 1825, was as bloody and warlike as ever for Ngapuhi and Hongi. Clarke left a vivid picture of Hongi's blind wife, Turikatuku, exhorting the warriors to acts of ruthless bravery before they left for battle, worthy of a rallying cry before Agincourt. They must "acquit themselves like men," remembering that "their wives and children . . . depended upon their valour and bravery."[20] The general Māori attitude to the mission was well summed up by the Māori who told John King that "white men never leave off praying. . . . New Zealand men never leave off fighting."[21] King recorded the practice of casting lots before going to war. A priest would use sticks to determine the omens: "the Priest cast(s) three small sticks, if the third (one) goes between the two former it is Ka Tika . . . a good omen, if not Kake . . . a bad omen."[22] The major engagement against the Māori leader Murupaenga became a great victory of the Ngapuhi, adding to the thousands slaughtered in the musket wars, who included Hongi's son. At Kerikeri it resulted in the missionaries being confronted with the severed heads of the vanquished. Clarke estimated a hundred of these grisly trophies, which were presented on poles to Hongi, as a kind of comfort for the death of his son: "poor, miserable comforters!" wrote Clarke. "Yet it is the only cordial they have for a departing spirit."[23] The missionaries looked on in horror as prisoners of war arriving in canoes were killed in cold blood, often by widows of the fallen warriors, urged on by Hongi's blind wife with her cry of "Spare not!": to Clarke, she was "implacable."[24] It was small wonder that in such a context the baptism of the dying chief, Rangi, was felt to be so momentous.

In the years that followed, CMS missionaries were to show great scrupulousness in their baptizing. Evidence of this appeared at once. Henry Williams, Charles Davis (a carpenter missionary who had arrived that year), and

19. G. Clarke Sr. Journal, 30 May 1824 (whistling god), 31 May 1824 (mission service), 3 December 1825 (Hongi assessment), Hocken MS 60-2.
20. Clarke Journal, 7 September 1825, Hocken MS 60-2.
21. King Journal, 6 February 1825, Hocken MS 73.
22. King Journal, 27 February 1825, Hocken MS 73.
23. Clarke to parents, 19 September 1825, ATL/MS 0250.
24. Clarke Journal, 8 December 1826 ("Spare not"), 13 December 1826 (implacable), Hocken MS 60-2; F. Hall Journal, 20, 21, 29 December 1821, C N/O 49/14; Kemp to Pratt, 19 January 1822 (cold blood), Hocken MS 70.

William Fairburn, after the careful questioning of the sick old chief, believed they had "satisfactory evidence" of genuine faith in Christ but not without some missionary heart searching. He was persuaded to take another name in addition to Rangi. Without overt reference to Bunyan, this became "Christian." William Puckey Jr., the most fluent in the Māori language, interpreted the baptism service from the *Book of Common Prayer* to the old man. Henry Williams commented: "the encouragement we have received is very considerable. We trust that a breach has been accomplished in the stronghold of the great enemy of souls," and, as we have seen, this encouragement extended to the mission at Wesleydale also.[25]

Almost at once, Henry Williams was hard at work undermining any false assurance held by Rangi's brother, Tioka. He assumed, far too easily for Williams, that he had the same heavenly destination as his brother. "You cannot go there," Williams told him, "except your heart is full of love to Jesus Christ"; and, more starkly, the alternative choice was to go to "the Reinga to dwell in everlasting fire . . . are you willing to go to the Reinga?" to which he replied (who would not? wrote Harrison Wright), "indeed no. I will go where my relation is gone. I will go to heaven."[26] The resort to hellfire preaching was common to both the CMS and their Wesleyan friends, although Earle wrote that it induced laughter and derision from Māori hearers and that a comparatively sympathetic visiting skipper from Salem, New England, regarded it as ineffective.[27] The standard belief in the hereafter for most Māori remained a kind of Valhalla of warriors, as expressed by Hongi to Richard Davis. Hongi had said of battle and potential death that "a man that has a large and loving heart for his friends who have been killed will bid the world farewell and jump from the precipice . . . if (warriors) be killed they will rejoice to go into the other world to be with their departed friends."[28] As this was volunteered at a general discussion between Davis and local chiefs, including Hongi, Rewa, Titore,

---

25. H. Williams to Coates, 10 September 1825, C N/O 93/8; see above, chapter 4, p. 39 and note 38; W. Williams, *Christianity among the New Zealanders* (London: Seeley, Jackson, and Halliday, 1867; rev. ed. 1989), pp. 62-63; Wright, *New Zealand, 1769-1840*; cf. R. Davis Journal, 9 September 1825: "my feelings (after the baptism) were such as I shall not attempt to describe," Hocken MS 66.

26. H. Williams to Bickersteth, 26 December 1825, C N/O 93/8; Wright, *New Zealand, 1769-1840*, p. 151.

27. A. Earle, *Narrative of a Residence in New Zealand* (1832), ed. E. H. McCormick (Oxford: Oxford University Press, 1966), p. 151; J. B. Knights, of Brig "Spy" Journal of 1832-34, Peabody Museum, Salem MS 656/1832 S: *"humility* and *self denial"* more winning than "the horrors and torments of a future state." See below for Earle in Bay of Islands.

28. R. Davis account of discussion with Hongi, Rewa, Titore, and other chiefs, 15 March 1825; R. Davis to Coates, 7 September 1825, Hocken MS 66.

and others, it can be taken as commonly held; at this stage, Valhalla prevailed over Christian heaven and hell as it had done for Norse warriors of the north for centuries. Davis, however, was also confronted with signs of dissatisfaction with traditional ideas: a group of twenty or thirty Māori had come three miles to hear of the "Great God," confessing that their "hearts were dark," and even the great Hongi himself had told Kemp that his people "should believe in that God of whom I had been speaking and . . . leave off their customs." Kemp on this occasion was "much pleased to hear Shunghee speak so favourably of religion."[29] Hongi reflected a certain religious schizophrenia among Māori in the Bay of Islands in the 1820s, with powerful undercurrents that occasionally broke the surface.

The arrival of William and Jane Williams in 1826, accompanied by the lay missionary James Hamlin, gave added impetus to the concentration on language and translation.[30] Henry Williams had already sent for a printing press in September 1825, and William Williams told Edward Bickersteth of the CMS that he was hard at work "at the New Zealand dictionary" while still onboard the *Sir George Osborne*.[31] After arrival at Paihia, he told the CMS that study of Professor Lee's orthography meant that they must disabuse themselves of their current thinking that "any person is fit for New Zealand while those who have received more advantages in education should be sent to the more polished natives of the East. The mind of the New Zealander is if I mistake not by no means inferior to that of the Hindoo and the language equally copious."[32] He wrote in his journal of June 1826 that the mission at Paihia planned two or three days per fortnight for language study, and by May 1827 he was revising a translation of the prologue to Saint John's Gospel with the comment, "there is so much in this language . . . that remains yet to be understood."[33]

A different form of initiative was Henry Williams's design and launch of the cutter *Herald*, intended to make the mission independent of commercial shipping from Sydney.[34] Marianne Williams left a description of the launch

---

29. R. Davis Journal, 10 July 1825, Hocken MS 66; Kemp Journal, 3 September 1825, Hocken MS 70.

30. H. Williams to Coates, 16 October 1826; "his mind has given fresh vigour" to language study and shows "rapid" advance.

31. H. Williams to Coates, 10 September 1825, C N/O 93/8; W. Williams to Bickersteth, 30 September 1825, C N/O 95/1.

32. W. Williams to Coates, 26 October 1826, C N/O 95/6; Fitzgerald, *Letters*, pp. 100-103 (Marianne Williams's description of the arrival).

33. W. Williams Journal, 11 June 1826, 5 May 1827, C N/O 95/177-9.

34. *Letters and Journals of Samuel Marsden*, p. 412; R. Campbell to Coates (from Sydney), 8 May 1826, C N/O 26.

of this vessel. Large numbers of Māori gathered on the beach anticipating rewards of pork and other remuneration for their help in the launch, only to find that "the dog-shores were knocked away (and) the ship glided down the ways into the water, to the utter amazement of the natives."[35] It did Henry Williams's *mana* no harm for Māori to witness the "wonderful genius . . . who only by knocking a wedge could launch such a large canoe."[36] The ship, however, brought Marianne the worst heartache of her life to that point in New Zealand as Henry sailed it away to Australia: "I seem to have been startled out of a dowry of eight years' happiness. And my heart has been assailed with a feeling of desolation it knew not before the depth of and shall not now I am resolved . . . sink under."[37] She and her seafaring husband agreed on a daily "Remembrance Diary," in which each day's absence would be marked by an entry of lines of verse or a message; her own began, "your absence, your long and bitterly felt absence."[38] She was, however, to be much cheered by the arrival of Jane Williams and her husband in the next month, with shared memories of life in Southwell.[39] The sea brought other visitors: the *Lambton* was the first effort of the New Zealand Company, of whom one founding member was J. G. Lambton, later earl of Durham, to bring emigrants from England. Its captain, however, judged the Māori too unfriendly to land his human cargo in safety, but it was a harbinger of things to come.[40]

The "stripping" of the Methodists in early 1827 meant that the year opened in catastrophe for the CMS mission also. False reports of Hongi's death circulated, which would have provided the Māori with every traditional reason for a fresh *muru* of those enjoying his patronage, for example, at Kerikeri. Stripping was a custom that had greatly puzzled William Williams on his arrival, because it was so often visited upon those already experiencing other misfortune; but Māori informants left the missionaries in no doubt that if Hongi died they could expect the worst. Consequently, even at Paihia Henry Williams buried money to the value of £50 in the garden and Marianne packed all their belongings, while at Kerikeri a preliminary evacuation was effected under cover of darkness, remembered by young George Clarke,

---

35. Fitzgerald, *Letters*, pp. 97-98 (letter of 24 January 1826).
36. Fitzgerald, *Letters*, p. 98.
37. Fitzgerald, *Letters*, p. 99; ATL/MS qms 2225-7 (20 February 1826).
38. Marianne Williams, "A Remembrance Diary," AML/MS 95/41.
39. ATL/MS qms 2225-7 (1 July 1826).
40. A. H. McLintock, *Crown Colony Government in New Zealand* (Wellington: R. E. Owen, 1958), p. 16; I. Wards, *The Shadow of the Land: A Study of British Policy and Racial Conflict in New Zealand, 1832-1852* (Wellington: A. R. Shearer for Historical Publications, Department of Internal Affairs, 1968), pp. 4-5.

then aged four, long afterward, as his canoe glided from the station with his mother onboard toward the comparative safety of Paihia; his memory also recalled the bleeding feet of Mrs. Turner, the Methodist minister's wife, on arrival from Whangaroa at Kerikeri after the *muru* there.[41] Hongi was indeed mortally, but not fatally, wounded by a musket ball in January 1827, and it was fortunate for the missionaries that his wound did not prove fatal immediately. For a time their situation was rightly described as a "tinder box" and "combustible," as Hongi's life hung "by a hair." William Williams took his medical skills to the chief, traveling to him by water because it was less dangerous than by land, but any hope that this would turn the wounded man religiously was disappointed: "Hongi's heart is as hard as flint," wrote Henry Williams.[42] At this point the total CMS party facing evacuation numbered fifty-nine and included ten women and thirty-six children.[43]

A visitor in 1827 who was to do much damage to the reputation of the CMS mission at home was the artist Augustus Earle, who left some abiding images of life in the Bay of Islands and published an account of his visit in 1832.[44] Earle, like Samuel Leigh before him, described Kerikeri as a neat English village, with "white smoke rising from chimneys of neat, weatherboard houses," but received, on his account, "a cold invitation to stay" overnight, despite a letter of introduction from John Hobbs of the WMMS. Paihia was no better, characterized by "coldness and inhospitality." He described the mission (inaccurately) as for "the greater part . . . hardy mechanics (not well educated clergymen) . . . a sturdy blacksmith . . . perplexing his own brains as well as those of his auditors with the most improbable and absurd opinions." He revealed his own limitations as an analyst of missionary method by criticizing the use of the Māori language; English should be the language of instruction. He had yet to see a "proselyte." It seems that Earle suffered from guilt by association and was kept at a distance because of his friendships with suspect whaling captains. Captain Brind and Captain Duke were *persona non grata* at Paihia because they were held to be personally involved in the prostitution of young Māori girls. Duke was a friend of Earle's, and Earle retaliated on the missionaries. Charles Darwin, a later visitor to Paihia on the *Beagle,* who was openly admiring of the missionaries' influence in New Zealand, held that it was "impossible to defend Earle," a position reinforced by Earle's modern edi-

---

41. Fitzgerald, *Letters,* p. 131 (William Williams); H. Williams to Coates, 17 January 1827 (*muru* danger); G. Clarke, *Notes on Early Life in New Zealand* (Hobart: J. Walch, 1903), pp. 13-14; Fitzgerald, pp. 128-29.

42. H. Williams Journal, 9, 13, 15, 19, 27 January (combustible), 18 May, C N/O 93/186-7.

43. *Letters and Journals of Samuel Marsden,* p. 445.

44. See n. 27 above.

tor, E. H. McCormick: "I am far less disposed than I was to take on trust Earle's facts and dates and assertions (especially those concerning the Anglican missionaries)." The importance of Earle's book is that he was one of the few Europeans of the time to live with Māori and give an account of precolonial New Zealand that combined something of the idyllic and the cruel sides of life. Through his relationship with Māori he was able to add to knowledge, discovering, for example, that Marion du Fresne's death was prompted by the unwitting breaking of *tapu* over a Māori burial ground, an account given to him by Te Ara ("George").[45]

A more welcome visitor was Samuel Marsden on the fifth of his voyages across the Tasman Sea. This visit, from 14 March to 18 April 1827, was the only one of which he left no journal record. The prospects for the mission were so uncertain that the idea (in part, put up by chiefs who were tired of war) of a Māori missionary settlement at Parramatta was discussed, an idea ultimately vetoed by the colonial authorities in New South Wales.[46] Marsden, greatly respected by the missionaries, found, however, that they did not agree with his views on the education of their children in "the colony," preferring to provide their own schooling for them. Nevertheless, to Marianne Williams Marsden was "a venerable and beloved friend," and William Williams wrote that "his interest for the welfare of New Zealand is not in the least diminished in strength," evidenced by his willingness to return again at "so advanced an age."[47] Even Hongi's blind wife had shown her respect for him by naming a child after him; Marsden was moved to see her at work with a spade, working as hard as any.[48] The first printing of Scriptures in Māori took place in Sydney in August 1827, 400 pamphlets that included Genesis 1–3, Exodus 20 (the Ten Commandments), Matthew 5 (the Sermon on the Mount), the Lord's Prayer, and some hymns.[49] This was the first fruits of the increased attention to language and translation that began in 1823. Henry Williams, cheered by another deathbed conversion of a young Māori man in August, was also cheered by

---

45. Earle, *Narrative*, pp. 73, 74, 86 (blacksmith), 133-34 (English), 157 (proselyte), 25 (Darwin), v-vi (McCormick), 130-31 (du Fresne), and n. 1. E. Markham, *New Zealand or Recollections of It*, ed. E. H. McCormick (Wellington: Alexander Turnbull Library, 1963), p. 46 n.

46. Fitzgerald, *Letters*, pp. 132-33, quoting a letter of William Williams, 28 April 1827.

47. M. Williams, 20 March 1830, ATL qms 2225-7; William Williams Journal, 5 April 1827, C N/O 95/179.

48. DUHO 176B, pp. 242-44.

49. *Letters and Journals of Samuel Marsden*, p. 492; Rogers, *Te Wiremu*, p. 70 n. 25; R. Davis to Coates, 17 September 1827 (from Sydney), Hocken MS 66; cf. 3 November 1827 from Paihia: "translation is going briskly on."

the "general improvement in language" that he thought "very wonderful" and led him to a wider general judgment: "I have never witnessed such interest as has been manifested lately — it is very encouraging."[50]

The long-awaited death of Hongi finally occurred on 5 March 1828. George Clarke wrote of him, "there were many things very interesting in poor Hongi though but a savage . . . a great respect for Europeans . . . on all occasions their friend" who might permit "petty robberies" against them but nothing more serious. He was, however, "desperate and cruel to his enemies . . . an active genius — whatever he was doing in the common cause of the arts it was sufficient he would do it and that in a way that was pleasing" (the reproductions of Hongi's carved self-portrait show the truth of this); but, wrote Clarke, he remained determined in his repudiation of the Christian gospel and was "full of native superstition."[51] Hongi had left dying instructions that missionaries were not to be assaulted. Frederick Maning was told by a chief of the Ngapuhi of Hongi's last charge: "children and friends . . . after I am gone be kind to the missionaries, be kind to the Europeans: welcome them, protect them, and live with them as one people," though he urged them to fight if any tried to dispossess them of their land.[52] True or not, no stripping resulted from his death, and his successor, Rewa, was a friend to the mission. Of him, William Yate, newly arrived as an ordained missionary, wrote: "his conduct, though not so refined and imposing as the great man . . . is certainly very pleasing."[53]

Rewa and Henry Williams joined forces in the important business of peacemaking in the wake of Hongi's death. This activity demanded some courage from Williams, sometimes standing defenseless between two warring parties, when a stray musket shot could have signaled the end. In this case he accompanied Rewa to Waikato in March 1828, and their efforts were crowned with success: some 150 Māori, armed with muskets, engaged in a peacemaking *haka*, sealed with a bloodless charge.[54] Peacemaking among war-weary tribes of the North Island has been identified as one of the factors making for progress in the mission's advance along with the increasing availability of

50. Henry Williams Journal, 11 August 1827, 3 September 1827, 14 September 1827, C N/O 93/187-8.

51. George Clarke, 31 March 1828, ATL/MS 0250.

52. F. E. Maning, *The War in the North of New Zealand* (1862), quoted in Fitzgerald, *Letters*, pp. 139-40.

53. Yate to CMS secretaries, 20 September 1828, C N/O 98/7.

54. Henry Williams Journal, 24 March 1828; Kemp Journal, 24 March 1828 (Williams's success), Hocken MS 70; R. Davis to Coates, 14 November 1827 (Wainui, a remarkable peacemaking Māori with Rewa and Williams), Hocken MS 66.

printed material to feed a growing appetite among Māori for literature and literacy. Henry Williams must have been saddened by the loss of the *Herald* at Hokianga and its plundering in May 1828, but the missionaries sensed change in the final years of the decade.[55]

Shepherd, who had experienced some of the privations and discouragements of the early pioneers and who himself had written in 1822 that "there is no good thing in the New Zealanders. They are altogether depraved," four years later told Bickersteth in London that he was "astonished" at the peace he was experiencing personally: "a very visible change for the better has taken place."[56] King had written in 1824, "for the past year they have been peaceable and quiet and have not robbed us as frequently."[57] Welcome as this was to beleaguered men, it was essentially a change from aggressive behavior rather than anything specifically religious. Social factors also entered in during the late 1820s: Owens pointed to the death of three leading and influential chiefs in Hongi, Muriwai of Hokianga, and Pomare, though he wanted to accept missionary influence too as a factor in changed attitudes.[58] The school at Kerikeri had doubled its numbers by late 1828,[59] a sign of increasing openness among Māori to *mihinare,* as they called the missionary life. A factor often neglected in studies (although not in the admirable research of Lila Hamilton) was the importance of the so-called domestic natives. These were Māori in direct contact with missionary households day in, day out. Kemp wrote in 1827 of "domestic natives (who) . . . read . . . write . . . (study) scriptures in (their) own language."[60] Richard Davis wrote of Taiwhanga, an employee of six months' standing in 1826, whom Hongi had tried to recruit for a fighting party. Taiwhanga was "loath to leave so valiant a man" but told Davis: "before you took me to live at your place I love my country and my customs but now I have a home and a good garden I love your manners and customs better than those of my own tapu and my heart is also very good for your prayers." Davis found this very encouraging but it did not satisfy him: "I wish I could say he

---

55. Henry Williams Journal, 8-13 May 1828, C N/O 93/191.

56. Shepherd to Pratt, 2 December 1822 (depraved); to Bickersteth, 5 November 1827 (change), C N/O 76/3; 76/10.

57. King Journal, 26 October 1824, Hocken MS 73.

58. Owens, in *The Oxford History of New Zealand* (Auckland: Oxford University Press, 1981), pp. 37-38; cf. Wright, *New Zealand, 1769-1840,* p. 43.

59. N. Easdaile, *Missionary and Māori: Kerikeri, 1819-1860* (Lincoln, NZ: Te Waihora Press, 1991), p. 69.

60. Kemp to secretaries, 6 November 1827, Hocken MS 79; L. Hamilton, "Christianity among the Māoris: The Māoris and the Church Missionary Society's Mission, 1814-1868" (Ph.D. diss., University of Otago, 1970).

THE CONVERSION OF THE MĀORI

was a converted man. Oh! This is the endeavour."⁶¹ Davis realized the significance of this community of Māori and wrote, "these poor natives who are living with us . . . their constant attendance on the means of grace. . . . I *do fully believe* (that) the natives who are living with us will be made partakers of divine grace."⁶²

Davis was aware of the strategy among some Moravian missions whereby indigenes were removed from their setting and placed in a Christian context. The idea of withdrawal appealed to Davis.⁶³ His Māori employee, Pita, was regarded by William Williams as a "proper subject for baptism" in 1829; with his wife, he had lived with Davis for four years. Davis was particularly joyous over the wife's conversion, though she was mortally ill. Taiwhanga, though not himself baptized, had written to Davis asking that his children might be.⁶⁴ In early 1830 Marsden was staying in the Kemp household, when a Māori woman, a seven-year employee, astonished both Marsden and Hongi's blind widow by praying extempore in their hearing: the widow cried, "astonishing! astonishing!" The Hamlin household also wrote of "native domestic servants . . . deeply impressed with the importance of eternal things."⁶⁵ Marianne Williams wrote of Pita's baptism, with his wife Meri, a ceremony shared with one of her own servant girls, who had given evidence of her conversion after some personal struggle: "she had thought of nothing else morning, noon and night . . . (has) only just become light within a few days." The girl told Marianne that her husband, named Poto, now prayed every night "from the heart" and not "from the book."⁶⁶ Marianne wrote of this baptism, held in early 1830, that "three of those who have lived longest amongst us and have been candidates for some months past" had been baptized as adults with four Māori children: she wrote, "these are the first we have beheld in full health and in the pride of life," and added, "one can say that my feelings were never so powerfully excited."⁶⁷

These baptisms, more than the dying Christian Rangi, were a sign of a de-

61. Davis to Coates, 27 February 1826, 10 March 1826, Hocken MS 66.
62. Davis to Coates, 3 November 1827, Hocken MS 66 (emphasis in original).
63. *Letters and Journals of Samuel Marsden,* pp. 496-97; Davis to Coates, 23 April 1832; Journal, 19 June 1840, Hocken MS M.166.
64. William Williams Journal, 19 July 1829, C N/O 95/185; R. Davis Journal, 23 June 1829, 25 July 1829, enclosed in Davis to Coates, 28 December 1829, Hocken MS 66.
65. Marsden Journal, 11 April 1830 (Easter Day); Hocken MS 176A, pp. 575-76, 573.
66. Marianne Williams, 16 February 1830, ATL qms 2225-7; cf. Fitzgerald, *Letters,* pp. 176-77.
67. Marianne Williams, 16 February 1830, ATL qms 2225-7. On "domestic natives" and their significance, see Hamilton, "Christianity among the Māoris," especially at pp. 47-51, and on Taiwhanga at pp. 81-92.

veloping Christian contagion emanating from the missionary households, which seem to have conveyed to Māori a desirable way of life. The result was to move beyond social change into something of a religious revolution, when the practices of the *tohungas* would be replaced.

CHAPTER 6

Methodist Mission Reestablished: Hokianga, 1827-1837

As Nathaniel Turner had promised in January 1827, the Methodist mission showed their determination to return to New Zealand later in the same year. Turner himself, however, although well prepared to serve again in New Zealand, was redirected by the New South Wales Methodists to Tonga, where it was judged his presence was needed. James Stack took up the chief Patuone's invitation to explore possibilities at Hokianga for a new station in July 1827, Patuone having befriended the dispossessed missionary party; he was older brother to Waka Nene, who was to have a considerable impact on New Zealand history through his interventions at the time of the treaty of Waitangi. After an earlier attempt in September, Hobbs and Stack finally sailed for Hokianga in the brig *Macquarrie,* commanded by Captain Kent, on 31 October 1827. After a first site had proved vulnerable to flooding, with Patuone's help they fixed on Mangungu, where the mission bought some 850 acres from the chiefs. By January 1828 the first wooden house had been built under Patuone's firm patronage.[1]

Without Turner, Hobbs became the leader, but he and Stack appeared to work well together in mutual appreciation. Hobbs was a gifted linguist, whose Māori hymns of 1825 are still used in traditional Māori Christian worship.[2] His musical abilities were reflected by the possession of a clarinet and an oc-

---

1. M. B. Gittos, *Mana at Mangungu: A Biography of William White, 1794-1875* (Auckland: St. Alban's Print, 1982), p. 36; G. G. Findlay and H. W. Holdsworth, *The History of the Wesleyan Methodist Missionary Society,* 5 vols. (London: Epworth Press, 1921-24), 3:198-200.

2. T. M. I. Williment, *John Hobbs, 1800-1883: Wesleyan Missionary to the Ngapuhi Tribes of Northern New Zealand* (Wellington: Government Printer, 1985), p. x.

tave flute; he also possessed a Greek lexicon and a duck gun.[3] In his life of Hobbs, Williment gives an interesting account of Hobbs's search for language equivalence. After many years spent trying to find a translation of the Christian understanding of sacrifice, he was told, on a trip in 1839 to Oruru, Whangaroa, of a practice of the Taranaki Māori: when besieged or surrounded, they had a custom known as *pita mata*, by which a living dog was fastened to a pole and left hanging to howl himself to death in order to gain favor with the gods. This was known as a "raw sacrifice" and provided Hobbs with an illustrative key, after many circumlocutions, to explain Christ's sacrifice on the cross.[4] By the time Hobbs reached New Zealand he had married Miss Jane Broggref and been ordained in New South Wales. In addition to his gifts as musician and linguist, he proved a pioneering horticulturalist, initiating Māori into the growing of fruit trees.[5] In regard to the CMS mission, which had showed friendship and practical assistance in reestablishing the station at Hokianga in November 1827, Hobbs was clear that "it is exceedingly important that we should all be *Methodists* in principle. Our church brethren are excellent men but they are fully grounded in Calvinism."[6] John Wesley's emphasis on the gospel offered to all was clearly important to him, though in practice there was little to choose between the two missions.

Hobbs and Stack, despite Patuone's support, met Māori resistance, criticism, and rebuff. Ironically, in March 1828, the month Hongi died, they were told that missionaries were of no use unless they brought muskets. Huta Kura, a Māori chief, also told Stack that missionaries who did not fight showed that they belonged to a tribe of old women. Another elderly Māori upbraided him over the rapacity of Europeans, in what may also have been a clash of understandings between the corporate, tribal possession by Māori people and the individualized ownership of the incomers: "before the white people came . . . the phlax grew and no one claimed personal right to it but since . . . the white people . . . these things are becoming valuable (and) everyone is laying claim to them but who has the *legal* right? Who amongst us has a right above another?"[7] The tragic suicide of Patuone's wife after the death of their son prompted Stack

---

3. William White ATL Papers MS 2368 Folder 3: a list of Hobbs's possessions is included.
4. Williment, *John Hobbs*, p. 128.
5. *DNZB*, 1:195; William White had played a part in advancing Hobbs's nuptials when visiting Ramsgate in February 1826 during his own search for a wife; White Journal, Kinder Library, St. John's Auckland, for 13 February 1826.
6. Hobbs Journal, 2 February 1828, MMS Microfilm Reel 18. White was also aware that Yate of the CMS read Romaine and Toplady, Calvinist writers. Cf. White to WMMS secretaries, 30 August 1831 (ref. as Hobbs).
7. Stack Journal, 27 March 1828, MMS Microfilm Reel 18.

to write: "the sin of suicide has lately been more and more frequent." Its frequency raises the question for the historian as to how far this represented a loss of racial confidence when confronted by European incursions, which in Hokianga meant the timber trade, whose solid support for the reestablishing of the mission had been given with undertakings on the control of drinking and the observance of the Sabbath by those so employed.[8]

Stack and Hobbs were also ridiculed for aspects of their message. Stack's teaching of the resurrection and the afterlife had been greeted with levity and disbelief, while an interested hearer, Te Ngau, had been told, "you were once a New Zealander and now you are a white man."[9] "I have preached the doctrine of the resurrection but at this they laughed," Stack wrote.[10] Against these rebuffs they had to take some comfort from the baptism of Hika, a relation of the chiefs Te Ara and Te Puhi, who had been impressed by Christian Rangi's composure in the face of death when in the care of the CMS: "the spirit of God came down from heaven to his heart and changed it and took away the fear of death," he told John Hobbs. He became the first Māori baptized at Mangungu, in 1830, but he died soon afterward.[11]

More alarming to Hobbs than Māori reactions was the news that William White was to return to New Zealand from England to resume leadership of the mission. Hobbs wrote in 1830 to the secretaries in London that he was unable to work with White: "his . . . natural disposition is to me, as it has ever been, quite contrary to my taste and feelings." Hobbs was willing to go anywhere in the world but would attain no "peace of mind" where White was. Turner, past superintendent, was by contrast a "*real* man," whose thoughts "matured before they were acted upon."[12] If White went to Tonga, Hobbs would stay, and Stack with him: "it is disturbing *always* to be under apprehensions of a fit of bad temper."[13] Stack may not have entirely shared Hobbs's view of White, and even Hobbs managed a show of diplomacy when White and his wife Eliza arrived in 1830: "(I) received joyful intelligence that Bro(ther) White had arrived at the Bay of Islands," Stack wrote. "I immediately dispatched a messenger to inform Bro(ther) and Sister Hobbs of the joyful news"; he added on 14 February in his journal, "Bro(ther) and Sister White received by Bro(ther) and Sister Hobbs with great joy." White had arrived in

---

8. Stack Journal, 30 April 1828; Findlay and Holdsworth, *History*, 3:198.
9. Stack Journal, 3 January 1829, MMS Microfilm.
10. Stack Journal, 7 April 1830.
11. Hobbs Journal, 21 March 1826; William White Journal, 17 January 1830; Williment, *John Hobbs*, p. 93; Findlay and Holdsworth, *History*, 3:202.
12. Hobbs Journal, 17 March 1830, 2 September 1830, MMS Microfilm Reel 18.
13. Hobbs Journal, 17 March 1830, 2 September 1830, MMS Microfilm Reel 18.

the middle of a tuberculosis epidemic among the Māori, whose "prevailing notion is that the Atua of the white people is killing them."[14]

Whatever the depth of the initial euphoria, which can be assumed to be genuine, by February 1831 Hobbs and Stack were writing that White had to go. Both were "decidedly of the opinion" of this necessity on account of his *"natural impudence"* and *"great irritability of temper"*; White was judged to be "not fit to labour on a *heathen* station," the logic being that he should "teach at home."[15] White, as might be expected, applied for Hobbs to be sent to Tonga. Hobbs he described as a good man but with a "peculiar propensity to censoriousness" and as guilty as anyone of anger with the Māori (on White's account, Hobbs had to be restrained by his wife on one occasion from shooting at a miscreant).[16] Hobbs and Stack did eventually leave for Tonga, but not before Stack had told the secretaries in London that, confronted by their departure, Patuone had told White that he should go and Hobbs and Stack should stay, adding that White was "no missionary" but a *"tangata tutu"* (an angry man).[17] For good measure Hobbs added, in a letter received at Hatton Gardens on 24 September 1831, that "it is surprising that the committee did not *keep* their *Resolution* of *never sending him out again.*"[18] Before they left for Tonga, they established the first Māori Methodist class meeting in 1831. Hobbs served in Tonga fruitfully from 1832 to 1838, before returning to New Zealand. Stack also returned after a visit to England, during which he joined the CMS mission, with whom he served from 1835 to 1845.

Reinforcement for William White came in the form of another Methodist minister, John Whitely. Like Henry, Marianne, and William Williams, he came from Nottinghamshire. He was ordained in 1832 and arrived in Mangungu in 1833. Whitely was a level-headed, responsible, and diligent missionary, who ultimately gave his life in the service of the mission during the troubles of 1869. White and he were joined in 1834 by William Woon, a Cornish printer who had served in Tonga and became a voluminous diarist in New Zealand, and by another married missionary in James Wallis. In 1835 Whitely felt fluent enough in Māori to open up a new station at Kawhia, Waikato, with the help of a Māori Christian collaborator, Te Awa-i-tara, baptized as William Naylor in 1836.[19] White believed that he had laid claim to the

---

14. Stack Journal, 31 January 1830, 14 February 1830, 5 April 1830, MMS Microfilm.
15. Hobbs and Stack to secretaries, 22 February 1831, MMS Microfilm (emphasis in original).
16. White to secretaries, 27 April 1831.
17. Stack to secretaries, 27 April 1831, Methodist Microfilm Reel 18.
18. Stack to secretaries, 27 April 1831 (emphasis in original).
19. *DNZB*, 1:443.

Waikato area for the WMMS in earlier journeys farther south, a claim disputed by the CMS missionaries, not least Henry Williams, who became exasperated by White and his missionary ambitions: "I view Mr White's as a dangerous character with whom we must not have intercourse"; and again, "Mr White is so strange and uncertain a man that he has withdrawn himself from the esteem of every one of us."[20] In the end, after consultations between the CMS and the WMMS in London, the Methodists generously conceded the area to the CMS, to White's disgust, a reaction supported later by the official historians of the society, who regarded it as a false exercise in comity.[21] Whitely returned to Hokianga but was able to reopen his station at Kawhia in 1839, where he proved successful.[22]

The saga of William White reached a form of closure in 1836, when White resigned from the mission to engage in the timber trade, his involvement in which (in part on behalf of the Māori and their interests) had led to bitter disputes with the Europeans involved, led by Lieutenant Thomas McDonnell, timber dealer and shipbuilder, as is well described by Gittos.[23] His involvement in trade led to the WMMS disconnecting him from the mission finally in 1838, after he had also faced charges of adultery with Māori women, evidence for which remained inconclusive.[24] Woon, initially a loyal supporter of White and his defender, by November 1836 believed the charges to be true.[25] Meanwhile, Nathaniel Turner had resumed leadership of the mission in the same year.

In such a complex account of the relationships within the mission and with the CMS mission, it would be too easy to overlook the much greater significance of the interaction with Māori society. The experience of the CMS mission after 1830 will be handled in the next chapter, but here the advance at Mangungu and its surroundings deserves notice. Gittos rightly saw 1830 as a year of no advance either in conversions or identifiable impact, but the teaching of Hobbs and Stack, and White and Whitely, was largely responsible for

---

20. Henry Williams to Coates, 12 September 1834, 31 August 1834, CMS: C N/O 93.
21. White to secretaries, 5 January 1835, MMS Microfilm; Findlay and Holdsworth, *History*, 3:211.
22. *DNZB*, 1:590.
23. Gittos, *Mana at Mangungu*, pp. 76-92.
24. *DNZB*, 1:589; Gittos, *Mana at Mangungu*, pp. 84-110.
25. Woon Journal, 25 April 1836: "Brother White is admirably qualified to conduct the affairs of the mission." Woon to Jabez Bunting, 14 November 1836: White was "guilty of some charges brought against him." Woon to Bunting, 3 January 1837: White is "a fallen man." MMS Microfilm Reel 19; cf. Gittos, *Mana at Mangungu*, p. 71, for "Woon's abject apology for his previous supposed lack of perception."

the same writer seeing 1833 as the year of "big changes in Māori attitudes."²⁶ White, whatever his failings, has to be given a share of the credit, whatever additional impact was made by disease and the experience of European technical superiority in the area of Hokianga. The availability of reading matter, through the work of the CMS, had a part to play: Hobbs had written from Hokianga that it had become fashionable for young Māori to learn to read, that they were also teaching one another and even translating portions of Scripture.²⁷ The advance was reported on by an independent observer in the Reverend J. Orton, invited by the WMMS to assess the state of the mission. He gave a favorable report of progress in a letter of 19 September 1833: 200 Māori were under instruction at Mangungu, where 150 were worshipers. Māori Christian leaders conducted worship daily at morning and evening prayers. He judged that there were some 3,000 Māori in the vicinity of the mission. He was aware of White's weaknesses, both in attracting "animadversion" from the timber merchants through his trading and through an "undisciplined mind," reflected in lack of time devoted to study and "want of system." Whitely he approved of in terms that hardly do justice to the modern ear: he was a "steady, docile, pious young man." Eliza White taught five days a week in school.²⁸ White had reported at length on the conversion and baptism of a dying chief, Hae-Hae, in 1832, but now baptisms began to multiply and White had forty-eight candidates and twenty-three baptisms in February 1834.²⁹ In July 1834 Woon recorded eighty-one baptisms at a single ceremony with White, Whitely, and himself officiating, a service attended by both Waka Nene and Rewa. Nene had been especially impressed, and by August 1834 both he and another chief "had declared themselves in favour of Xtianity [sic]."³⁰ Woon's journal of 1834 greeted Māori response enthusiastically, comparing it to his experience in Tonga and so to "a rich harvest."³¹ On Christmas Day 1834, 1,000 Māori worshiped at the Mangungu chapel. Woon said Māori responses in worship "have a striking effect and like time in music kept with

---

26. Gittos, *Mana at Mangungu,* pp. 42, 68; M. B. Gittos, *Give Us a Pakeha* (Auckland: Privately published, 1997), p. 5, on 1833 as a hinge year.

27. Hobbs to secretaries, 24 January 1833, from Hokianga MMS Microfilm Reel 19.

28. Orton to secretaries, 19 September 1833, MMS Microfilm Reel 19.

29. For White's somewhat formulaic account of Hae-Hae's deathbed conversion, see *MR* (1833), p. 517; for further baptisms, including a Chief Matangi, see White to secretaries, 4 February 1834, MMS Microfilm, see Reel 19.

30. Woon Journal, 27 July 1834, extract in Woon to secretaries, 30 November 1834, MMS Microfilm Reel 19; Woon Journal, 25 August 1834, ATL/FMS 263.

31. Woon Journal, 25 August 1834, 2 and 7 September 1834, ATL/FMS 263; Woon to secretaries, 31 August 1834, MMS Reel 19.

great exactness.... I have never heard anything like it except the chanting of the choristers in the cathedral of St Paul's at home."[32] Such Māori resonance was and is memorable.

This picture of increasing impact continued in 1835. Woon recorded an occasion in April 1835 when White claimed 1,000 Māori attended an open assembly, though Woon felt he exaggerated. In this event, a Christian Māori known as "Simon Peter" addressed the crowd on the advantages of the Christian religion, supported by two other converts, "Noah" and Ngaro. After these speeches, White himself called on the whole company to "turn to God." Whatever the effect, it was an example of the effectiveness of Māori speaking to Māori in the cause of the mission and appeared to have one identifiable and welcome result: various chiefs pledged themselves (after running to and fro in Māori rhetorical style) to "cease from war." "Simon Peter" then preached to another chief in Woon's hearing, an address that included the approved missionary references to the fall of man, the love of God, and the gift of Christ: on Woon's account, the chief's attention was "riveted." In a private letter to Mr. Briggs, Woon wrote: "there is a general stir among the people... about *karakia* (prayer and worship). I hope some are sincere."[33] Whitely too wrote of "Simon Peter" as a "chief of great eminence... of great renown as an old warrior and cannibal, universally respected by the people here."[34] Woon wrote of three more chiefs being baptized in 1835 and of William Naylor, a baptismal name, another chief of eloquence who gave an address at his baptism and assured Woon of his sincerity by setting aside several wives.[35] Waka Nene, whom Woon perhaps underestimated as a "mean, insignificant looking man but a desperate savage when excited" in June 1835, was baptized by the Methodists, while, as a deliberate symbol of unity, his older brother Patuone sought baptism from the CMS: both had declared for Christianity in November 1834.[36]

By the time Nathaniel Turner returned to the mission, it had seventeen Māori assistants and 500 "scholars."[37] There was truth both in Woon's assessment of White, as a man peculiarly fitted to his task as a missionary, who adapted to the Māori both in knowledge of their language and understanding

---

32. Gittos, *Mana at Mangungu*, p. 75; Woon to secretaries, 3 May 1834, MMS Microfilm Reel 19.
33. Woon to Briggs "Private," 21 April 1835 ("exaggerated"); Woon to secretaries, 14 May 1835 *(karakia)*, MMS Reel 19.
34. Whiteley to Beecham, 4 October 1835, MMS Reel 19.
35. Woon to Beecham, 8 February 1836, MMS Reel 19.
36. Woon Journal, 18 June 1835, ATL/FMS 263; Williment, *John Hobbs*, pp. 124-25.
37. *MR* (1837), pp. 162-63.

of their habits, and in the judgments of the "docile" Whitely of White's "unfitness for the post he now occupies." One sign of this was White's discourtesy to Orton, and another was that Whitely and Wallis were plainly at their wits' end as to how they could still proceed at Mangungu.[38] White's letter of resignation of 3 May 1836 must have brought relief to his colleagues[39] and would have secured Hobbs's return to the mission from Tonga in 1838 when beset by the illness of his wife. Turner, after years of absence, wrote in July 1837 that "Christianity has effected a considerable change amongst them," the occasion being the kind of local argument that some years before would have resulted in a "clamour" for a "brother's blood."[40] *Utu* and *muru* as customs were being reexamined in the light of Christian teaching. Woon too had heard certain "responsible merchants" speaking in "glowing terms" of "much real change."[41] Turner's report of the mission of 1837 recorded the addition of "310 souls" to the mission, a total of 256 baptisms, 620 meeting in class at Manungu, 300 at two other centers of Waingaroa and Waiharakeke, and 2 Māori martyrs, shot and killed when attempting to reach other Māori with the missionary message.[42]

---

38. Woon to secretaries, 2 December 1834, MMS Reel 19; Whitely to Beecham, 3 February 1835, MMS Reel 19.

39. Gittos, *Mana at Mangungu*, p. 89. Turner refused to reopen White's membership to the mission in 1836, returning a letter from White unopened: Turner to White, 8 December 1836, MMS Reel 19.

40. Turner to secretaries, 16 July 1837, MMS Reel 19.

41. Woon to editor of the *Watchman*, 10 May 1836, MMS Reel 19.

42. Turner's Report on 1837 dated 30 September 1837 (written with Whitely), MMS Microfilm: the story of the two martyrs Matiu and Rihimona, shot by Chief Kaitoke (and his subsequent conversion), is told in Findlay and Holdsworth, *History*, 3:212-13.

CHAPTER 7

Change, Scandal, and Expansion, 1830-1838

For New Zealand's future, the 1830s were significant for more than the progress of mission at Hokianga. The missionaries became increasingly anxious over the issue of lawlessness in places where Europeans congregated like Korareka (Russell), and their anxieties were shared by the colonial authorities in New South Wales. One particularly shocking action by a European skipper called Stewart occurred in 1830 when he aided Te Rauparaha, the wily Māori chief based at Kapiti, in a treacherous assault across the Cook Strait, which resulted in the torture and death of the Ngai Tahu chief, his wife, and his daughter who had been lured onboard with Stewart's connivance. It was an outstanding example of the need to bring the rule of law to bear on New Zealand, which was beset also by the activities of a number of escaped convicts from the colony who, with other lawless Europeans, earned the soubriquet "devils" from the Māori, a class of persons they were careful to distinguish from the missionaries, although there were occasions, as in the case of Patuone with William White, when the categories began to overlap.

Lawlessness and some fear of the "tribe of Marion," as the Māori called the French with memories of Marion du Fresne, along with some missionary prompting, resulted in a petition from the chiefs to King William IV for British protection in 1831. Immediately before his journal entry relating to the chiefs' petition,[1] William Williams noted the presence of a French corvette in Sydney harbor in September 1831. In 1833 James Busby arrived as British resident, but he was dependent for both money and troops on Governor Bourke in New South Wales. He was charged with keeping the peace between Māori

---

1. William Williams Journal, 27 September 1831, 4 October 1831, C N/O 95/191.

and Europeans and with counteracting European lawlessness. Busby was well described as a "man-of-war without guns," but he took various initiatives that he hoped would strengthen stability. He designed a flag for New Zealand shipping, which was accepted by both races in 1834, and wrote a declaration of independence, initially supported by thirty-four chiefs and later by a total of fifty-two (including both Patuone and Waka Nene), which made a renewed application for protection from the British Crown, one factor being the expected arrival of the Frenchman Baron de Thierry in Hokianga, who was known to have wider ambitions toward French influence in New Zealand. Associated with the declaration were proposals for a regular assembly at Waitangi in which both races would make laws. Although this failed to materialize, the initiative was a step toward the treaty eventually made at Waitangi in 1840.

The CMS had grown in missionary numbers by 1830. To the original veterans, Kemp and King and William Puckey, with Shepherd, were added, in a second phase, George Clarke, Henry Williams, Richard Davis, William Williams, and James Hamlin. After 1828 another six men were added: Charles Baker; William Fairburn (whose daughter Elizabeth was to marry William Colenso and become a notable missionary in her own right); Alfred Brown, whom G. A. Selwyn was to make an archdeacon along with the Williams brothers; James Preece; Richard Taylor; and William Yate. Baker gave long service from his arrival in 1828 to his retirement in 1865; his initial reaction was of "brightening prospects" and "natives" who "treat us with all possible respect and kindness" in the Bay of Islands. He wrote of order being kept in school and Māori willingness to accept criticism or "plain speaking," which had not been true previously. He saw an "increasing desire in our settlement natives to read the scriptures," and "a great change" between 1830 and 1832; by 1835 he could write that "the day of redemption has dawned upon us," the evidence for which was considerable advance in Paihia where young Māori men were active "in the spiritual and moral welfare of their countrymen," rendering "considerable assistance in visiting the outposts" of the mission. In addition to this Māori-to-Māori lay ministry, which was to prove so potent a form of expansion between 1835 and 1845, in November 1835 he wrote, "many of the poor New Zealanders are moving towards making a surrender of themselves to Christ . . . many who are making a profession of religion . . . love our Lord Jesus Christ in sincerity." Missionaries of both missions were ever on the watch for an outward conformity unmatched by inner commitment.[2] Cer-

2. Baker to secretaries, 14 April 1829, 6 September 1830 (plain speaking), 2 November 1835, C N/O 18/1-9.

tainly Baker's experience here was in sharp contrast to that of Kemp and King in the early days. Fairburn too, a layman and schoolmaster, who had spent some years in New Zealand before joining the mission, also wrote of "much brighter prospects" in 1828 and of "natives" who "are materially altered in their behaviour towards us," even if they confess that "often our hearts are dark and we forget what you have said." Fairburn moved from Paihia to Puriri and found that there many Māori "acknowledge the correctness of the Christian religion but at the same time frankly declare (that) they dare not break through certain of their own customs lest they die through the anger of the Atua." He gave evidence of the physical demands of the missionary life, on one journey "travelling through swamps for hours together soaked through from head to foot and at night to sleep in a wet tent and damp bed . . . the path of duty." Like the Methodist Hobbs in 1833, Fairburn found that reading was keenly pursued at Puriri and had become fashionable; "it seems to have superseded the more favourite game of draughts."[3]

Alfred Brown, who served the CMS in New Zealand for fifty years (1829-79), was impressed by the baptism, soon after his arrival in Paihia, of a Māori warrior who admitted to seizing a wife in battle whose children, by a previous husband, had been killed and eaten by an enemy; no wonder Brown referred to such as "wild, untamed savages," in this case to be regarded as a Christian "trophy." Brown, too, found that Māori Christianity was not formal and outward; before he retired to bed one night he overheard one man praying extempore before sleep, "give me a clean heart, give me the Holy Spirit." Brown's first year was a year of sickness in the Bay of Islands: "the Natives around us are dying fast," he wrote. The issue of peacemaking (and its concomitant of war weariness, identified as a reason for change in Māori life and welcome to the missionary message) arose in 1831 when a chief told him: "we do attend to what you say in making peace with one another but we cannot understand your *karakia*." Rewa, Hongi's successor, however, told Brown and Henry Williams that the god Wiro would not be broken *(wati)* while he and the old chiefs lived, but probably young men and slaves "would become believers"; but a Māori who recounted the myth of Maui fishing up the North Island on a hook "could not help joining in our laugh at his ridiculous superstition." Brown witnessed a Māori ceremony in which a dead body was conveyed by canoe; he decided that the *tapu* seemed to be removable at the will of the chiefs, "sacredness being taken away by the passing of a piece of bread under the thigh and eating it," accompanied by much "mumbling" of words, all very

---

3. Fairburn to Coates, 24 March 1828; to Jowett, 24 June 1834 (custom); to Jowett, 5 May 1835 (Puriri Māori); 23 June 1837 (swamps); 30 April 1838 (draughts); C N/O 39/1-11.

indistinct. Brown was present for the arrival of Busby (5 May 1833) and at a large gathering of Europeans for "divine service," followed by a gathering of chiefs (17 May 1833) to whom a letter from King William was read. Brown was fulfilled in his calling; he wrote in 1833, "I can only add that the happiest period I have known during my pilgrimage on earth has been from the time that I exchanged the society of those who are entwined with the dearest affections of my heart to dwell amongst a race of cannibals who are enveloped in a darkness which 'may be felt.'"[4]

William Yate had traveled out with Richard Taylor, but Taylor had initially remained in New South Wales. Yate's is a special case in missionary history, whether or not through notoriety. For the CMS 1830-36 were years inevitably associated with Yate, whether in giving evidence to the parliamentary commission on aborigines in London; printing the first collections for the mission in Sydney; writing the first missionary book on New Zealand, his *Account of New Zealand* of 1835; or answering potentially criminal charges brought by Bishop Broughton against him in 1836 (more on which below). By 1836 a whole cluster of new recruits had been added to the CMS ranks: Thomas Chapman (arrived 1830); James Stack, previously with the WMMS; Joseph Matthews (1832); John Morgan and John Wilson (1833); William Colenso the Cornish printer (1834); and Robert Maunsell, Irishman, talented linguist and scholar of Trinity College, Dublin (1835). All contributed to the growing impact of the mission as it spread to Puriri (1833), north to Kaitaia (1833), and south and east in the North Island to Tauranga (1835) and stations in Matamata, Rotorua, and Thames (1837) and Waikato. Stack, after years of sterling and isolated service, became mentally unhinged in his exposed and frightening situation among warring tribes in the East Cape and Hicks Bay. Joseph Matthews struck up an influential and long-standing missionary partnership with William Puckey Jr. at Kaitaia, where they worked together for many years, while Puckey himself, born and nurtured in New Zealand and with a familiarity with Māori language unique in the mission, was of invaluable help to William Williams as chief translator of the Māori New Testament, 5,000 copies of which were finally printed by Colenso in December 1837 after extended labor upon it.

4. On war weariness see J. Metge, *The Māori of New Zealand* (London: Routledge and Kegan Paul, 1967; rev. ed. 1976), p. 30, where similar views in the works of Harrison Wright and J. M. R. Owens are adduced: Brown to secretaries, 30 April 1831, may confirm *karakia;* on disease as a factor, Brown to secretaries, 27 November 1830, 30 April 1831; Brown to Coates, 23 March 1830 (cannibalism, extempore prayer); Brown to secretaries, 26 February 1833 (Rewa); 16 September 1833 (canoe, *tapu*); 31 May 1833 (Busby); Brown to Jowett, 16 September 1833 (happiness); C N/O 24/1-18.

Like William Fairburn and Charles Baker, the Reverend Thomas Chapman wrote encouragingly to the CMS on arrival: for this mission "the days of mourning" were over, he wrote, though he admitted that the reception of the message could be "to coldly assent to what you advance" even if "the chain of superstition is certainly broken." By 1837, writing from the Tauranga station, he told the CMS secretaries that "in this district many in every quarter are enquiring after salvation" and added that this was observable as also a "spirit of enquiry amongst young men."[5] Joseph Matthews, who had visited a slave market while coming out via Rio de Janeiro, which he had found in "weekly" operation in 1831, deemed the god of war the prevailing influence among the Māori: "they are a people that delights in war," he wrote. He added, when he reached his northern outpost of Kaitaia, that he regarded the Māori proneness to polygamy, theft, lying, adultery, and suicide as "Egyptian darkness." Nevertheless, by 1836 local Māori had built a chapel seating 800 to which they "poured in" from distances of four, six, and eight miles, willing to make a sixteen-mile round trip for the teaching. Pane, a local chief who in 1833 had refused to forsake polygamy when challenged to do so by the Christian Māori Titore, became a candidate for baptism with his one wife on 21 November 1836 and proceeded to engage in "several evangelistic visits to his tribes." Samuel Marsden, aged seventy-two, visited the Kaitaia mission ("a venerable person") in the same month (April 1837) that a Māori man had been so impressed by the persistence of a slave girl in reciting her catechism and praying when threatened with death that, Matthews wrote, "his *heart* was *touched*. He repented and is now a slave of God," the comparison with the slave status of the girl being deliberate. At Kaitaia, the seven adult baptisms of 1834 grew to sixteen in 1837 and sixty in 1839.[6]

The Reverend John Morgan was equally sanguine to William Jowett when writing from Puriri in 1834: "New Zealand never before saw such a day; the island (meaning the North Island) is now opening before us and it is a duty and privilege to lay ourselves out and ... to go up and possess the good land," even though he was realistic enough to recognize that in the first instance the Māori wanted missionaries "not for the spiritual but the temporal things." In giving an account of his 100 nights in a tent and some 1,500 miles of travel by foot and Māori canoe, often, like Fairburn, wading through swamps and being wet through and through, he bore witness to the physical hardness of his

---

5. Chapman to secretaries, 5 September 1831, 10 July 1837, C N/O 28.
6. Matthews to secretaries, 28 May 1831 (Rio); to Jowett, 8 June 1834 (Wiro); 24 January 1835 (darkness); 6 March 1836 (chapel); 22 November 1836 (Pane); cf. to Coates, 11 April 1833 (polygamy); 7 April 1837 (slave girl); 8 April 1837 (S. Marsden); C N/O 61/1-13. Report on the Kaitaia Mission of 1834, 1837, 1839, C N/O 61/57-111.

life in 1835. He left a graphic account also of the ravaging of his station at Matamata in September 1836, with an eyewitness account of an unwilling observer of a victorious cannibal feast, with the women "collecting wood" to cook their awful repast and the men, with "blood-stained bodies," "hatchet in hand," bringing in and cutting up "the legs, the arms, the trunks . . . to the place selected for cooking," along with the heads "stuck on poles as trophies of victory." He wrote: "I have known 60 bodies cooked in one day," children being fetched from school to join in the feast. Yet with all this horror, to which he added gruesome details of torture on other victims, he saluted the endurance not least of the missionary wives: "I never heard any of the wives of the missionaries regret that they had left their native land, the comfort and quiet of the family circle, to engage as missionaries."[7] J. A. Wilson, at Tepuna, also witnessed Māori cruelty in battle and showed impatience with advocates of the "noble savage": "what the wise of the world extol and philosophers . . . deem noble . . . is all of nature's rudeness, vileness and depravity." Wilson, who had served in the navy before his wife Anne had been largely responsible for his change of life, was in touch through his wife with a social circle including "her relation, Lady Wood," in Yorkshire. Anne was admired by the missionary party both for her Christian conviction and for her beauty of person and manner but was to die an agonizing death from cancer in 1838, after confessing of life in Puriri, "this exile is extremely painful." Wilson's comments on Māori practices were prompted by the sending of pieces of slaughtered enemy chiefs to the victors' allies in other parts of the island.[8]

William Colenso and Robert Maunsell were both to leave a considerable mark on Māori life, Colenso through his expertise as a printer and Maunsell through scholarly work on the Māori Bible. Before the production of the Māori New Testament in 1837, Colenso had printed 2,000 copies of Philippians and Ephesians, followed, one year after his arrival, by 1,000 copies of Luke's Gospel. "I cannot bind them fast enough for the natives." One Māori wrote to him: "Sir . . . for me one gun (meaning a book) to enable me to shoot Hiro (the evil spirit)," about which Colenso commented: "the natives call a

---

7. John Morgan to Jowett, 29 April 1834; 2 October 1835 (tent); to secretaries, 14 September 1836 (Matamata robbery); C N/O 65/1-17; Morgan to George Staples and Thomas Morgan, 1 November 1849, Part 1. C N/O 65/109.

8. J. A. Wilson to secretaries, 29 January 1834; Journal, 9 May 1836, C N/O 97; cf. C. R. Ross, "More Than Wives? A Study of Four Church Missionary Society Wives in Nineteenth Century New Zealand" (Ph.D. diss., University of Auckland, 2003), pp. 12-13; C. R. Ross, *Women with a Mission* (Auckland: Penguin, 2006). Journal of Anne Wilson, ATL Papers MS 5512-09, which includes an account of her death written by Charlotte Brown, Alfred Brown's wife, dated November 1838; cf. R. Taylor Journal, 19 April 1839, AIM/TS vol. II.

Bible or Gospel 'a gun,'" while transliterating the Māori message: "e kara, e pexa — maku te tahi pu hei puphi mo hiro." Māori could see the Bible in the way that Celtic Christians saw the cross, as a powerful, sacred tool against unseen spiritual forces. By 1838 Colenso had bound 5,000 copies of the New Testament, before turning his efforts toward prayer books and hymnals. He himself hankered after a preaching and teaching role: "if God can call for herdsmen, a printer too," he wrote, alluding to the prophet Amos. Colenso was an acute student of Māori life and in later life contributed a frequently quoted article, "On the Māori Race of New Zealand" (1868). As an anthropological observer, he wrote in it, "religion . . . they had none," but he discussed *tapu, karakia*, the *reinga*, and belief in the *atua* (to him a malignant demon) and the various divinities; to die at home was the work of Whiro; at sea, of Tawhiramatea; in war, of Tu. On the Māori language, he specified its complexity, brevity, and yet copiousness, though he found no equivalents in it for hope, gratitude, or charity, and indeed saw ingratitude as a prevailing vice in the race. As we shall see, Colenso also wrote the best contemporary record of the proceedings at Waitangi in 1840.[9]

Robert Maunsell, who had won a prize for Hebrew in his student days, gave early notice of his scholarly intentions by writing from Waimate in June 1836 of his need for a Hebrew concordance, also for a Vulgate version of the Bible. Although unable to make a contribution to the Māori New Testament, he was to make a considerable one to the Māori Bible, and served as one of a team of translators brought together by G. A. Selwyn, which included the Cambridge-trained bishop, the Oxford-trained William Williams, Maunsell from Dublin, and the fluent Māori linguists William Puckey Jr. and James Shepherd, the first born and nurtured among Māori and the second acquiring the language through long residence and innate capacity; both had given much assistance to William Williams on New Testament translation. Maunsell gave one more instance of a "domestic native" becoming a Christian when he baptized a young man who had been a member of William Fairburn's household as what he called "the first fruits of the southern mission," writing by then from Manukau. He showed himself to be one of a number of CMS missionaries who disapproved of the "laxity" of the Methodist missionaries over baptismal discipline and would have assured himself of the reality of this man's profession. He also, however, admired Nathaniel Turner as both an excellent man and as superinten-

---

9. *DNZB*, 1:87-89: Colenso to Coates, 16 March 1835 (2,000 copies); 7 January 1836 (binding, gun); to secretaries, 24 March 1838 (5,000 copies, herdsmen), Hocken MS M.1/63 A. *TPNZI*, 1:339-443; see pp. 374-75, 385.

dent of his mission. On a bleaker note, he wrote to Dandeson Coates on the subject of Māori infanticide: "while war kills in its tens, mothers kill their hundreds."[10]

One attempt to acquire understanding of one aspect of Māori belief was the journey by William Puckey Sr. and others in December 1836 to the extreme northern point of the North Island, North Cape, where Te Reinga was situated. Here the spirits of the departed were understood to descend to the underworld *(po)* by means of a tree known as *aka*, projecting from a rocky promontory, which was believed to act as a kind of ladder to the abode of the departed. Puckey found the place "calculated to inspire the soul with horror" and was not surprised that "the New Zealanders choose such a situation as this for their hell," not strictly their view of *po*. William Williams included some of this account in his later work *Christianity among the New Zealanders*. Puckey gave the remark of an elderly Māori, faced with the alternative eschatology of the missionaries: "it is all very well for you to go to Rangi (the church's heaven) but let us have something to hold on by as we descend, or we shall break our necks on the precipice." He feared that Puckey and others might remove the *aka*. There were, however, other Māori who said, "what of it if the ladder is cut away? It is a thing of lies and the spirits were never there."[11]

The Case of William Yate

Yate had initially been warmly welcomed both as man and as preacher by his fellows.[12] To George Clarke he was "an excellent young man"; to Richard Davis (who later claimed he had never liked Yate) "a brother indeed" and "valuable," though he wished Yate would visit Māori in the villages more than he

---

10. *DNZB*, 1:285-86; Maunsell to Jowett, 4 June 1836 (Hebrew); n.d. March 1838 (baptisms); to secretaries, 26 October 1838 (N. Turner); to Coates and secretaries, 5 March 1838 (infanticide); CMS C N/O 64/1-8.

11. W. Puckey MS, "A Journal of an Expedition to Explore the Reinga," C N/O 72/35; William Williams, *Christianity among the New Zealanders* (1989), pp. 205-8. *The Letters and Journals of Samuel Marsden, 1765-1838*, ed. J. R. Elder (Dunedin: Collins, Somerville, Wilkie, 1932), p. 41 (Puckey's background).

12. For documentation on the case, see *DNZB*, 1:611-12 (J. Binney); cf. J. Binney, "Whatever Happened to Poor Mr Yate? An Exercise in Voyeurism," *NZJH* 9, no. 2 (1975): 111-25, and see also Professor Binney's excellent introduction to the 1970 edition of Yate's *An Account of New Zealand* (London: R. B. Seeley and W. Burnside, 1835; Dublin: Irish University Press, 1970); like Kendall, Yate has inspired a good novel in Annamarie Jagose, *Slow Water* (Wellington: Victoria University Press, 2003).

did. William Williams wrote, "in Mr Yate I am persuaded we shall have a valuable fellow labourer."[13]

Yate came from Bridgnorth in Shropshire. A grocer's apprentice in early life, he can be fairly placed among those for whom missionary service was a route to enhanced social status.[14] He was intelligent, however, trained at the CMS institution in Islington, and was ordained in 1826 for New Zealand, where the missionary community perceived him to have gifts as a preacher. For his part, he was optimistic for the mission when he arrived in 1827, and found forty-eight boys and girls at school in Kerikeri and the schools "going on *well.*" The mission he considered strongly united. By 1829 he was confiding to his journal that "our very enemies are compelled to say that we are making rapid progress in New Zealand."[15] He left evidence of his own catechetical method with the Māori chief Tute, who claimed that "his old heart was gone and that a new one was in its place. Gone where? It is buried. I have cast it away from me. How long has it been gone? . . . Four days. Like what was your old heart? Like a dog — like a deaf man it would not listen . . . nor understand. . . . What is your new heart like? Like yours, it is very good. Where is its goodness? It is altogether good. It tells me . . . to sleep all day on Sunday and not to go to fight. Does it tell you to pray to Jesus Christ? Yes it tells me I must pray to him when the sun rises, when the sun stands in the middle of the heavens and when the sun sets. When did you pray last? This morning. What did you pray for? I said Oh Jesus Christ give me a blanket that I may believe." Yate commented, "I fear your old heart still remains." The exchange illustrates both the "blanket" economy with which the missionaries had tried to replace muskets and the nearly universal Māori understanding of Christianity being bound up with doing nothing on Sunday, deeply inculcated by the missionaries of both missions.[16]

In 1830 Yate went to Sydney, a place he heartily disliked, for the printing of mission materials. He obtained a printing press and, after a visit to Tonga, began to print in New Zealand from translations prepared by William Williams, William Puckey, and himself at Waimate, including a substantial section of Saint Matthew's Gospel. Edward Parry Hongi, a young Māori man, helped Yate

---

13. George Clarke to his father, 4 February 1829, ATL/MS 0250; Davis to Coates, 14 November 1827 (brother); 31 January 1829 (valuable); Hocken MS M.1, 66; William Williams, 12 March 1828, C N/O 95/13.

14. S. Piggin, *Making Evangelical Missionaries, 1789-1856* (Appleford: Sutton Courtenay Press, 1981), pp. 124-34; N. Gunson, *Messengers of Grace: Evangelical Missionaries in the South Seas, 1797-1860* (Melbourne: Oxford University Press, 1978), pp. 153-64, 341-55.

15. Yate to Coates, 9 February 1828 (schools, unity); Journal, 9-10 December 1829; C N/O 98/5, Journal C N/O 98/47.

16. Yate to secretaries, 3 February 1829, C N/O 98/9.

with translation and accompanied him to Sydney in 1833, where some 1,800 pieces of mission printing were produced, including liturgy, hymns, and catechisms.[17] By then he was not the only missionary pressing for a move to the south of the North Island, and he was a pioneer at Puriri in 1833 when he and William Williams conducted a Christmas Day service at the first of the CMS stations in the south. William Williams reported on the positive Māori reception of Yate's printed materials.[18] Yate left for England in 1834, and during the voyage drafted his book *An Account of New Zealand and of the Church Missionary Society's Mission in the Northern Island*. This appeared in 1835 and ran to two editions in the same year, making Yate something of a celebrity, though the book was not well received in New Zealand by the mission, any more than was his evidence to the House of Commons Select Committee on aboriginal peoples of 1836. Of this Henry Williams wrote to Dandeson Coates: "that portion given by Yate is what might have been expected, a tale made up for the most part false and in many parts glaringly," while Coates's own evidence was "very correct and clear." Of the book, George Clarke wrote: "in reading the work we were convinced that there must have been something incorrect in the spirit of the author and irreconcilable with Christian simplicity." Richard Davis hoped that some of it had been written "through ignorance"; to Charles Baker it was a "source of grief" and "misleading to the public"; while for William Wade it was misleading.[19] All these judgments would have been colored by Yate's disgrace.

In February 1836 Yate sailed for New Zealand with his sister. Among the passengers was the missionary Richard Taylor, who had commented favorably on a sermon preached by Yate before departure, and a lawyer called Armistead. During an extended stay in Sydney as a temporary chaplain, Yate was accused of homosexual practices both with Māori young men and, by Taylor and Armistead, with Edward Denison, third mate of the *Prince Regent*, in which they had all sailed. Charges were laid before Bishop Broughton in Sydney. Sodomy was an offense punishable by death, and Broughton inhibited Yate from ministering while the charges were investigated. After agreeing with Yate to

---

17. Yate to secretaries, 16 March 1830 (dislike), 2 January 1833 (printing, E. P. Hongi), 22 March 1833 (1,800 copies).

18. William Williams Journal, 25 December 1833 (Puriri), C N/O 95/198; "the natives generally are much pleased with our new native book which has just arrived from the colony by Mr Yate." C N/O 95/197; Yate to secretaries, "we *must* form settlements to the southward"; "we are too many in the Bay of Islands"; C N/O 98/38.

19. Henry Williams to Coates, 11 January 1838, C N/O 93/66; Clarke to secretaries, 25 October 1836, C N/O 30; R. Davis, 20 August 1836, Hocken MS M.1, 66; Baker to secretaries, 5 September 1836, C N/O 18; Wade to Coates, 7 September 1836, C N/O 91/7; PP (1836) VII (538) 1586-1871 (Yate), 4269-4348 (Coates).

hold a consistory court, when the charges could be answered, Broughton decided that he did not have the constitutional powers necessary. Yate was encouraged to return to England, though on arrival he found that the CMS had disconnected him, probably on the advice of Samuel Marsden, who was convinced of his guilt. In New Zealand, Richard Davis for one was convinced that Yate had indulged in indecent acts with a number of Māori, and George Clarke also believed evidence from Māori to that effect.[20] Dr. Philip Parkinson's researches in New South Wales have confirmed Professor Binney's view that in the strict sense of sodomy Yate was not guilty but that the missionaries' less specific views were accurate enough.[21] In the mission the cataloguing of these practices between a missionary and Māori men induced a sense of horror. Baker experienced "gloom"; Maunsell felt that the mission at Paihia and its successful schools had been "crushed" by that "wretched man Yate"; Ashwell found Yate's very name was subject to evasion as "justly abhorred in New Zealand."[22] For the mission the episode culminated in a day of fasting (19 October 1836) and the shooting of Yate's horse as a final act of dissociation.

Factors for Change

The details of the case of William Yate should not deflect us from careful consideration of the significant factors that made the period 1830-38 so important. From around 1833, in both missions, a growing sense of change was em-

20. Marsden was convinced by J. Polack's investigation with his weight of Māori evidence: see *Letters and Journals of Samuel Marsden*, p. 518 n.: he advised Yate to "quit the colony" by the earliest boat. R. Davis Journal, 4 October 1836, who gleaned that homosexual practice was not unknown to Māori and habitual in Yate, Hocken MS M.1/66; G. Clarke, 25 October 1836, "habitually indulging in impurities too gross to name," C N/O 30. R. Taylor Journal, 10 January 1836: "Mr Yate gave an excellent sermon at St. Dunstan's"; AIM/TS p. 78; cf. entries for 21, 29, 30 April and 12, 15, 30 July 1836 for Taylor and Armistead's part in the case; AIM/TS pp. 117, 120, 128-35.

21. P. Parkinson, "Our Infant State: The Māori Language, the Mission Press, the British Crown and the Māori 1814-1838" (Ph.D. diss., Victoria University, Wellington, 2003), pp. 294-316. Dr. Parkinson records a letter from William Williams to Samuel Marsden held in the New South Wales Colonial Secretaries' correspondence in the State Records Office (4/2357-1, File 37/9199) that used Williams's medical knowledge to specify mutual masturbation and oral sex without the addition of *per anum* sodomy. A Māori deposition by Samuel Kohi also gave a "graphic description" of attempted seduction by Yate (p. 312).

22. Baker to secretaries, 6 September 1837, C N/O 18; Maunsell to Coates, 5 November 1838, C N/O 64; William Williams Journal, 19 October 1836 (fasting), C N/O 95/204; Yate failed to obtain exoneration from the CMS but found employment as a seamen's chaplain in Dover, 1846-77; *DNZB*, 1:611-12.

braced by the Māori. Richard Davis recounted a meeting with the chief Te Morenga in March 1833: "we are wicked, but few people become believers, but I believe the time is coming . . . when we shall all believe." Davis added longingly: "Oh that the language of this . . . savage may be prophetic." In April 1833 he found little parties of Māori on the move who "told [him] that they were hurr(y)ing after the word" on their way to the chapel at Waimate.[23]

One new factor in the period was the growth of literacy and the availability of literature. James Kemp wrote in 1832: "the desire to learn to read is growing more and more among the natives at *large*," and there was "considerable thirst for knowledge, in learning to read and write." In terms of supply, this was the time when William Williams was translating New Testament books such as Acts (1832), Ephesians and Philippians (1835), and 1 Peter (1836). In the same year he was at work on Mark's Gospel (first eleven chapters) in June; Titus, Philemon, James, Hebrews, 1 John, and Genesis in July, September, and October; and Jude and Revelation in November. Yate and Colenso produced printed versions, as already related, and the missionary Benjamin Ashwell, who had arrived in New Zealand in 1835 after service with the CMS in Sierra Leone, could write in 1836 of a chief who had requested eight copies of a translated Gospel for his eight sons, "for they would do them more good than guns."[24] Although the new literacy and book culture among young Māori was welcome to the missionaries, it destabilized the traditional authority of the chiefs, many of whom would be outstripped by the expertise of the rising generation. Nevertheless, Gunson is surely right that throughout the Pacific "there was a kind of magic appeal about the printed book," and that, with any destructive tendencies, there went the positive influence of "the preservation of the language (as) a modifying force."[25] Shepherd expressed the force for change: the wish to read the gospel in their own tongue had become strong enough by 1838 to displace the usual evening entertainment of dances and "obscene songs" at Kerikeri; instead, the time was spent in "reading the scriptures and repeating the catechisms."[26]

If reading was a positive factor for change, disease may have played its part

23. R. Davis Journal, 31 March 1833, 4 November 1832, Hocken MS M.1/70.

24. Kemp to secretaries, 3 January 1832, 4 November 1832, Hocken MS M.1/70. William Williams Journal, 25, 30 June 1832; 19-21 February 1835; 24-26 May; 18 June; 2-5 July; 18 July–19 September 1836; 25-30 September; 2-7, 16-21 October; 4, 20-25 November 1837; C N/O 95/193-206. Ashwell to Jowett, 2 February 1836, C N/O 17/2.

25. Gunson, *Messengers of Grace,* p. 266; P. Adams, *Fatal Necessity: British Intervention in New Zealand, 1830-47* (Auckland: Oxford University Press, 1977), p. 46: "scriptural texts were in demand as religious texts *per se.*"

26. Shepherd to Jowett, 23 March 1838, C N/O 76/35.

in causing Māori to reach out for new sources of supposed psychic resistance to evil. Some Māori, at least, saw epidemics as the work of the European *atua* and concluded that they must fight like with like. Davis spoke of widespread "pulmonary consumption" and voiced fears of Māori extinction. He believed that 50 percent of the Māori with whom he had been in contact had died during the fourteen years of his residence. George Clarke wrote of influenza epidemics in both 1837 and 1838, and Davis's fears of extinction of the race were shared by the trained surgeon Samuel Ford in September 1837. Clarke's "very considerable" epidemic of 1838 had caused Ford to treat 800 cases after dealing with 1,200 cases in the Paihia area in December 1837. Ford wrote: "you may look far and wide . . . and you can scarcely point out a single instance of a New Zealander being free from disease." He found "they are greatly alarmed . . . and attribute these new diseases to our 'Atua or God.'" Nor were the symptoms confined to the Bay of Islands. James Stack had told Ford that the 1838 epidemic was making "great ravages" farther south. It was common in the Pacific that immunity to European disease was absent; populations were often decimated, and in New Zealand a contributory factor for tuberculosis and flu was the replacement of traditional dress by the much prized blankets, often worn wet or damp by Māori susceptible to lung infections.[27]

A sign of a society subject to flux, here as elsewhere in the Pacific, was the emergence of a syncretistic cult, owing something to missionary teaching but also incorporating traditional elements. This was Papahurihia, first known to the missionaries in 1833, inspired by a young *tohunga*, from whom it took its name. Henry Williams wrote that a lizard figure was displayed, to which they gave the name Nakahi. To Davis, Te Atua Wera was "an old god in new dress." Henry Williams found a chief, Warepoaka, who declared his belief in the cult, and he wrote to Coates outlining its tenets. These included observation of the Sabbath on Saturday (members saw themselves as "Jews"), a form of baptism, and some adherence to the Bible: "they pretend to know the scriptures." William Williams met it at Te Puna, where the chief Waikato, bitterly opposed to missionary instruction though courteous to missionaries in person, was a supporter of the "new superstition" and of its teacher, described by Williams as "a very young man."[28]

---

27. Davis to Jowett, 18 November 1834 (pulmonary), Hocken MS M.1/66. Clarke to secretaries, 19 September 1837; to Coates, 30 May 1838, C N/O 30. Ford to Coates, 26 September 1837 (far and wide), 4 June 1838 *(atua)*, 29 August 1838 (ravages); report to CMS, December 1837–June 1838 (1,200 cases), C N/O 41/3, 5, 6, 11; for a moderating view see J. Belich, *Making Peoples: A History of the New Zealanders from Polynesian Settlement to the End of the Nineteenth Century* (London: Allen and Unwin, 1990), pp. 175-78.

28. J. Garrett, *To Live among the Stars: Christian Origins in Oceania* (Suva and Geneva:

There are signs that war weariness was a further factor for change. In his travels in the south of the North Island, Alfred Brown met a chief who told him that a missionary was needed and should bring some Ngapuhi chiefs with him to Waikato, "that they might be friends." This chief, Waharoa, whose motives Brown questioned, was followed in 1834 by a more dependable ally, Werowero, who was very desirous of missionaries not least on the grounds of potential mutual extermination by warfare. Brown saw this as a "severe reproof" to the church in its tardiness to provide a remedy: "we shall continue to destroy each other till missionaries do reside with us" was the plea. The missionaries were cast in the role of peacemakers, as Henry Williams had been in March 1828, observed by Augustus Earle, and now Brown, Fairburn, and Wilson conducted a peacemaking mission to Rotorua in April 1836.[29] George Clarke found the Māori "tired of war" after the loss of fifty fighting men in July 1837, and Kemp found Christian Māori reluctant to join the war parties in March 1838, although, as Shepherd had discovered earlier, great pressure could be brought to bear on the men by appeals to their original dedication ("baptism") to the god of war. Such vows should be honored.[30]

Finally, there was the positive attraction of Christian faith allied to a desire for religious change, shown in the increasing occurrence of Māori acting as purveyors of the new religion to their own race, a factor of importance as the mission moved farther south. On a missionary voyage of 1832, Henry Williams freely admitted Māori proficiency in the leading of prayer: "many of the youths discharge this important duty far better than we can . . . having a greater command of language," "imploring the Divine presence to go with us . . . for the spread of the gospel." William Williams took a Māori Christian with him to Wangai as an additional evangelist and recognized that a Māori like the Christian Ripi had an understanding of custom unmatched by Europeans, resulting in enhanced effectiveness.[31] He took this a stage further by leaving

---

WCC and Institute of Pacific Studies, University of the South Pacific, 1982, 1985), pp. 69-70; R. Davis Journal, 11 July 1833, 3 August 1833, and 7 August 1835 (old god), Hocken MS M.1/66; H. Williams Journal, 10 August 1834, C N/O 93/204; H. Williams to Coates, 17 June 1834 (Sabbath, baptism), C N/O 93/49. See J. Binney, "Papahurihia," in *DNZB*, 1:329-31; William Williams Journal, 14 March 1835 (Waikato), C N/O 95/201.

29. A. Brown Journal, 17 November 1833 (Waharoa), 24 March 1834 (Werowero), C N/O 24/104-5. H. Williams Journal, 17, 22, 24 March 1828, C N/O 93/190; A. Earle, *Narrative of a Residence in New Zealand*, ed. E. H. McCormick (Oxford: Oxford University Press, 1966), p. 148; A. Brown Journal, 17, 18 August 1836, C N/O 24/110.

30. Clarke to secretaries, 29 July 1837, C N/O 30; Kemp to CMS, 23 March 1838, Hocken MS M.1/70; Shepherd to Bickersteth, 7 September 1830, C N/O 76/21.

31. H. Williams Journal, 3 January 1832, C N/O 93/199; W. Williams Journal, 9 January 1830, 5 December 1832 (Ripi), C N/O 95/186, 196.

Christian Māori at stations that he hoped Europeans would occupy in time. At Puriri in 1833, according to Morgan, the missionaries arrived to find that Christian worship had already been initiated by a "domestic native" of Alfred Brown's household in the Bay of Islands, so that a "small party" assembled for daily prayers. Māori youths who had been enslaved by raiding parties and taken back to the Bay of Islands from the east coast were rescued by missionaries and later returned to Tauranga and Waikato, taking Christian impressions with them. The new stations at Waimate (1831); Te Puna (1832); Kaitaia (1833); Puriri (1833); Matamata, Te Papa (Tauranga), and Rotorua (1835); and Thames (Maraetai) (1837) were a sign of spreading influence, often in response to urgent requests from chiefs. William Williams, pressed like others for resident missionaries by local chiefs, judged that they were motivated by more than material advantages: "chiefs have come the distance of 200 miles . . . asking for missionaries . . . persuaded that there is something, a certain indefinable something which the missionary is able to communicate to them." In the same letter he spelled out to the London administrators the new distances involved, of Puriri to Waikato (he estimated 46 miles) and Puriri to Rotorua, which he judged to be 60 miles, with Waiapu 120 miles east; there was need for at least three ordained missionaries to cover the developing mission.[32]

The European population increased from around 150 nonmissionary personnel in 1830 to some 2,000 in 1838.[33] Despite the welcome presence for the missionaries of James Busby, the influence of colonial or imperial Britain was minimal on Māori life, though many Māori knew the colony of New South Wales at first hand and, as we have seen, a few also knew London. Missionaries were undoubtedly wary of the French (it was, after all, only fifteen years after Waterloo, and Napoleon's shadow still loomed), and they welcomed any willingness by the Crown and the colony to shoulder responsibility for law enforcement. Māori would have been aware of European technological superiority and beset by European-inspired diseases, but it would be a mistake to discount the effect of the missionary message, expressed through the often self-sacrificial labors of the missioners; nor to think that the passion for the book, which was real enough, meant that the printed materials were read only for their usefulness as reading primers. Māori were to show repeatedly their

32. J. Morgan to Thomas Morgan and George Staples, 1 November 1849, C N/O 65/109. William Williams to secretaries, 20 February 1834: an important letter in which he estimates the Māori population of the north island at 106,000, of whom 12,000 were in the Bay of Islands area, 6,000 around Hokianga: but to the south and east large concentrations of 18,000 (Waikato), 15,600 (Bay of Plenty to Hicks Bay), and 27,000 (Hicks Bay to Hawkes Bay) — a strong case for reinforcement.

33. Metge, *Māori of New Zealand*, p. 30.

ability to acquire, retain, and deploy scriptural materials in religious debates, a facility that the arrival in 1838 of an alternative form of Christianity through Bishop Pompallier and the Marist missioners was to provoke on numerous occasions. Probably William Williams described better than any the motivation at work in many Māori outside the immediate vicinity of the Bay of Islands: a search under the various pressures of their life for "a certain indefinable something which the missionary is able to communicate to them."

CHAPTER 8

The Marists in New Zealand, 1838-1842

The arrival of Bishop Pompallier and the Marists in 1838 at Hokianga requires some background explanation. In 1816 a French priest, Jean-Claude Colin, had founded the Society of Mary in Lyons as a religious order. At much the same time, the order known later as the Picpus Fathers (the Congregation of the Sacred Heart of Jesus and Mary) was confirmed as a missionary congregation by the pope in 1817 and given responsibility for Catholic mission in Oceania by Propaganda in Rome in 1825. In return for receiving recognition from the pope as an order, the Society of Mary also accepted responsibility for missionary work in Oceania. By agreement with Rome the Marists were to concentrate their efforts in the west, a field that included the islands of Wallis, Futuna, and Tonga as well as the larger field of New Zealand.[1]

Whereas the Anglican CMS and the Methodist WMMS also carried the name of societies, they operated under a different structure. The two Protestant societies were effectively independent bodies with their own executives in Salisbury Square and Hatton Gardens. The CMS sat comparatively loose to their ecclesiastical superiors, though significant denominational figures like Archbishop Howley could influence their decisions. The WMMS was more closely integrated into Methodism and its governance. Colin and the Society of Mary had a measure of independence, but after their approval as a missionary congregation in April 1836 for work in Oceania, they were also re-

---

1. "Marists," in *Oxford Dictionary of the Christian Church*, 3rd ed., pp. 1037-38; John Hosie, S.M., "Colin, Jean-Claude Marie," in *Biographical Dictionary of Christian Missions*, pp. 144-45; R. M. Wiltgen, *The Founding of the Roman Catholic Church in Oceania, 1825-1850* (Canberra: ANU Press, 1979).

sponsible to Propaganda in Rome, the missionary directorate set up in the seventeenth century, whose current head was Cardinal Fransoni, and through him to the pope.

Missionary history was shot through with tension between the religious orders (Jesuits, on whom the Marists modeled their approach, Franciscans, Dominicans, Capuchins, and others) and ecclesiastical authority. Pompallier himself had never taken final vows as a Marist, but he had been closely associated with the order, and he and Colin began in firm and united zeal for the Marist mission. But in a case that had marked resemblances to the Anglican bishop Selwyn's strained relationship with the CMS in the 1840s, after his appointment as bishop of New Zealand in 1841, separate foci of authority led to tension. Colin, as superior general of the order, was looked to as the religious superior of the Marists, both priests and lay brothers or catechists. It was to Colin that they looked for religious counsel and in whom they confided the problems that arose in the field. Pompallier, however, carried the responsibility for the day-to-day running of the mission, toward which he expected ecclesiastical obedience from priests and lay brothers. Their allegiance, however, was as much to their order as to their bishop. Selwyn faced a similar, if different, tension between his wish to determine where missionaries served and the jealously guarded prerogative of the authorities of the CMS on "locations." Whether in orders or societies, dual foci of authority made for irritants, to which the vexed questions of finance and the control of funds were an added component. Sadly, by 1842 Colin had decided to send no more Marists to work with Pompallier.[2]

Bishop Pompallier (1801-71) was a tall, distinguished-looking man, easily perceived by Māori as a *rangatira*, who was also able to earn the respect of Europeans both within and beyond his own religious affiliation. He had served as an officer in the dragoons in the French army of the post-Napoleonic period and may have worked also in a silk firm in Lyons before ordination in 1829. As a missionary leader he showed something of the courage and dash of a cavalry officer, if also a streak of imprudence that could accompany these virtues. His association with the Marists comprised seven years spent in the archdiocese of Lyons. After Colin accepted responsibility in the Pacific, he

---

2. K. J. Roach, "Venerable Jean-Claude Colin and the Mission in New Zealand 1838-1848" (Louvain diss., Pontifical Gregorian University, Rome, 1963), and "J-C Colin and the Foundation of the New Zealand Catholic Mission," *NZJH* 3, no. 1 (April 1969): 74-83. For Selwyn and the CMS, see T. E. Yates, *Venn and Victorian Bishops Abroad* (Uppsala and London: Swedish Institute of Missionary Research and SPCK, 1978), pp. 51-62; on Pompallier, see L. Keys, *The Life and Times of Bishop Pompallier* (Christchurch, NZ: Pegasus Press, 1957); E. R. Simmons, *Pompallier, Prince of Bishops* (Auckland: CPC Publishing, 1984).

chose Pompallier as his bishop. Pompallier regarded himself as a Marist in all but name, but, as he had never professed, he owed obedience strictly only to the pope, whereas had he been a "religious," it would also have been owed to Colin as superior. Colin offered to surrender his own authority over the missionaries to Pompallier, but it appears that at this stage Pompallier saw strengths in the dual system. Even so, it seems that Colin encouraged the Marists to regard Pompallier as both their religious and ecclesiastical superior; Colin's part was to supply the mission with workers in the field. Toward this role Colin accepted provicariate status from the Propaganda in a letter to Cardinal Fransoni of 25 May 1837.[3]

Pompallier sailed for Oceania via Le Havre and Valparaiso with four priests and three lay brothers. Of these, Pierre Chanel (1803-41) became a Marist martyr on the island of Futuna; Pierre Bataillon was placed on Wallis (Uvea), where his mission proved successful; one priest died on the voyage; and Pompallier arrived with L. C. Servant at Hokianga on 10 January 1838. Later in the same year a further party of three priests, Frs. Baty, Épalle, and Petit, with three lay catechists, sailed as reinforcements. Pompallier established himself in Russell (Kororareka), the main mission center, in July 1839, leaving Servant at Hokianga.[4]

Servant showed himself to be an acute observer of Māori life in the comparatively short time he spent in New Zealand; he moved to Futuna to replace the martyred Chanel in 1842. His work *Customs and Habits of the New Zealanders* is still regarded as one of the most authoritative accounts of Māori life of his region at that time. Despite minor inaccuracies, such as his belief that Māori used bows and arrows (introduced later by Europeans), the book provided a detailed portrait of Māori life, with the correct terms for their clothing, homes, diet, rights of ownership, planting, fishing, tattooing, dancing, and singing. He balanced his picture of their goodness, humility, and gentleness with a frank admission of their cannibalism: "there is no dish considered more delicious for these tigers than eating human flesh," and he recognized that "an insult is never forgotten." He understood Māori birth, marriage, and burial ceremonies, the deposition of the corpse in the *atamira* (cemetery), the dismissal to *po,* and the eventual *hahunga,* as well as aspects of Māori life such as the oracles, prayers, and healings practiced by the *tohunga*. The treatment of the sick obviously appalled him, and it was indeed a point of sharp contrast with Christian practice: "the sick person must simply

---

3. Roach, "Venerable Jean-Claude Colin," pp. 4-31.
4. Keys, *Pompallier*, pp. 89-113; Simmons, *Pompallier*, pp. 25-34; "Chanel" and "Bataillon," in *Biographical Dictionary of Christian Missions*, pp. 47-48, 125.

await death; he is pitilessly abandoned and deprived of any kind of food," a practice that Marsden encountered at Ruatara in 1814 and we see was still prevalent thirty years later. He knew the Māori respect for dreams, the practice and fear of sorcery *(makutu)*; and he gave an account of the "departmental" gods of Wiro, Taniwa, and Tawaki, and of the myth of Maui, Taki, and Hina in relation to origins. He knew of Te Reinga and judged that "there is no doubt whatsoever about belief in a future life amongst the natives." Insults, he wrote, produced bursts of anger "like the explosion of a volcano," but the violence in anger was matched, as he saw it, by the ardor and affection a person expresses "for those he loves." Servant left to posterity a well-grounded, empirical account of Māori life as he experienced it; and, against the prevailing tendency of outright dismissal on both sides of the missionary divide, he was willing to make use of William Yate's *Account of New Zealand* of 1835.[5]

In his correspondence to France, Servant described other aspects of life. Tobacco smoking was nearly universal among Māori, and tobacco became a form of currency.[6] Māori courtesy was to touch the hand and "sometimes to rub nose to nose." In contrast with Protestant missions, "a beautiful statue of the Virgin" was displayed, a reminder of the Society's patron and an icon that "greatly attracted the New Zealanders." They were also greatly attracted by the chanting of traditional Catholic pieces like the Miserere; they enjoyed chanting. He recorded fifteen baptisms, among them a chief of Hokianga, and twelve weddings, and found that "a great number of chiefs" were "very favourable to the catholic religion" in 1838.[7] He told Colin that another chief insisted on living alongside Pompallier's residence, urged the Catholic religion on his friends, and assisted at mass. Māori had gravity and vigor but also "terrible ferocity towards enemies and slaves." They were offering to build a Catholic chapel.[8] One chief had shown what was expected of a missionary when he said: "true missionary, we are evil, speak, speak for peace"; peace was achieved on this occasion following an insult, if with difficulty. He told Colin that the Māori were "avid" for the word of God and that to meet demand

---

5. L. C. Servant, *Customs and Habits of the New Zealanders*, trans. J. Glasgow with foreword by E. R. Simmons (Wellington: Reed, 1973), especially pp. 4, 6, 16, 19, 41-48.

6. Servant to parents, 22 May 1838. I am indebted to Fr. Charles Girard for the gift of his multivolume collection of Marist correspondence, *Lettres reçues d'Océanie par l'administration generale des pères maristes pendant le generalat de Jean-Claude Colin* (Rome: Centre d'études maristes, 1999), referred to here as CG with volume and page. Servant's letter is CG/I/pp. 153-56.

7. Servant to du Treuil, 22 May 1838, CG/I/pp. 166-68.

8. Servant to Colin, 14 August 1839, CG/I/pp. 225-28.

Pompallier had commissioned him to transcribe pages of instruction and prayers. There was urgent demand for more priests.[9]

To his friend Terraillon he described aspects of the Māori culture, their lack of musical instruments except for a "miserable flute," which was compensated by their modulated, softly sung, poetic chanting of traditional songs, monotonous to the European ear but full of charm to themselves because it expressed their affection for parents, friends, and tribe. They told stories with vivid expression of emotion, striking their thighs in an animated manner and incorporating the impersonation and mimicry of characters in the narrative. He dwelt on the authority of the great chiefs, who possessed rights of life and death over slaves or over adulterous wives and their paramours. Such chiefs were greeted with extreme courtesy: "Haere mai, Haere mai." He described a *haka* and the gender distinctions of tattooing, women having only slight tattoos on upper and lower lips. They were happy people but more reflective and serious than some others in the tropics. They had their amusements, of which war dances were a favorite, but they could display affecting emotion in the face of death, with their "very melancholy chanting" to accompany a bier ornamented with carved figures "made with great regularity."[10]

Two further letters to Colin raised the perennial issue of Protestant "heretics," as virulently hostile from one side as the other. In debate he used an illustration that occurred frequently in such affairs: the true tree was Roman Catholic religion and church, of which the Anglicans and Wesleyans were less than satisfactory offshoots or decayed branches. The contrast of approach, particularly in relation to objects of devotion (seen as idolatry by his opponents), was seen here as he commended the use of tableaux, medals, and visual reminders of the saints, which he felt to be equivalent to carvings of the ancestors killed in battle in the Māori *pa*s and which he found appealed not least to Māori women. His fellow missionary, Fr. Garin, left an unforgettable picture of Servant, ascetic and bookish, in debate with the robust Henry Williams: "Father Servant, thin, tall, dry, emaciated and pale as a sheet seemed a runt alongside the large and fresh-faced Williams . . . a prosperous looking, well-fed father of ten children." Servant was honored to accompany Pompallier to the treaty negotiations at Waitangi, at which he observed the eloquence of the Māori participants, while emphasizing the apolitical nature of the mission whose preoccupation was the *royaume* of Jesus Christ. By 1840, however, he was also aware with his fellow missionaries of Pompallier's failings as a leader: his lack of business sense, his prodigality toward the Māori when his

---

9. Servant to Colin, 15 October 1839, CG/I/pp. 297-301.
10. Servant to Terraillon, 15 October 1839, CG/I/pp. 302-5.

own priests were short of basic provisions to live on, and his occasional acts of high-handed authority that caused Servant, after consultation with Baty, Petit, and Épalle, to air his criticisms to Colin. It was by no means the last letter of its kind to reach Colin from the Marist group, a practice Pompallier tried to control by ensuring that no sealed letters went to France from the missionaries without his oversight, not least also to obviate unauthorized excerpts appearing in Propaganda's *Annales* and its accounts of missionary work.[11]

By May 1840, soon after this letter was written to Colin, Pompallier had been able to spread the mission from Hokianga, where Baty and Comte were stationed, to Whangaroa (Frs. Épalle and Petit-Jean) and Tauranga, where he had placed the future bishop Philippe Viard and Kaipara (Fr. Petit), with himself and Servant still in the Bay of Islands. The French settlement of Akaroa was a special case. Prior to the Treaty of Waitangi, French hopes of laying claim to the South Island of New Zealand, cherished, among others, by Napoleon's onetime marshal, Soult, now French Minister of Marine, had meant that there was a French naval presence under the command of an officer called Lavaud, who had attempted to direct the missionaries, leading to one major confrontation with Comte. Ultimately, somewhat disgusted with the lack of support from the resident French community, Pompallier withdrew the Marists from Akaroa, and after Waitangi, French hopes were dashed by Governor Hobson successfully laying claim to the South Island. In this letter explaining his dispositions, Pompallier made exaggerated claims that some forty tribes now gave allegiance to the Catholic faith and that instead of seven priests he needed fifty priests for New Zealand. By then his facility for language, both English and Māori, had led to a Māori catechism entitled *Ho nga pono nui oti haki katorika romana;* as no printing press had yet arrived from France, he asked Colin to produce 1,000 copies. Before long he asked for two printing presses, one for each island, a sign that, like the Protestants, he was aware of the Māori appetite for literature, toward which he prepared a Māori grammar and a Māori-Latin dictionary for use by the Propaganda. He himself was known as "Epicopo" by the Māori, and Roman Catholic Māori were *pikopo,* as earlier Christians had been known as *mihinare.*[12]

---

11. Servant to Colin, 5 March 1840, CG/I/pp. 344-45 (debate), 349 (medals), 354 (Waitangi); A. M. Garin's description as rendered by E. R. Simmons in *DNZB*, 1:390; Servant to Colin, 26 April 1840, CG/I/pp. 368-71.

12. Pompallier to Colin, 14 August 1839 (catechisms), CG/I/pp. 223-45; Pompallier to Colin, 18 August 1839 (presses), CG/I/pp. 245-53; Viard to Noailly, 6 January 1840, where a chief with a sick daughter instructs "go find Epicopo," CG/I/pp. 320-21 (translation from the French throughout is by the author).

Whatever his faults, Pompallier was able to win the respect of both Māori and English settlers. As his Marist priests pointed out, winning the respect of the latter was no mean feat in a colony that was English in government and Protestant in religion. He managed to allay suspicion of himself and his party as French subversives. More than once the confidence he inspired in the financial houses of New Zealand rescued the mission from total insolvency, threatened as it was by the failure of a bank in London (Wright's) and delay in European funding; the mission was kept afloat by English Protestant bankers.[13]

By 1839 Pompallier had plans for a college, a church, and a Catholic cemetery that involved land purchase and building; he wanted also to purchase a vessel to help him visit the islands of Wallis and Futuna where Chanel and Bataillon were working, respectively. He saw the need for printing presses and asked his benefactors to supply one for each island. It was to be a continual cry from the Māori, not least Protestant Māori to Catholic Māori: "Where are your books?" The concentration of the CMS and WMMS on the supply of Bibles and other printed religious literature, combined with the Māori appetite for the written word, had made this a test of seriousness in missionary endeavor for Māori.[14] The bishop's claims in May 1840 of widespread Māori response to the Catholic faith were, however, extravagant. He told Colin that there were now 25,000 to 27,000 Māori Catholics and that he needed fifty priests, not his current seven, for his mission. Pompallier and Servant had attended the treaty negotiations at Waitangi, on which the former reported in a letter to Colin of 14 May 1840, in which he emphasized his political neutrality: salvation was his concern, not who signed the treaty or did not. He welcomed the new governor's religious inclusivism, however hard Henry Williams had found this to swallow in drafting the treaty according to Hobson's directions: "God be blessed, the new English authorities appear impartial."[15] On the same date, however, Maitrepierre was making a digest of documents from the mission in Oceania for Colin as superior that showed deep unease. The mission was difficult and extravagant, and in Pompallier had a vicar apostolic who in-

---

13. Garin to Colin, 30 November 1842 (French Catholic clergy, English Protestant colony), CG/II/p. 532; Roach, "Venerable Jean-Claude Colin," pp. 115-16 (Wright's bank); Pompallier to Lyon Propaganda Association, 6 November 1842 (Protestant bankers), CG/II/pp. 464-65.

14. Pompallier to Colin, 14 August 1839, 18 August 1839, CG/I/pp. 233-53; Perret to Colin, 19 August 1842 (demand for books), CG/II/pp. 336-37.

15. Pompallier to Colin, 14 May 1840 (two letters), CG/I/pp. 385-416: for numbers p. 388; stations p. 391; Hobson pp. 398, 399; Waitangi negotiations p. 400; the next chapter gives a fuller treatment of Waitangi.

creasingly regarded the religious society as an obstacle to the dependency and obedience of his priests, who in turn were losing confidence in their bishop. The memorandum was already proposing measures to meet this crisis: a provincial visitor should be appointed by the order to meet the needs of the priests, and both prudence and fresh administrative direction were needed; the "actual state of the mission" demanded an injection of moral strength "accompanied by prudence."[16]

The purchase of a vessel of 120 tons for 25,000 francs, whose crew cost an additional 1,250 francs per month to retain, held by Pompallier to be "indispensable" to both Colin and Propaganda, did nothing to allay fears in Lyons. Relationships in the missionary body were soured by Pompallier insisting that the priests and the lay brothers eat separately, a source of humiliation to the latter according to disapproving priests.[17] The priests themselves were inadequately housed, short of food, and often hungry, while Pompallier continued to be prodigally generous to Māori in gifts. At Akaroa, Fr. Tripe (who eventually became sufficiently disenchanted to leave the mission) realized that the bishop greatly exaggerated when he claimed 35,000 Māori for the Catholic faith; by contrast, Tripe knew of 300 baptisms.[18] Comte, who was with Tripe in Akaroa, realized that Pompallier had damaged relations with Tripe by discouraging comments, but wrote that, despite the bishop's great zeal "for the salvation of souls," when confronted by advice or criticism, he took refuge in the "inexperience" of other missionaries,[19] a charge Pompallier did repeat in letters to Colin when he urged the superior not to encourage insubordination from inexperienced young priests, who owed their bishop the obedience that the captain of the ship might expect. His actual vessel was the cause of great anxiety to him without funding, as he was paying interest of 10 percent on the principal and faced expropriation if nothing was paid to the bank in Kororareka by 1 June. He complained also that in defiance of his earlier instructions, sealed letters were still going to Europe.[20] Colin, on his side, was given cause for anxiety by Fr. Baty, who wrote of isolation at Te Auroa. By then, Pompallier had eleven stations to staff, but Colin and the Congregation were firmly of the opinion that priests should not work alone, which the bishop himself had recognized early in the

16. Maitrepierre digest for Colin of Pompallier documents, 14 May 1840, CG/I/pp. 425f.
17. Pompallier to Colin, 30 July 1840 (vessel purchase), CG/I/p. 452; Pezant to Colin, 4 September 1840, CG/I/p. 486 and n. 4; cf. Garin to Colin, 22 September 1841, CG/I/pp. 746-47.
18. Tripe to Colin, 30 March 1841, CG/I/pp. 566-71; p. 570 for numbers.
19. Comte to Colin, 25 April 1841, CG/I/pp. 573-76.
20. Pompallier to Colin, 17 May 1841, CG/I/pp. 583-603; cf. p. 591 (inexperience).

mission by refusing to leave Servant, although anxious to visit Chanel and Bataillon in the islands.²¹

The year 1842 was decisive for the Marist mission in New Zealand. Pompallier was absent from the Bay of Islands on a visit to the islands from 19 November 1841 to 25 August 1842. The visitor proposed in Maitrepierre's memorandum to Colin arrived in the person of Fr. Forest. His first letter to Colin of 3 April 1842 demonstrated his analytical skills. He gave figures of population for Port Nicholson (Wellington) as 6,000, Nelson as 1,200, Auckland as 600. He described the progress of the Protestant missions since 1814, with their fifty-four schools, and noted the significance of the New Zealand Company and what it represented for further European immigration. By May 1842 he had time to take stock of the Marist mission and reported somberly on what he found. It was "in the most miserable state . . . critical . . . our poor fathers suffer much." The bishop's ship was very costly at 400 francs per day; debts had arisen from bad administration. The bishop refused to withhold anything from any supplicant, making also grand promises and regarding expressions of Māori affection *(moi picopo)* as conversion. None of the stations were solidly based, although there were securely grounded Catholics at two or three of them. The Marist priests had reacted against the bishop's view that all, like himself, owed obedience to Rome alone (so bypassing the Society of Mary), which was an attempt to have sole authority. The situation had been exacerbated by inopportune purchases of land that could have been obtained at cheaper rates. No one, with the possible exception of Épalle, possessed administrative capacity (Viard was in Europe), and the priests were experiencing hunger and privation. In a further collective letter from them, signed by Forest, they asked "with one voice" for good administration.²² Colin was told by Fr. Petit-Jean, writing from Sydney, that the affairs of the Society in New Zealand were well known and that there was a danger of "dishonour of our little society"; he wrote also that Pompallier's claims of 15,000 catechumens and 15,000-20,000 Catholics were a fantasy "which costs Monseigneur dear."²³

Well before these disturbing reports reached them, Colin and Poupinel (secretary of the missions) had conferred in Rome for three months (28 May

21. Pompallier to Colin, 4 September 1838, CG/I/p. 215; Baty to Colin, 25 October 1841; Baty to Girard, 25 October 1841; CG/I/pp. 759, 763.
22. Forest to Colin, 3 April 1842, CG/II/pp. 92-95 (first impressions); 22 May 1842, CG/II/pp. 215-18; collective letter, 22 May 1842, CG/II/p. 220 (privations), p. 221 (good administration). As well as Forest, signed by Épalle, Garin, Petit, Petit-Jean.
23. Petit-Jean to Colin, 8 July 1842, CG/II/pp. 259-69; 28-31 July 1842, CG/II/pp. 284-320; cf. p. 260 (dishonor), p. 286 (fantasy).

to 28 August 1842). To meet their fears over the isolation of priests, Propaganda passed a decree that insisted on a "companion" at least, a brother if not a priest, and had agreed that every four or five years at least one priest would be recalled to report on the mission both to the Society and to Propaganda. Cardinal Fransoni, who had earlier commended Colin's moderation in dealing with Pompallier, now acted to restrain the superior from overreacting to the bishop's letter of 15 November 1841, which told Colin bluntly, "further evils will be your responsibility." By 1842, Fransoni had been persuaded by Colin that a new vicariate of Central Oceania was needed to obviate Pompallier's long absences in the islands, and by August 1842 Bataillon had been appointed and approved by the pope. The final straw for Colin appears to have been Pompallier's letter of 6 November 1842 (received June 1843), in which the bishop was perceived by the Society of Mary of accusing them of failing to convey the full amount of Propaganda's grants to New Zealand. Fransoni discerned that any difference was accounted for by fares and goods for outgoing missionaries. Pompallier's suggestion of funds being "lost" was mistaken.[24] By then, Colin had already decided that further relationship with Pompallier was against the interests of his Marist protégés and the seventh party of Marists who left Lyons in August 1842 were to be the last to serve under Pompallier in New Zealand. Colin had supplied fifty-two personnel over five years for Pompallier's sphere of responsibility, of whom thirty-five served in New Zealand.[25]

---

24. Roach, "Venerable Jean-Claude Colin," pp. 160-71, 185-98, 285-318.
25. CG/II/p. 378 and n. 4; Roach, "Venerable Jean-Claude Colin," pp. 125-32.

CHAPTER 9

The Treaty of Waitangi, 1840

In the 1830s the colonization schemes of Edward Gibbon Wakefield began to mature. Wakefield had a disreputable past (he had twice abducted teenage heiresses and spent time in prison), but he possessed powers of persuasion that amounted to near genius. A pilot scheme in South Australia, whereby 35,000 acres were sold to colonists at £1 per acre, led to the formation of the New Zealand Association in 1837. His brother, Arthur Wakefield, visited the CMS on 6 June 1837 to enlist support, and Wakefield himself published *The British Colonisation of New Zealand,* illustrated by Augustus Earle in the same year. He also persuaded J. G. Lambton, later Lord Durham, to lend his name and capability to the association. James Stephen, the influential civil servant of the Colonial Office, opposed Wakefield's ideas, as submitted to him by the then prime minister, Lord Melbourne, on the grounds that they required the acquisition of the sovereignty of New Zealand and possible extinction of its inhabitants, and because they were "so vague as to defy contemplation." Both missionary societies in London strongly opposed the schemes, and Dandeson Coates of the CMS and John Beecham of the WMMS wrote pamphlets against the proposals.[1] Wakefield pictured the Māori as strongly desiring colonization. Although the New Zealand Association was wound up

---

1. P. Burns, *Fatal Success: A History of the New Zealand Company* (Auckland: Heinemann Reed, 1989), pp. 28-54; D. Coates, "The Principles, Objections and Plan of the New Zealand Association Examined" (1837); J. Beecham, "Colonisation: Being Remarks on Colonising in General with Examination of the Principles of the (New Zealand) Association" (1837); J. Stephen in Colonial Office 209/2, pp. 386-87; cf. A. H. McLintock, *Crown Colony Government in New Zealand* (Wellington: R. E. Owens, 1958), p. 38; "unprincipled genius" (E. G. Wakefield) "appalled him" (James Stephen).

in July 1838, in the next month Wakefield had formed the New Zealand Company for the same purposes.

While Lord Normanby, now in charge of the Colonial Office as colonial secretary, hesitated, Wakefield decided to preempt government inhibitions. On 12 May 1839 his brother William Wakefield, his nephew Edward Jerningham Wakefield, and the naturalist Ernst Dieffenbach sailed in the *Tory* with a party of 704 steerage passengers and 152 so-called capitalists. It was rightly described by a select committee of the House of Commons as conduct "in direct defiance of the authority of the Crown" and "highly improper." William Wakefield arrived in Port Nicholson and acquired large tracts of land, amounting to twenty million acres, from the Māori, using as his chief negotiator Richard "Dicky" Barrett, an interpreter with limited grasp of Māori, even though a young Māori, Ngaiti, was at hand on the *Tory*. Land was also acquired at Queen Charlotte's Sound and Taranaki. It was a prelude to the arrival of the thirteen shiploads of immigrants between May 1839 and July 1840.[2] This was the situation that confronted Captain Hobson, who arrived in the Bay of Islands on 29 January 1840, representing the authority the Wakefields had defied.

Whole books have been written on the Treaty of Waitangi, and its provisions are still the subject of legal debate in the twenty-first century. In this study of the conversion of the Māori, we will concentrate on the missionary involvement in the treaty and Māori reactions. A very important starting point is that all three missions, as has been shown, saw considerable response in the north of the North Island well before British colonial rule. Insofar as conversion has been discerned by some to be a search for power, in which European religion, medicine, and technical superiority were components, among, for example, the Ngapuhi in the 1830s, accompanied by increasing awareness among Māori of the wider implications of British influence through their knowledge of New South Wales and even London in some cases, it might appear that power expressed through government was a leading factor in the response to the missions between 1830 and 1840. This does not seem to be true for the period under discussion. Other questions handled here are how far the missionaries were covert imperialists and, associated with that, whether their influence on the Māori participants in the negotiations was decisive. A further question that will remain is how far political authority should be seen as a factor in Māori response to Christianity in areas of the country touched after 1840.[3]

---

2. Burns, *Fatal Success*, pp. 77-123; "Barrett, Richard," in *DNZB*, 1:19-20; E. J. Wakefield, *Adventures in New Zealand from 1839 to 1844* (1845) (Christchurch, NZ: Whitcombe and Tombs, 1908); McLintock, *Crown Colony*, p. 122 n. 2.

3. T. L. Buick, *The Treaty of Waitangi* (Christchurch, NZ: Capper Press, 1976); C. Orange, *The Treaty of Waitangi* (Wellington: Allen and Unwin, 1987); *The Illustrated History of*

In the late 1830s, missionaries had expressed their anxiety about land purchases and immigrants. Charles Baker had applauded the "spirited opposition" of the CMS in London to the plans of the New Zealand Association; the missionary body in New Zealand had approved them.[4] As early as 1836 Richard Davis had written to Dandeson Coates in London about the arrival of "very many settlers," who had introduced "much wickedness," while trying to set the Māori against the mission.[5] Davis recorded the presence of Baron de Thierry and wrote, "I fear the country is equally in danger from the French nation." His apprehensions were deepened by the presence of the "Popish" mission.[6] "*If the country is to be colonised let it be by the British government and by it alone*" (emphasis in original). Davis fully reflected what John Darch has aptly termed the "incidental imperialism" of the missionaries: they had no great wish for colonial incursions, gave reluctant recognition that such was proving necessary and preferred British to French rule. French naval intervention at Tahiti provided a warning, and the influx of Europeans wanting to purchase land was an aggravating factor. Davis himself had tried to intervene to ensure just purchases.[7] Henry Williams wrote to Coates: "I do not hesitate to say that, unless some protection be given by the British government the country will be bought up and the people pass into a kind of slavery or be wholly extirpated. The European settlers are making rapid advances and beginning to hold out threats": "the English government should take charge of the authority as guardians of New Zealand . . . chiefs should be incorporated into a general assembly with an English governor at the head . . . the natives have many years since proposed this should be done and have repeated their demand from time to time."[8]

John King added the factor of general European lawlessness. Land sales to Frenchmen, Spaniards, and convicts meant there would be war unless "some overwhelming power . . . repudiate . . . the affairs of the country" and in par-

---

the *Treaty of Waitangi* (Wellington: Bridget Williams Books, 2004); on power see McLintock, *Crown Colony*, p. 119; J. D. Y. Peel, *Aladura: A Religious Movement among the Yoruba* (London: Oxford University Press for International African Institute, 1968), pp. 216-17; M. P. K. Sorenson, in *Oxford History of New Zealand* (Wellington: Oxford University Press, 1981), p. 171: "Māori had to discover the sources of secular power of the Europeans."

4. Baker to CMS secretaries, 26 November 1838, C N/O 18/30.

5. Davis to Coates, 9 February 1836, Hocken MS 1.66.

6. Davis to Coates, 9 March 1837 (de Thierry), 6 December 1838 (French, RC Mission), Hocken MS 1.66.

7. Davis to Coates, 22 March 1839 (Tahiti), 15 November 1839 (Europeans), Hocken MS 1.66; J. Darch, *Missionary Imperialists? Missionaries, Governments, and the Growth of Empire in the Tropics, 1860-1885* (Milton Keynes: Paternoster, 2009).

8. Henry Williams to Coates, 11 January 1838, C N/O 93/66.

ticular apply judicious government to secure the rights of the Māori in these purchases.[9] Henry Williams told Coates that he was less ready than Coates "to give to these gentlemen (of the New Zealand Association) . . . full credit for the purity of their motives and benevolence of their intentions," which in his view were "somewhat to themselves alone."[10] His brother wrote: "if any step be taken to better the condition of the New Zealanders . . . it will be done by the British government" and, whatever James Busby might opine, the missionaries would be the indispensable link to the Māori, as indeed they proved to be. He found dissatisfaction with the purchases and the nature of the contracts proposed to Māori after the arrival of the *Tory:* a British governor was needed with powers to resolve the problems.[11]

Hobson arrived with instructions from Lord Normanby to negotiate a transfer of sovereignty with the "free and intelligent" consent of the Māori and to protect their interests. Māori chiefs were invited to a meeting at Waitangi on 5 February. Meanwhile Hobson, Busby, the missionary A. N. Brown, and the shipowner and American consul (though English) J. R. Clendon worked on a draft treaty, which Henry Williams and his son Edward eventually translated into Māori and another missionary from the CMS, Richard Taylor, engraved onto parchment.[12] William Colenso, who was present, left a graphic account of the meeting in *The Authentic and Genuine History of the Signing of the Treaty of Waitangi, New Zealand, February 5 and 6, 1840.*[13] A large marquee had been set up, decorated with flags and bunting, with a platform for Hobson, Busby, and others. To this "spacious tent" Bishop Pompallier arrived, "dressed in canonicals" and attended by a priest (Servant). Hobson then addressed the assembly through Henry Williams as interpreter (p. 16) and read the proposed treaty in English before Henry Williams read it in Māori (p. 17). The treaty consisted of three articles, which, in its English form, laid down the following: first, that the chiefs ceded to the queen

9. King to William Jowett, 2 January 1840, C N/O 55/33.

10. Henry Williams to Coates, 18 June 1838, C N/O 93/68.

11. William Williams to secretaries, 14 November 1838, C N/O 95/57; 31 December 1839 (land purchases), C N/O 95/67.

12. Orange, *The Treaty of Waitangi,* pp. 36-39; *Illustrated History of the Treaty of Waitangi,* pp. 19, 24, 30-32; I. Wards, *The Shadow of the Land: A Study of British Policy and Racial Conflict in New Zealand, 1832-1852* (Wellington: A. R. Shearer for Historical Publications, Department of Internal Affairs, 1968), p. 42 and n. 1; J. Belich, *Making Peoples: A History of the New Zealanders from Polynesian Settlement to the End of the Nineteenth Century* (Auckland: Allen Lane, 1996), pp. 187-97.

13. W. Colenso, *The Authentic and Genuine History of the Signing of the Treaty of Waitangi, New Zealand, February 5 and 6, 1840* (Wellington: R. C. Harding, 1890). Page references have been placed in the text.

"without reservation" all the rights and powers of sovereignty; second, that the queen guaranteed the full, exclusive, and undisturbed possession of lands, estates, forests and fisheries, and other properties to the chiefs, with a Crown right of preemption on any lands that they might wish to "alienate"; and third, that the queen extended protection to them and the rights and privileges of British subjects.[14] Colenso recorded the initial and somewhat devastating response of Te Kemara to these proposals: "Health to thee, O Governor. . . . I am not pleased towards thee. I do not wish for thee . . . my land is gone, gone, all gone. The inheritance of my ancestors, fathers, relatives, all gone, stolen, gone with the missionaries . . . that man there, the Busby and that man there, the Williams, they have my land . . . (pointing to the Rev. H. Williams) thou, thou, thou bald-headed man — thou hast got my lands, O governor" (pp. 17-19). Rewa, who was a confidant of Pompallier, also expressed this view: "the country is ours but the land is gone," and went on to accuse Richard Davis and George Clarke of the CMS of removing it. Kawiti called on the governor to "go back, go back, we are free: let the missionaries remain but as for thee return to thy own country" (pp. 18-20, 22).

Colenso recorded numerous speeches by Māori chiefs, but the assembly was swayed by the contributions of three who had been closest to the missionaries, Tamati Waka Nene, his brother Patuone, and Hone Heke. Waka Nene's impassioned advocacy, probably arising from the conviction of John Hobbs, his Methodist missionary mentor, that British government would be beneficial to the Māori, was held later by Felton Mathew, who was present, to be decisive: "Nene spoke in a strain of fervid and impassioned eloquence such as I never before heard and which immediately turned the tide in our favour."[15] Woon also wrote that Hobson had said again and again, that without the intervention of "Walker [sic] Nene" he would have returned empty-handed.[16]

Hobbs wrote a letter after the event that reflected his views at the time: British law among the Māori would promote their welfare,[17] and his biographer quoted a leader from the *New Zealand Herald* of 3 August 1923, which claimed that "behind the (speech) of Tamati Waka Nene . . . was the *mana* of John Hobbs."[18] In a lesser key, the same could be said of Henry Williams's in-

---

14. Orange, *The Treaty of Waitangi*, p. 258, for English text of the treaty.
15. T. M. I. Williment, *John Hobbs, 1800-1883: Wesleyan Missionary to the Ngapuhi Tribes of Northern New Zealand* (Wellington: Government Printer, 1985), p. 147; F. Mathew and S. Mathew, *The Founding of New Zealand* (Wellington: A. R. Shearer for Historical Publications, Dept. of Internal Affairs, 1968), p. 143.
16. Woon to WMMS secretaries, 20 April 1840, MMS Microfilm.
17. Hobbs to WMMS secretaries, 25 January 1841, MMS Microfilm.
18. Williment, *John Hobbs*, p. 146; and Samuel Ironside, in T. A. Pybus, *Māori and Mis-*

fluence on Patuone and Hone Heke, both supporters of the treaty even if less influential than Nene, who was reported to have spent many hours of consultation with Hobbs before the negotiation. Certainly, Hobson thanked the WMMS subsequently for its "powerful aid."[19] Nevertheless, as the historian of New Zealand, Michael King, wrote in 2003 on the charge of Waka Nene "parroting" the views of his Wesleyan mentors, such considerations "have no relevance": "these *were* his views on the day. And he carried sufficient *mana* among his own people as a former fighting chief and more recently as a peacemaker for his arguments to be taken seriously."[20]

Extensive discussions among Māori participants followed during the night, but although Hobson had originally suggested meeting on 7 February, the Māori wanted a conclusion on 6 February. Before the final signing Pompallier intervened and asked Busby for an undertaking that Māori who became Roman Catholic be given the protection of the British government. Henry Williams was charged with conveying Hobson's agreement to this proposal. No lover of Rome, Williams wrote later that he found this "somewhat of a tough morsel, requiring care," and gave Hobson a piece of paper that read: "the governor wishes you to understand that all the Māories [sic] who shall join the Church of England, who shall join the Wesleyans, who shall join the Pikopo church of Rome, and those who retain their Māori practices, shall have the protection of the British government," which Hobson accepted. Williams then read this, and after he heard it, Pompallier "rose, bowed to the Governor and retired from the meeting." When Busby called up Hone Heke to begin the signing, Colenso asked the governor whether he believed the Māori really understood its implications, to which Hobson replied that he had done all that he could and that if the chiefs did not know the import of the treaty, "it is no fault of mine." Colenso still demurred, but Busby referred him to Heke's own speech of the day before about having to trust the missionaries. Heke then signed, as did Te Kemara and eventually Rewa, whom Colenso, almost certainly unjustly, believed Pompallier had tried to prevent from agreeing to do so. Forty-five chiefs signed on that day, and on Colenso's account the total number from the three centers of Waitangi, Hokianga (where Hobbs acted as interpreter), and Waimate was 120.[21]

---

sionary: *Early Christian Missionaries in the South Island of New Zealand* (Wellington: A. H. and A. W. Reed, 1954), p. 179: "if ya think so, say so" (Ironside to Waka Nene).

19. Williment, *John Hobbs*, pp. 146, 150.

20. M. King, *The Penguin History of New Zealand* (Auckland: Penguin Books, 2003), p. 162, emphasis in original.

21. Colenso, *Authentic and Genuine History*, pp. 33 (Hobson), 34-36; Orange, *The Treaty of Waitangi*, p. 61.

If evidence were needed of the missionaries' importance to the process, it can certainly be found in what followed. Hobson experienced a stroke within weeks of the meeting at Waitangi, but Henry Williams and others were indefatigable in scouring the country for signatures. In the Tauranga area, Alfred Brown collected 21, while William Williams gathered 25 more in the area of East Cape to Napier and another 10 at Waiapu. Robert Maunsell collected 32 around Waikato Heads, though not all of the leading chiefs; among these, Te Wherowhero, paramount chief of Waikato, was one who refused. Henry Williams, however, was successful with Te Rauparaha at Kapiti and reached a total of 132 chiefs from Otaki, Waikanae, Wanganui, and Manawetu. Claudia Orange wrote of Henry Williams, "Williams' success must be attributed solely to his own persuasion. That he was a man of considerable *mana* among the Māori was undoubtedly significant," and she added, "generally missionary influence was significant simply because the Māori trusted the missionaries' good intentions."[22] One missionary, J. A. Wilson of the CMS, who, like Henry Williams, had a services background, refused to take part in the process as a "servant of the government," which he probably saw as an improper role for a missionary.[23] Of the others, Whitely and Wallis of the WMMS, James Stack, Thomas Chapman, and John Morgan were all involved, with varying levels of success, some of it not recorded. Te Rangihaeata, ally of Te Rauparaha, signed, and in the north at Kaitaia the paramount chief Nopera Panakareao also signed. He was a very influential figure and was among 60 chiefs who signed, telling his wife in May 1840 that "the shadow of the land goes to Queen Victoria but the substance remains with us," a judgment he had reversed by January 1841, a somber juxtaposition with which Ian Wards began his study.[24]

Missionary influence may have informed an understanding of the treaty that had general links with Christian teaching. Both Hone Heke and Patuone had spoken of the covenant and sacred compact aspect of the treaty at the negotiations.[25] This understanding was to cast a long shadow into the future, allied as it was to a sense of personal relationship to the Crown and the queen, which Patuone had expressed by the gift of a *mere* for her possession: "sacredness" may have helped the missionaries to hold both Crown and Māori to the treaty's observance later, but the personal compact aspect made it hard for

22. Orange, *The Treaty of Waitangi*, pp. 66-73, 90.
23. Orange, *The Treaty of Waitangi*, pp. 85-86.
24. Wards, *Shadow of the Land*, pp. i-ix; Orange, *The Treaty of Waitangi*, pp. 69-90.
25. Orange, *The Treaty of Waitangi*, p. 57; Wards, *Shadow of the Land*, p. 37; King, *History*, p. 164. Cf. J. Metge, *The Māori of New Zealand* (London: Routledge and Kegan Paul, 1967), pp. 38-49, on Māori reinterpretation; P. Adams, *Fatal Necessity: British Intervention in New Zealand, 1830-47* (Auckland: Oxford University Press, 1977), pp. 11-15.

Māori to adjust to the impersonal nature of the Crown-in-parliament format of the British constitution when confronted with it later in New Zealand history. Again, Henry Williams's ambiguous use of Māori terminology to convey terms like sovereignty (he used as a Māori word *kawanatanga* from Māori *kawana* [governor]) has been judged since to have had the effect of emphasizing Māori independence and toning down loss of self-determination. When British colonial law was applied later not only to Europeans but also to Māori, this did not necessarily comply with how Māori had understood the treaty.[26] There was a clash between an essentially protectorate view and what actually transpired.

In terms of the conversion of the Māori, while noting again that there had been substantial response before 1840, the context of British government as a form of European ascendancy was likely to have had some influence. Whereas Pompallier shrugged off the political, in what was at one level an admirable neutrality allied to missionary concentration, some of his priests were probably more aware than he of the long-term implications for the French Marist mission of the new colonial context; Fr. Comte for one did not share his bishop's optimistic detachment on the subject.[27] Hobson caused Busby to declare Crown sovereignty over the South Island, as earlier over Stewart Island, and he moved fast when confronted by moves toward independence by settlers at Port Nicholson, which he regarded as treasonable, the sovereignty declaration of 21 May being followed quickly by action there on 25 May.[28] He completed his commission from Lord Normanby when Crown sovereignty was gazetted in London on 2 October 1840.[29] The treaty was therefore in place when fresh shiploads of New Zealand Company personnel, amounting to some 1,350 more immigrants, arrived by July 1840.[30] Joseph Matthews of the CMS found that Hobson impressed the Māori, and Robert Maunsell found him admirable at conciliating Māori opinion, when confronted with the large numbers of incomers.[31] Hobson appointed George Clarke, another CMS veteran, as Protector of the Aborigines, which accorded with his instructions

---

26. Orange, *The Treaty of Waitangi*, pp. 33, 46; King, *History*, pp. 164-65; Belich, *Making Peoples*, pp. 194-96.

27. Comte to Colin, 25 April 1841, in Fr. Charles Girard, *Lettres reçues d'Océanie par l'administration generale des pères maristes pendant le generalat de Jean-Claude Colin* (Rome: Centre d'études maristes, 1999), 1:579-80.

28. Wards, *Shadow of the Land*, pp. 46-48.

29. Wards, *Shadow of the Land*, pp. 47-48; Orange, *The Treaty of Waitangi*, pp. 83-85.

30. McLintock, *Crown Colony*, p. 122 n. 2.

31. Matthews to William Jowett, 29 June 1840, C N/O 61/24; Maunsell to secretaries, 12 September 1842, C N/O 64/29.

from Lord Normanby; and a Land Claims Commissioner to assess the validity of purchases, filled later by William Spain. Hobson ruled through a legislative council of six, of which he was executive, which after 1841 included New Zealand's first chief justice, William Martin, and three others. His governorship was cut short by his death in September 1842 a few days short of his fiftieth birthday.[32] His successor, Robert Fitzroy, was to call the Treaty of Waitangi the "Magna Charta" of New Zealand, by scrupulous adherence to which alone the cooperation and fidelity of the Māori subjects of the Crown were to be retained.[33]

32. *DNZB*, 1:196-99.
33. Colonial Office 209/49, p. 446; Wards, *Shadow of the Land*, p. 42 n. 2; R. Fitzroy, *Remarks on New Zealand as a Colony in 1846* (London: W. and H. White, 1846), p. 10.

CHAPTER 10

Expansion of a Mission: Māori Initiatives and the CMS, 1834-1842

Although the Bay of Islands gave the early signs of change and movement of response to the missions ("the Christian natives now form a great body," wrote George Clarke in March 1837), it was in what happened farther south and particularly in the East Cape that gave evidence of what New Zealand historians have called (surely rightly) a "mass movement."[1] As early as 1834 William Williams and William Yate were showing signs of impatience with the missionary community in the Bay of Islands. Yate wrote: "we are too many in the Bay of Islands" and "we must form settlements in the southward," the word "must" having a threefold underlining in the original.[2] William Williams, who estimated the whole Māori population of the North Island at 106,000, realized the weight of numbers farther south, which he estimated at 4,800 in the Thames area, 18,000 around Waikato, 15,600 in the Bay of Plenty with Hicks Bay, and another 27,000 between Hicks Bay and Hawkes Bay.[3] He and Yate paid a preliminary visit south in 1834, and he wrote in June that the possibilities had generated "excitement" in the CMS mission as they discovered a "degree of intense interest" from Waikato through to Waiapu. They planned for Alfred Brown to go to Tauranga and also to reach Puriri and Rotorua, where Yate had visited. William Williams sketched a mis-

---

1. W. H. Oliver and J. M. Thomson, *Challenge and Response: A Study of Development of the East Coast Region* (Gisborne, NZ: East Coast Development Research Association, 1971), p. 32. Chapter 2 of this work is a fine historical analysis of mission developments; G. Clarke Sr. to secretaries, 31 March 1837, C N/O 30.

2. Yate to CMS secretaries, 27 January 1834, C N/O 98/38; cf. William Williams Journal, 8 April 1838, C N/O 95/207.

3. William Williams to secretaries, 25 February 1834, C N/O 95/35.

sionary strategy in this letter not dissimilar to Roland Allen's *Spontaneous Expansion of the Church* or the more contemporary ideas of Henry Venn, with missionaries acting as initiators before moving on to unevangelized fields, while leaving the building of the church to indigenous converts.⁴

In this case, however, the Māori were the initiators rather than the missionaries, who "discharged a rather more humble role than is customarily accorded to them" and who "ratify change quite as much as they initiate it."⁵ The missionaries themselves were aware of this aspect. Henry Williams wrote of these unevangelized areas: "it was extremely pleasing to observe in these wild settlements where no European has ever been before" Māori voices giving "responses in choir services." On the 1834 visit, William Williams had been responsible for the return of certain Ngapuhi captives from the north, among them Taumata-a-kuri, "a man who had the best claim to be considered the pioneer evangelist of the East Cape."⁶ As well as his evangelistic exploits, this man took part in a siege in the Bay of Plenty in 1834 at Toka-a-kahu, when he was reported to have led the attack with a book in one hand and a musket in the other. He was looked upon as a Christian *tohunga*, who taught reading as well as Christianity, one "possessed of occult powers."⁷

Taumata was not alone because, as we have seen, William Williams had left a number of Māori teachers in strategic positions. In 1838, on a return visit, the missionaries discovered that Sunday observance had been established in Hicks Bay, at least in terms of naming the day, and at Tokomau and Turanga it was a day without work. Up to this point there were clear signs of Māori change, not least in the demand for books, reading, and writing, but "from 1838 conversion became a mass movement," "sweeping almost the whole population along in its fervour."⁸

Māori initiative may have been at its strongest in the East Cape, but there were also signs elsewhere. In 1839, from quite a different quarter, a deputation to the Bay of Islands from Te Rauparaha's base at Kapiti, consisting of Tamihana Te Rauparaha and Matene Te Whiwhi, the first being the chief's son, managed to persuade the missionary community to release the newly ordained Octavius Hadfield, ordained by Bishop Broughton of Sydney in the Bay of Islands in 1838, to work among the people around Otaki. Here, once more, the way had been

---

4. William Williams to secretaries, 2 June 1834, C N/O 95/36.

5. Oliver and Thomson, *Challenge and Response*, p. 28; cf. R. Lange, "Indigenous Agents of Religious Change in New Zealand 1830-1860," *JRH* 24, no. 3 (October 2000): 280.

6. Henry Williams to Dandeson Coates, 23 January 1840, C N/O 93/75; Oliver and Thomson, *Challenge and Response*, p. 29.

7. Oliver and Thomson, *Challenge and Response*, p. 30.

8. Oliver and Thomson, *Challenge and Response*, p. 32.

prepared and was assisted later by a returned captive and slave, Ripahau, who had known the Williams brothers and taken with him excerpts of the New Testament and the *Book of Common Prayer*. Hadfield was further assisted by Riwai Te Ahu, who became a lay reader at Waikanae, and before long the mission was in touch with some 7,000 Māori, with a congregation of 500 at Kapiti in July 1840.[9] Similar numbers were reported by Richard Davis in the far north at Kaitaia, where he joined a congregation of 600 in 1838.[10]

William Williams and Jane took up residence permanently in Turanga in 1840. Jane wrote from Poverty Bay to Marianne Williams, from whom she had become separated after fourteen years together in Pahia: "at every place William visited in the East Cape district he found a chapel. None but the native teachers have as yet been resident there, but so blest have their labours been, that he finds many whom he considered fit subjects for baptism," and we know that her husband had quite strict requirements for this.[11] He himself wrote of the "astonishing" movement in the east coast in his journal of February 1840, and later: "the reason under God why the successes were so great on this eastern coast was because we had a number of natives from this part of the island who had been christened in the Bay of Islands. The people seemed much more inclined to listen to them than to us."[12] He set about capitalizing on Māori teaching and communication skills by training teachers at Poverty Bay, who were deployed in Turanga, Uawa, Rangitakia, and Kawakawa; "local agents everywhere naturalized the new religion. Conversion was an experience of whole societies."[13]

By 1841 congregations numbering in the thousands were recorded: 3,200 at Waiapu, 2,500 at Uawa and Turanga. High proportions of the total Māori population in these places were regarded as Christian, by CMS missionaries always reluctant to credit professions. So, in Turanga and Mahia, of a total of 10,000 Māori, some 6,000 were regarded as Christian; of 4,000 at Uawa, some 2,300; of 6,000 in East Cape and Waiapu, 4,300. William Williams appeared to echo Luther, who claimed that the word triumphed while he sat and drank Wittenberg beer: "the Word has only been preached by Native Teachers. We have literally stood *still* to *see the salvation of God*" where Luther and Moses combined.[14]

---

9. B. Macmorran, *Octavius Hadfield* (Wellington: Privately published, 1971), pp. 8-23; *DNZB*, 1:179.
10. Richard Davis Journal, 18 July 1838, Hocken MS M.1 66.
11. Jane Williams to Marianne Williams, 18 May 1840, ATL collection qms 2225-7.
12. William Williams Journal, 5 February 1840, C N/O 95/208.
13. Oliver and Thomson, *Challenge and Response*, p. 33.
14. Oliver and Thomson, *Challenge and Response*, p. 29; cf. William Williams to secretaries, 26 July 1841 (stood still), C N/O 95/77; cf. Exod. 14:14 (NRSV): "The LORD will fight

A year earlier he had estimated average congregational numbers in the CMS stations at 1,020 at Kaitaia, 1,940 in the Bay of Islands, 1,000 at Turanga, 700 at Thames, 1,200 in East Cape, 1,000 at Poverty Bay, 1,400 at Rotorua, and 500 at the Bay of Plenty, with a need for 33,000 prayer books with hymns, while he anticipated contact with 36,000 people in the general Tauranga area, where he had 20 Māori teachers to help.[15] It was from this period 1839-41 that the frequently cited figure of 30,000 worshipers in CMS churches alone occurs: Henry Williams gave it as such to Coates in July 1840 as "30-40,000 per Sabbath," and William Williams used the same figure in his *Christianity amongst the Māoris*.[16] He wrote there of the Tauranga area of the time: "the whole fabric of native superstitions were gone, whether relating to the living or the dead, the old priests being as fond to take this step (i.e. baptism) as any others . . . the change was apparent to the casual visitor of the natives."[17] There were cases of tribes following the chiefs, and he noticed that elderly Māori responded quite as much as their juniors, although someone like Rewa in the Bay of Islands had said that this would not happen: "the old men including the leading chiefs are among the foremost to receive the gospel, not only giving up . . . their former practices but submitting with a wonderful simplicity to that . . . instruction required by their teachers . . . eager to be possessed of the sacred scriptures for which in most instances they are ready to pay." In this annual report to the CMS of 1841, worshiping numbers in Waiapu, Turanga, Table Cape, and the other centers were put at 8,680, with 2,115 baptisms in the year, of which 839 were adults. He had spent 102 days of the year in travel.[18]

Writings of other missionaries gave ample evidence of this wealth of Māori initiative. John Morgan, who was to serve at Puriri and Mangapouri (1834), Matamata (1836), Tauranga (1838), and Otawhao, and would experience the destruction of the station at Matamata in tribal warfare, referred initially to the whole area, in a phrase strangely reminiscent of David Brainerd's visit to the Delaware Indians of 1 May 1744, as a "waste howling wilderness." After the initial reconnaissance by Henry Williams, Morgan, Brown, Fair-

---

for you . . . you have only to stand still" (Moses to the Israelites at the Red Sea). Journal, 12 March 1840 (placing of Māori teachers), 11 June 1841 (one such called "Marsden," "a steady consistent native much looked up to by the people"), C N/O 95/208, 209.

15. William Williams to secretaries, 12 November 1839, C N/O 95/65.

16. Henry Williams to Coates, 25 July 1840, 10 October 1841, C N/O 93/79, 92; William Williams to secretaries, 21 December 1846, C N/O 95/106, and in *Christianity amongst the New Zealanders* (London: Seeley, Jackson, and Halliday, 1867), p. 279.

17. W. Williams, *Christianity among the New Zealanders*, p. 289.

18. William Williams, Annual Report to CMS, C N/O 95/233.

burn, and Baker had made the missionaries "hopeful for the south," Morgan reported that by March 1835, under Māori ministry, there had been widespread "surrender . . . to Christ."[19] George Clarke, veteran missionary and future Protector of Aborigines, reported on Māori teachers going to the East Cape with a "strong desire" for Turanga and Waiapu, while William Fairburn reported "many baptised natives" who were "going forth," some "to Coromandel."[20] G. A. Kissling, who was inclined to compare New Zealand as a field unfavorably with his previous setting in Sierra Leone, was now suitably impressed with congregations at Hicks Bay of 400 in the morning and 500 in the evening where "no European teacher or missionary had been except natives." William Williams recorded one such teacher, who was copying out manuscript hymns and prayers for use in the absence of books; he had 20 Māori teachers at work by 1839.[21] He found a Māori Christian *pa,* where a community had separated themselves off in order to live Christianly with guidance from Māori Christian leaders from Kerikeri.[22] After moving to Turanga in 1840, he called the movement on the east coast "astonishing," discerned its roots as beginning in what had transpired at Rotorua farther south in 1835-36, and later, in his book, raised what might be called the Constantinian issue, whereby rather than personal conviction, for "the multitude," "it was becoming the general religion of the country." After 1840 the possibility that the Treaty of Waitangi had a similar effect on state alignment as the battle of Milvian Bridge had for the "multitudes" of the Roman Empire cannot be neglected, even if the signs of much religious conviction had been shown. By 1853 the first few Māori teachers left at the East Cape in 1839 had grown in numbers to 114 for the Turanga district.[23]

What was true of the East Cape area was true also, if less spectacularly, of the Thames-Waikato set of stations. Fairburn gave evidence of an infant church brought into being by a Māori chief at Thames in 1833.[24] Robert

---

19. Morgan to secretaries, 25 March 1833 (waste howling wilderness), 14 September 1836 (destruction of Matamata), C N/O 65/2, 9; Baker to secretaries, 22 January 1835, 2 November 1835 (surrender), C N/O 18/20, 22.

20. Clarke to secretaries, 28 November 1838, 1 June 1839, C N/O 30; Fairburn to W. Jowett, April 1840 (Coromandel), C N/O 39/14.

21. G. A. Kissling, Hicks Bay Report for quarter ending 25 June 1843, C N/O 56/9; W. Williams Journal, 3 February 1840, C N/O 95/208; to secretaries, 28 August 1839 (teachers), C N/O 95/65.

22. W. Williams Journal, 23 March 1838, 7 April 1838 (luggage bearers asked to be paid in prayer books), C N/O 95/207.

23. W. Williams Journal, 5 February 1840 (astonishing); cf. to secretaries, 3 June 1839, C N/O 95/208, 63; *Christianity amongst the New Zealanders,* pp. 211 (Rotorua), 279.

24. W. Fairburn Journal, 17 November 1833, C N/O 39/22.

Maunsell, who could be critical of Māori, wrote of the "intellectual power" of the Māori teachers, among whom was a chief's son called "Jowett." Maunsell was as surprised as William Williams at the progress of the mission in his area, after a first convert at Maraetai, and at the accompanying decay of Māori religion and custom, witnessed to him by a dying chief at a *hahunga* surrounded by mourning relatives, whom Maunsell asked about the possibility of cure through the ministrations of a *tohunga*. "Of what avail was that misuse?" was the reply, accompanied by a profession of faith in Christ, which in this context Maunsell found to be a "declaration . . . as unexpected as it was gratifying" in 1841. By 1849 Maunsell held that the essential basis of conversion of the Māori was over and had taken place from 1840 to 1849; now the need was for *education,* on which subject, he may have felt, as John Morgan certainly did, that the CMS was much less enthusiastic than it was for primary evangelism and church planting, essential as it had become.[25] Benjamin Ashwell reported on imaginatively led public worship by Māori at Owai, and in a journal entry again emphasized how Māori-led Christianity occurred in the Wellington (Port Nicholson) area "long before Europeans" initiated anything. Like Maunsell, he noted the decay of Māori custom: William Tawaihai "was resolved to abandon the old customs" "by cutting off his hair (sacred) and throwing it in a fire on which his slaves (were) cooking fish" in turning to Christ, a major break with tradition that Ashwell noted put the slaves' lives at risk from angry chiefs aware of the sacrilege involved.[26] Hamlin, a careful student of Māori custom, also found inquirers making themselves *noa* by hair burning as part of their response; one chief, Rewatahi, told him in March 1837 at Mangapouri that he and his tribe, the Ngatiteata, "had come to a determination to have nothing more to do with their native superstitions," but Hamlin found that the chief relapsed when he was ill and the tribe relapsed with him.[27] Alfred Brown, who had regarded the Waikato as an area where "a darkness may be felt" and experienced the destruction and abandonment of Matamata in 1836-37, was making the 500th entry into the baptismal register by 1841, a year in which 269 baptisms (190 being adults) were recorded for

---

25. R. Maunsell, March 1838 (Maraetai convert); to secretaries, 2 February 1843 (Jowett); to William Jowett of CMS, 21 September 1839 (intellectual power); to secretaries, 10 April 1841 (dying Māori); to Henry Venn, 9 February 1849 (conversion, education); to secretaries, 27 December 1844 (surprise), C N/O 64/5, 15, 25, 30, 35, 53; John Morgan to Venn, 2 September 1850 (educational grant's withdrawal), C N/O 65/45.

26. B. Ashwell Journal, 27 October 1837 (Tepuka at Owai), C N/O 17/94; later entries (Port Nicholson, customs), C N/O 17/96, 98.

27. J. Hamlin Journal, 21 June 1836 (hair), 13 March 1837 (Ngatiteata), Hocken MS M.1 68-69.

Matamata, Taupo, Rotorua, and Tauranga, largely as the result of work by Māori teachers, of whom there were two in Otawhao in September 1839 and, by January 1841 and the 500th entry in the register, another seventeen over a wider area.[28]

On the Thames-Waikato area in the period 1833-40, K. R. Howe has raised interesting issues. He has showed how the various factors used by Harrison Wright to explain the spread of *mihinare* religion in the Bay of Islands are largely absent in this region. There were no epidemics, in the way disease was held to be a factor in the north. Involvement by Europeans, as in the East Cape, was minimal, as were the cultural dislocation and moral difficulties they brought. Hongi's muskets had done damage here, and there was a wish for peace among the chiefs. But the more important factor was Māori interest, even excitement, over the new ideas on offer. Māori leaders like William Broughton, Wiremu Tamihana, and Solomon "were sufficiently imbued with Christian doctrine by 1838 to believe that Christianity, as they understood it . . . would be beneficial to the Māoris" and were "largely responsible for . . . spreading the gospel after the missionaries left Matamata." The mistake is to view the Māori as passive recipients of missionary work; the evidence here shows that they were active propagators of the message. Howe's picture is of a Māori mental world with "great capacity to accept change" coupled with a strong desire "for mental excitement" where they found ideas that were "novel and interesting." J. W. Stack, sometime Methodist, had noticed the Māori facility for picking up Christian teaching and not only to "talk about it" but also to practice it, with a skill he found "really astonishing" — Howe wrote that the demand for baptism preceded the demand for Bibles and that there was no sign that Christianity had to "penetrate the shell of Māori resistance," as Wright had suggested for the Ngapuhi. Māori embraced change in customs over burial practices and attitudes to their chiefs' head and hair, as Hamlin had observed.[29]

28. Brown to Jowett, 16 September 1833 (darkness); to secretaries, 21 April 1837 (Matamata); Journal, 26 September 1841 (baptisms); to secretaries, 8 September 1841 (190 adults); Journal, 19 September 1839 (Otawhao teachers); 9 January 1841 (17); C N/O 24/18, 27, 120, 35, 116, 119; R. Lange, *Island Ministers: Indigenous Leadership in Nineteenth Century Pacific Island Christianity* (Canterbury, NZ: MacMillan Brown Centre for Pacific Studies, 2005), p. 153. "Matiu, Tahu and Ngakuku were three of Brown's trusted Māori teachers": a reference back to main text, p. 135, and his use of such.

29. K. R. Howe, "The Māori Response to Christianity in the Thames-Waikato Area 1833-40," *NZJH* 7, no. 1 (April 1973): 28-46; on "excitement," see Maunsell to CMS secretaries, 27 December 1844: "I never expected the excitement which the first influx of gospel truth caused would continue." C N/O 64/35. Cf. P. Adams, *Fatal Necessity: British Intervention in New Zealand, 1830-47* (Auckland: Oxford University Press, 1977), pp. 47-48.

From Kaitaia in the north to Otaki in the south, CMS writings gave evidence of many Māori initiatives. At Kaitaia Joseph Matthews wrote in March 1839 of Chief Noble as a man who was "steady, thoughtful and persevering" as a preacher of the Gospels and hence "a great blessing," a view confirmed by William Puckey, who saw him as a very effective evangelist who "has been the instrument under God's hand of causing many tribes to join us."[30] In the Rotorua-Taupo area, Henry Williams recorded a group of Rotoruan Christians who had emerged prior to any European presence. Thomas Chapman, who had experienced at first hand the destruction of Matamata in September 1836, had an encounter with a *tohunga* who was disgusted at the Christian progress by 1846-47: "you study, we kill." This was followed by a concession that the future lay with the *mihinare:* "shaking his whole frame by the violence of his anger he added 'But history goes straight on now — all our sacred ways are gone — and you (addressing a Māori boy of Chapman's) will go on ... breaking all our sacred rules until you exasperate us beyond forbearance: go and let us see your faces no more.'"[31] Taupo had its early Māori martyrs, Manihera and Kereopa of the Ngatiruani tribe, who mounted a fatal Christian mission to hostile Māori and whose end was chronicled by William Williams.[32] Farther south, Hadfield too recorded rapid progress, with Te Rauparaha's nephew as one of the chief instigators, while C. L. Reay wrote of Māori initiatives in the South Island from his station in Nelson: Tahama Hone and other teachers from Nelson preached in the North Island along the coast to Taranaki.[33] Henry Williams wrote of his own and the new bishop Selwyn's experiences of finding Christian response in places no European had visited: "the greatest growth arising from knowledge having found its way in a silent manner unknown to any missionary, as I find its effects where no European had ... gone before. ... I speak mainly of what I was eye witness to ... the same has been seen through the southern island by the Bishop."[34] Significant as the missionary contribution had been, in the spread of the new religion to the south and east the Māori contribution was more so and the judg-

---

30. Matthews to Coates, 5 March 1839, C N/O 61/21; W. G. Puckey Jr., 21 September 1839; cf. 12 June 1840, C N/O 72/14, 15. Matthews and Puckey had nineteen "appointed" Māori teachers by February 1841, Matthews to Jowett, 17 February 1841, C N/O 61/26.

31. Henry Williams Journal, 12 December 1839, C N/O 93/207; T. Chapman, 12 September 1836 (destruction); cf. 8 October 1836, Journal, May-October 1848, sec. 9.

32. W. Williams, *Christianity among the New Zealanders,* pp. 324-25.

33. Hadfield to Coates, 1 February 1841: "rapid ... yet a steady progress" based on the work of Ripahau, C N/O 48/3; A. Brown Journal, 13 August 1839 (nephew), C N/O 24/116; Reay to secretaries, 3 September 1844, C N/O 73/3.

34. H. Williams to Coates, 20 August 1844, C N/O 93/109.

ment that the missionaries "discharged a rather more humble role than is customarily accorded to them" is one that they themselves had also recognized. One outstanding example was the evangelistic sortie, prompted by Octavius Hadfield certainly but by then a Māori enterprise, when Te Rauparaha's son, Tamihana, and his cousin, Matene Te Whiwhi, made a journey of a thousand miles in a small open boat to act as apostles to the Māori of the South Island, who included the former enemies of Te Rauparaha, the Ngai Tahu, thus risking their lives in the cause while giving reassurances of peace along with general Christian exhortation. Such activity exceeded the expectations of their missionary mentors again and again.[35]

---

35. See articles in the earlier *Dictionary of New Zealand Biography,* ed. G. H. Scholefield, especially "Te Rauparaha, Tamihana or Katu," pp. 202-3; *DNZB*, 1:507-8: "he (Tamihana) and Matene zealously studied the gospel and became the first native apostles to the south island" (p. 202).

CHAPTER 11

Indigenous Agents: Teachers, Catechists, and Martyrs

Although the last chapter concentrated on Māori initiative arising from the work of the CMS, indigenous agents were also widely used in both Roman Catholic and Methodist missions. Our understanding of this widespread use of Māori teachers has been much enhanced by Raeburn Lange in his recent work *Island Ministers,* and in an earlier article specifically on Māori.[1] His magisterial book has placed the phenomenon in the wider context of Polynesian and Melanesian ministers and missionaries throughout the Pacific, where, for example, it is known that the LMS missionary John Williams placed Tahitian teachers on Samoa and a gifted Tongan, Joeli Bulu, was active and effective on Fiji from 1838. Tahitian teachers had also been active in Tonga itself, the site of a successful WMMS mission begun in the 1820s.[2]

Certain factors discerned in Lange's work deserve special notice in New Zealand. First, native teachers (*kaiwhakaako* to Māori) were valued not least for their skills in teaching reading and literacy, as Māori reached out for the sources of European power and wealth.[3] Second, the teachers "did take on at

---

1. R. Lange, *Island Ministers: Indigenous Leadership in Nineteenth Century Pacific Island Christianity* (Canterbury, NZ: MacMillan Brown Centre for Pacific Studies, 2005); Lange, "Indigenous Agents of Religious Change in New Zealand 1830-1860," *JRH* 24, no. 3 (October 2000): 279-95.

2. Lange, *Island Ministers;* I. Breward, *A History of the Churches in Australasia* (Oxford: Oxford University Press, 2001), pp. 29-38, 59-64 (Joeli Bulu); Timothy Yates, *The Expansion of Christianity* (Oxford: Lion Hunter, 2004), pp. 146-65; C. W. Forman, *Island Churches of the Pacific* (New York: Orbis, 1982).

3. Lange, "Indigenous Agents," p. 283.

Indigenous Agents

least some aspects of the role of religious experts in the traditional order,"[4] so that their religious leadership did not represent a clean break from the roles of the *tohunga* and, in one or two cases, Christian teachers retained an interest and expertise in traditional schools and genealogies. Such men (the record has no women, though some Māori priestesses were a feature of traditional life) had "deep roots in the Māori social and religious world."[5] Third, although many of the teachers were ex-captives, often of the Ngapuhi, and owing their Christianity to residence in Hokianga, the Bay of Islands, and Kororareka, the distinct loss of *mana* that resulted from their captive status was overcome through their recognized skills in reading and teaching and their religious awareness.[6] For G. A. Selwyn, who reached New Zealand as Anglican bishop in 1842, the teachers' power and influence often exceeded that of the tribal chiefs.[7] Lange judged that "in the dissemination of new religious ideas, the bridging of the gap between British and Polynesian religious concepts, and the insertion of Christianity into Māori culture, Māori initiatives were no less significant than the much chronicled deeds of the missionaries from Britain and Europe."[8]

Although Roman Catholics appeared to lay less emphasis on indigenous agents, their use of Māori catechists, noted by Lange,[9] was more widespread than often appeared in the records, partly because, as E. R. Simmons has written, missionary accounts were constructed for those who had an interest in figures they knew in person, which meant concentration on the European missionaries.[10] For this reason, he wrote, it is all too easy "to forget the part the Māoris played in their own conversion. . . . the story of the New Zealand church in its earliest days is primarily a Māori story not a European one . . . change of mind and heart that created a Catholic church in New Zealand was essentially the work of Māori to Māori."[11] Lange mentioned by name the leading Māori catechist Romano,[12] and Simmons mentioned the "foremost catechist" Werahiko[13] but admitted that few of the names were available of those

---

4. Lange, "Indigenous Agents," p. 290.
5. Lange, "Indigenous Agents," p. 295.
6. Lange, *Island Ministers*, p. 152.
7. G. A. Selwyn, *A Charge Delivered to the Clergy of the Diocese of New Zealand . . . 1847* (London: Rivington, 1849), p. 61; Lange, "Indigenous Agents," p. 288.
8. Lange, "Indigenous Agents," pp. 280, 283.
9. Lange, "Indigenous Agents," p. 280.
10. E. R. Simmons, *Pompallier, Prince of Bishops* (Auckland: CPC Publishing, 1984), p. 36.
11. Simmons, *Pompallier*, pp. 36-37.
12. Lange, *Island Ministers*, p. 155.
13. Simmons, *Pompallier*, pp. 36-37.

to whom so much was owed. A young chief, Tupara, was the Catholic apostle in Rotorua, where there was a community of 300-400 Roman Catholic Christians; Mohi Tuhimete of Pokau and Hakaria Te Hura were two among many who strengthened work in the Waikato district that led to 1,110 baptisms.[14]

Father Pézant, somewhat outstanding as a Marist missionary and later a parish priest, whose work "won universal respect even from Protestant missionaries,"[15] wrote a *mémoire* of his time in the Waikato district based at Rangiawhia from 1841, in which there is frequent reference to catechists. They supply his language deficiency on arrival at Tauranga,[16] prompt baptisms at Kawhia, in the case of Hakaria Te Hura visit three tribes with him on a journey ending at Taranaki, and even, in the case of Moise Tuhinete ("one of the best Catholics of the island"), assist in a debate with the CMS missionary, John Morgan, helped by a group of "quelques autres des meilleurs catéchistes." Pézant reported on his station to Colin, which included 80 baptisms "by the New Zealand catechists." His final comment on them as a class was that they were well enough instructed to "confound the protestant ministers" and were "very attached to our holy religion."[17] The whole piece serves as a reminder of how important, if often anonymous, the work of the RC catechists was in the Marist mission. Both Lange and Simmons recalled that when Pompallier came to set up his seminary at St. Mary's North Shore in Auckland, he was able to select fifteen of the pool of catechists, whom he plainly judged to be suitable candidates for priesthood, even if the plan never reached fruition.[18]

In turning to Methodists, Lange has held that the WMMS was perhaps more deliberate in the use of Māori agents than the CMS, though this has to be qualified by what has been shown of William Williams's determined strategy in the East Cape and the fact that, as Lange recognized, the CMS issued formal licenses to Māori teachers from 1840.[19] Methodist historians have identified three Māori teachers from as early as 1839 in John Lee Tutu, Taurua (also known as Richard Watson), and Moses Rewa.[20] A group of teachers at

14. Simmons, *Pompallier,* pp. 60, 87.
15. *DNZB,* 1:341.
16. Pézant, *Mémoire,* in Fr. Charles Girard, *Lettres reçues d'Océanie par l'administration generale des pères maristes pendant le generalat de Jean-Claude Colin* (Rome: Centre d'études maristes, 1999), 3:521-73; 524 (language).
17. Pézant, *Mémoire,* pp. 551, 556, 563-64 (debate), 564 ("quelques . . ."), 556, 572.
18. Lange, *Island Ministers,* pp. 170-71; Simmons, *Pompallier,* p. 127.
19. Lange, *Island Ministers,* p. 153.
20. W. A. Chambers, *Samuel Ironside in New Zealand, 1839-1858* (Auckland: Ray Richards and Wesleyan Historical Society, 1982), p. 62; T. G. Hammond, *"In the Beginning": The History of a Mission* (Auckland: Methodist Literature and Colporteur Society, 1915), pp. 35-36.

Mangungu in 1839-40 produced two Christian martyrs, Matiu, an ex-slave and evangelist, and Rihimona, both killed in a Christian approach to the hostile chief Kaitoke, an encounter that left a third teacher, Wiremu Pantene, son-in-law of Waka Nene, with four bullet holes in his blanket but his body intact.[21] Among a group of chiefs who had responded to the WMMS in the 1830s were Simon Matangi, William Barton, and Abraham Taonui. Matangi accompanied John Whiteley to Kawhia and, according to the missionary, was as universally respected as a Christian teacher as he had been dreaded as an adversary in his pre-Christian past.[22]

In the Taranaki district, the outstanding Māori Christian leader was Wiremu Nera (William Naylor), who worked with another, Hohana.[23] According to T. G. Hammond, Nera claimed the honor of being "the first evangelist of the Māoris of South Taranaki." John Whiteley had taken him with him to the Taranaki coast and "Wiremu Nera became the recognised native minister of the area," Hammond wrote,[24] in which role he taught a class of Māori for two years before seeking baptism for them.[25] John Skevington, who came as a Methodist missionary to serve in Nera's district in April 1842, wrote that Nera had preached to nearly all the South Taranaki tribes "before a single European had been near them"; despite being unable to read, he appears to have been an effective evangelist who prepared the way for European missionaries and became an official Wesleyan teacher.[26] The two Methodist missionaries, Bumby and Hobbs, went south on a missionary journey to Port Nicholson (Wellington), taking with them six Māori teachers and volunteers who were to be left there on 7 June 1839, two of them from Mangungu (More, Minarapa), four from Waimate (Reihana, Hemi, Ngaroto, Waka),[27] one of whom, Reihana, had been baptized by the CMS missionary, Richard Davis.[28] John Bumby, who was current superintendent of the WMMS mission, was to die tragically by drowning soon after this expedition on 24 July 1840.

In the South Island, Methodist use of indigenous agency was possibly even more striking in the 1840s. James Watkin had been appointed to the lonely station of Waikouaiti, Otago, and arrived from Sydney in 1840, isolated from his Methodist brethren farther north. Watkin's journal and letters are

---

21. Chambers, *Samuel Ironside*, p. 66 and n. 11; Hammond, *"In the Beginning,"* p. 15.
22. Lange, *Island Ministers*, p. 153.
23. *DNZB*, 1:312; Chambers, *Samuel Ironside*, pp. 69, 79.
24. Hammond, *"In the Beginning,"* pp. 14-18.
25. Chambers, *Samuel Ironside*, p. 79.
26. *DNZB*, 1:312-13.
27. Chambers, *Samuel Ironside*, p. 96.
28. Chambers, *Samuel Ironside*, p. 99 n. 31.

no guide to his worth as a missionary; in these he often appeared in despair of the country, its inhabitants, and his situation among them. His letter of 15 September 1840 to the secretaries at home gave a picture of deep depression amounting to self-loathing, and his journal of 1841 showed him wanting to leave New Zealand in January and May.[29] Nevertheless, in the view of the historian T. A. Pybus, "seldom has a missionary accomplished so much in one year as Watkin . . . in 1840," and this was particularly the case in relation to Māori teachers, where his training "stood out as a marvellous achievement."[30] Of these, Joseph (Hohepa) was "a typical Māori teacher . . . one of a band of travelling preachers,"[31] and Horomona Pohio, who came from Ruapuke Island, became its first teacher and pastor, a highly valued chief who also taught on Stewart Island (Rakiura).[32] The Māori church at Otakou had two teachers who were reported to be good preachers in Hoani Wetere Korako and Tare Wetere Te Kahu,[33] while another man, Rawiri Waitere Manaru, who had become a Christian through the work of John Whiteley, was active as a class leader.[34] An interesting figure was the ex-*tohunga* Matiaha Tiramorehu of the Ngai Tahu: he was a chief who taught for the mission, retaining his interest in Māori traditional learning and forming later a Māori academy *(wharekura)*. He was baptized by Watkin in 1843, and both Watkin and J. W. Stack acknowledged him as the best authority on Māori tradition and genealogy in the South Island.[35]

One reason for the progress in Māori teaching and preaching was Watkin's practice of gathering teachers, as many as twenty-six of them, for regular training sessions; this practice was also followed in the extreme north of the North Island by Joseph Matthews of the CMS, who offered two to three hours of instruction to intending preachers on the Saturday before their engagements.[36] Among Watkin's protégés was Matiu, chief and *tohunga*, who became, in Pybus's phrase, a Christian *tohunga*.[37] A less appealing side to the

---

29. MMS Microfilm, Watkin to secretaries, 15 September 1841; Journal extracts, 8 May 1841.

30. T. A. Pybus, *Māori and Missionary: Early Christian Missionaries in the South Island of New Zealand* (Wellington: A. H. and A. W. Reed, 1954), p. 16.

31. Pybus, *Māori and Missionary*, p. 21.

32. Lange, "Indigenous Agents," pp. 282, 285; Lange, *Island Ministers*, p. 153.

33. Pybus, *Māori and Missionary*, p. 45.

34. Pybus, *Māori and Missionary*, p. 26; Chambers, *Samuel Ironside*, p. 98.

35. *DNZB*, 1:540-41; Pybus, *Māori and Missionary*, p. 66; Lange, "Indigenous Agents," pp. 285, 290; Lange, *Island Ministers*, p. 153.

36. Pybus, *Māori and Missionary*, p. 44; S. C. Matthews and L. J. Matthews, *Matthews of Kaitaia* (Dunedin: Reed, 1940), pp. 105-7.

37. Pybus, *Māori and Missionary*, pp. 159-60.

evangelistic sortie (noted at the end of the last chapter) by Tamihana, Te Rauparaha's son, and his friend Matene was their attempts to undermine Wesleyan work. Hadfield, their mentor, was known, like Selwyn, to have reservations about the Methodists and a strongly Anglican ecclesiology, which his Māori followers may have imbibed; Pybus pointed out rightly that teachers like Pohio had acted as evangelists in the south of the South Island long before this foray, which was impressive but by no means pristine in either Ruapuke or Stewart Island.[38]

A chief and *tohunga,* who was a skillful worker in the highly prized greenstone *(poenamu)* called Korako, who was not a Christian teacher, paid suitable recognition to Watkin's work before he left for Port Nicholson in 1844: he had "put an end to the vile butcheries inflicted upon the native race ... (to) cannibalism and other evils."[39] Whatever Watkin's own assessments of his life in Otago, frequently bleak and depressed, he left a firm foundation for his successor Charles Creed, not least of Māori workers, which included those at Port Levy (Koukourarata), Ta Awao, who evangelized the Ngai Tahu after 1839, and Hohepa Korehi.[40] Both were active more widely in the Canterbury area. Creed himself took three other Māori teachers on a missionary journey in September 1844: Hohepa Maru, Wiremu Pantene Te Aowangai, and Rawiri Te Maire. Once more, however, the advent of the European missionary postdated services being conducted by Māori Wesleyan leaders, as discovered, for example, by the Frenchman from Akaroa, Lavaud, who found a group of forty engaged in worship, using "prayers taught them by a Protestant native pastor."[41]

In addition to Watkin and Creed, another notable Methodist pioneer and missionary, Samuel Ironside, came to Cloudy Bay in December 1840. His precursor had also been a Māori teacher, Wiriamu, who, when the New Zealand Company's ship *Tory* had been moored nearby, had assembled the Māori Christians onboard for acts of worship.[42] Ironside appointed Māori catechists, who included Puaha, a close relation of both Te Rauparaha and Te Rangihaeata, whose class meeting was said to have had "long term effects" on the life of the Ngati Toa.[43] Ironside also used some thirty Māori teachers in the district areas of Punkura, Rangitoto, and Motueka, holding regular teachers' meetings to support what they did in local *maraes* by preaching, teaching,

38. Pybus, *Māori and Missionary,* pp. 50-60.
39. Pybus, *Māori and Missionary,* p. 29.
40. Pybus, *Māori and Missionary,* p. 68; Lange, *Island Ministers,* pp. 151-52.
41. Pybus, *Māori and Missionary,* p. 89 and n. 1.
42. Chambers, *Samuel Ironside,* p. 98.
43. Chambers, *Samuel Ironside,* p. 106.

and exercising pastoral care.[44] Among them was one Naohu, who prepared forty candidates on d'Urville Island at Horea for a baptism on 30 July 1842.[45] The arrival of 450 New Testaments, products of the BFBS, in Cloudy Bay, the "Holy Book" or *Pukapuka Tapu*, caused "all to be full of repressed excitement" and resulted in a huge feast.[46] Ironside left Cloudy Bay in July 1843 to establish work in Nelson and Marlborough. In the so-called Wairau Massacre, which resulted from the land hunger of the New Zealand Company and in which Te Rangihaeata's wife was shot and Captain Arthur Wakefield and other Europeans killed in response, Ironside was the minister responsible for burials.[47]

In writing of Roman Catholic experience in the north, E. R. Simmons wrote perceptively of both the perils and the advantages of religious change for the Māori. His judgments extend beyond the field of Roman Catholic mission while also providing a helpful introduction to the final chapter of this book. The stages of Māori change are well described:

> at first, they tried to accept the benefits of European trade and contact without changing their ancestral way of life too much; and during this period . . . Christianity made very slow progress. But in the space of a single generation the Māoris were faced with their own special version of an old dilemma: they could gain the European world only at the loss of their own soul. If they accepted the new material advantages it meant that their closely knit world, in which the land, the ancestors and the spirits were interwoven . . . must be broken up to allow entry of European ideas and values. If they paid attention while Europeans poured scorn on Māori myths and religion, they stood to lose their sense of personal identity and worth. Yet how could they refuse the very real advantages Europeans offered?

The chosen people of the Old Testament could provide a fresh *whakapapa* (ancestry) "larger than the Māori race," and "in Christ they could find the hero ancestor of the new tribe of Christians and could find their own identity in that tribe . . . and find that wholeness which was given by the religions of old. . . . by the 1830s some Māoris were beginning to see the attraction of Christianity in precisely these terms (though) . . . obviously the material

---

44. Chambers, *Samuel Ironside*, pp. 120-21, 127: this writer names twelve of the thirty Māori at p. 121.
45. Chambers, *Samuel Ironside*, p. 116.
46. Chambers, *Samuel Ironside*, p. 114.
47. DNZB, 1:209-10.

things were important considerations. But it seems that the attraction of Christianity at the time was an important factor. It does have something to offer that was — and still is — important to the Māori people." Whereas many Europeans were "totally devoid" of a sense of the sacred, this was not true of the Māori, for whom a spiritual dimension to the whole of life was generally assumed and accepted; so, "Māori Christianity (became) . . . better Christianity than that of European settlers."[48]

---

48. Simmons, *Pompallier*, pp. 12-15.

CHAPTER 12

Conversion: An Analysis

Herbert William Williams, grandson of William Williams and, like his grandfather, Anglican bishop of Waiapu and Māori scholar, wrote a perceptive article on Māori-dom in the *Journal of the Polynesian Society* of 1935, entitled "The Reaction of the Māori to the Impact of Civilization."[1] After commending Raymond Firth's work *Principles of Economy of the New Zealand Māori,* Williams noted the passing of the *tohunga,* who "is no more," and of *tapu* and *makutu,* while at the same time putting questions against the view that missionaries were responsible for their decay.[2] In the conclusion of his paper he wrote: "we may accept as substantially correct Bishop Selwyn's statement that in 1842 he found the whole Māori race converted to Christianity."[3] The early 1840s were to see many changes in New Zealand society, including colonial government in the persons of Governors Hobson (1841-42), Fitzroy (1843-45), and George Grey (1845-53) and a move from mission to church, symbolized by the arrival of G. A. Selwyn as the first Anglican bishop in 1842. But this judgment of religious change by Selwyn, endorsed by Williams, is highly significant.

Before examining the position taken up by such varied writers as Harrison Wright, Judith Binney, J. M. R. Owens, K. R. Howe, and James Belich on the question of Māori conversion, some more general consideration may be needed. In the New Testament, as expounded by Bishop Lesslie Newbigin, conversion is made up of three aspects: a personal relationship to Christ by an

---

1. H. W. Williams, "The Reaction of the Māori to the Impact of Civilization," *JPS* 44 (1935): 216-43.
2. H. W. Williams, "Reaction of the Māori," p. 226.
3. H. W. Williams, "Reaction of the Māori," p. 241.

"inner turning of the heart and will"; membership in a visible community; and commitment to a pattern of behavior and action.[4] Important twentieth-century studies of the phenomenon of conversion have been made by William James in his *Varieties of Religious Experience* of 1902 and by Raoul Allier in *La Psychologie de la conversion chez les Peuples non-civilisées* of 1925, which drew extensively on mission literature, particularly that of the Paris Evangelical Mission and its *Journal des Missions Evangéliques,* with additional material from the Swiss *Mission Romande* and Moravian writings.[5] Allier made a good deal of the resistance of tribal societies to change, including what he called *endurcissement* (hardening); conversion here involved pain, made up both of the pain of converting and, quite as much, of the pain of not converting. A sense of an obligation to change was matched by a sense of responsibility for being in a state that was condemned.[6] He specified the use of the terminology of the "two hearts" by Māori, Kanaks, and Africans of the Zambesi equally, an example being the great African chief Moshesh of the Lesotho, who told David Livingstone's father-in-law, Robert Moffat, the pioneer missionary: "before I listened to you I had only one heart, now today I have two."[7] For Allier, as for William James, conversion was a kind of death as well as a way of release after what Allier termed "La Crise," which led to a "new orientation of deep emotions" and "changes of tastes and aversions."[8]

Of great value to the present study is a full-scale examination of conversion in a Polynesian society very similar to the Māori made by Sir Raymond Firth in his *Rank and Religion in Tikopia: A Study in Polynesian Paganism and Conversion to Christianity* of 1970. Here, religion not only provided basic notions of ultimate reality but was supremely about power and the "ability to control."[9] For this purpose certain techniques were available; as with Māori, the *ariki* handled *tapu* and would often be chiefs. The *atua* were amoral but also raised questions of power and control.[10] Like the Māori, the Tikopians were slow to change: a mission begun in 1901 reached the point of nine adult baptisms in 1919.[11] Firth

---

4. L. Newbigin, "Conversion," in *Concise Dictionary of the Christian World Mission*, ed. S. C. Neill et al. (London: Lutterworth Press, 1971), pp. 147-48.

5. On Allier, see my essay in M. Percy, ed., *Previous Convictions* (London: SPCK, 2000), pp. 124-36, and in *Mission Studies* 13, nos. 1 and 2 (1996): 306-19.

6. Allier, *La Psychologie de la conversion chez des Peuples non-civilisées* (Paris: Payot, 1925), 1:328-30.

7. Allier, *La Psychologie*, 1:351, 365-66.

8. Allier, *La Psychologie*, 1:531, 548-49.

9. R. Firth, *Rank and Religion in Tikopia: A Study in Polynesian Paganism and Conversion to Christianity* (London: Allen and Unwin, 1970), p. 18.

10. Firth, *Rank and Religion*, pp. 110f.

11. Firth, *Rank and Religion*, pp. 37-38.

took issue with Allier over the view that conversion involved suffering, though he agreed with Allier's emphasis on the significance of dreams in conversion and, while accepting the importance of economic factors and those of social status, felt that these could be overplayed.[12] For one significant Christian convert and chief, the reason for seeking conversion was the welfare of the land.[13] Firth saw conversion as having to do with problems of meaning and power "in subtle conjunction."[14] Tikopians who became preachers gained status and power and Christianity lessened violence,[15] but the old ways lived on, too. The *ariki*, Tafia, baptized in 1924, "had not forsaken the old gods though he worshipped the new" and still made offerings to the *atua*.[16] Firth held that, despite the importance of economic benefits, personal conviction over Christian theology and its moral system was not to be overlooked: though "rarely alone . . . nevertheless its importance should not be underestimated."[17]

In a more recent study of a quite different tribal society, J. D. Y. Peel found that the Yoruba of modern Nigeria also demonstrated that the key to religion and religious change was the quest for power; prayer here also was a technique, a "technical instrument" toward control.[18] Like Firth, Peel thought there was a danger of underestimating the influence of the missionaries and their message, whether (in West Africa) the missionaries were Christian or Muslim. Like Firth, too, Peel was wary of those like the Comaroffs, who in their study of the Tswana under the influence of the London Missionary Society had heavily emphasized economic and technical benefits.[19] There were undoubted links between Christianity and "civilization," but for Peel they were contingent and subject to strains. Much more signifi-

---

12. Firth, *Rank and Religion*, p. 326; cf. Allier, *La Psychologie*, 2:326f., and note on Allier by Firth at p. 325 n. 1; on the importance of dreams in conversion, see Allier, 1:373-74, confirmed among Māori by the naval surgeon W. B. Marshall, *A Personal Narrative of Two Visits to New Zealand* (London: J. Nisbet, 1836), pp. 96-97.

13. Firth, *Rank and Religion*, p. 328.
14. Firth, *Rank and Religion*, p. 407.
15. Firth, *Rank and Religion*, pp. 407-8.
16. Firth, *Rank and Religion*, p. 309.
17. Firth, *Rank and Religion*, p. 321.
18. J. D. Y. Peel, *Religious Encounter and the Making of the Yoruba* (Bloomington: Indiana University Press, 2000), pp. 90, 92.
19. John L. Comaroff and Jean Comaroff, *Of Revelation and Revolution: Christianity, Colonialism, and Consciousness in South Africa* (Chicago: University of Chicago Press, 1991), is the first volume of a trilogy on the work of the London Missionary Society among the Tswana people. This influential study emphasized the "colonizing of the mind" of the Tswana, a position that was held by others to preclude any "free response and appropriation, let alone independent agency to indigenous actors." B. Stanley, "Conversion to Christianity: The Colonisation of the Mind?" *IRM* 92, no. 366 (July 2003): 317.

Conversion: An Analysis

cant was the adoption of the Christian story: "Christian mission is about the effective telling of a story and conversion occurs when people are prepared to take that story as their own."[20] As with Māori, originally political calculation was involved and white men were acquired as objects of prestige, while their missionary character was largely ignored.[21] The book, as with Māori, was seen as the key to Christianity, and it amazed the Yoruba that by the techniques of the white man not only the aged and experienced but also women and children could be initiated into such learning.[22] Essentially, the Yoruba believed the new religion supplied them with power for the needs of this world and the next.[23]

One influential writer on conversion was Robin Horton, who interacted with an earlier study of the Yoruba by Peel; Africanist scholars saw this people "struggling" to adapt inherited concepts of control to the new situations of modernity.[24] Horton felt this could too easily and glibly be referred to as "conversion," which he saw, surely correctly, as a multilayered and complex phenomenon. One major factor at work was the impact on traditional cosmology of Christianity and Islam through the work of missionaries, whereby the lesser spirits gave way to supreme being.[25] Horton judged that there was no *immediate* abandonment of the tribal "explanatory system"; he put as much emphasis on the general context of change as on the religious solvents. For him, Christianity benefited from the fluctuating context. For others, as David Maxwell pointed out in a helpful overview, the danger of the approach of some anthropology, including that of the Comaroffs, was that "their work left little room for consideration of religious ideas and narratives, the indigenous agents who transmitted them and the converts who adopted them."[26] Peel's *Religious Encounter and the Making of the Yoruba*, by contrast, had asserted the "importance of indigenous or local narratives, which receive and re-pattern missionary signs and symbols."[27] Rather than a "colonisation of consciousness" by Europeans, the reality was that Christianity had "already

---

20. Peel, *Yoruba*, pp. 3-6 (strains), 310 (story).
21. Peel, *Yoruba*, p. 128.
22. Peel, *Yoruba*, p. 225.
23. Peel, *Yoruba*, p. 265.
24. R. Horton, "African Conversion," *Africa* 41, no. 2 (April 1971): 92; see also Horton, "On Rationality of Conversion," *Africa* 45, no. 3 (1975): 219-35 and 373-99.
25. Horton, "African Conversion," pp. 102ff.
26. Horton, "African Conversion," p. 104; David Maxwell, "Writing the History of African Christianity: Reflections of an Editor," *Journal of Religion in Africa* 36, nos. 3-4 (2006): 382-85.
27. Maxwell, "Writing the History," p. 385.

been appropriated" and native agency and indigenization were doing "most of the proselytism" — more than the missionaries.[28]

What then of those who have more particularly addressed the Māori between 1814 and 1842? For Harrison Wright, factors of social dislocation predominated; he instanced the presence of epidemics, assigned to the power of the European *atua;* the collision with modernity in European technical superiority, shown as iron tools replaced greenstone adzes; and a combination of disease and war weariness inducing "apathy" among Māori.[29] J. M. R. Owens put the emphasis on the power of ideas to initiate change by way of the missionary preaching and teaching; the contrast with Harrison Wright is not dissimilar to that between Peel and the Comaroffs. Owens held that to argue that the Māori "turned to Christianity as a solution to the problems introduced into their lives" is too negative an approach; it "denies the freedom of choice" and appropriation.[30] He pointed also to the increased efficiency of the mission after 1830 and the spread of literacy as the means of turning the tide after the initial lack of success. Judith Binney made an influential and important reply to Owens. She pointed to the common pattern of response in Pacific communities, of initial resistance followed by eventual breakthrough, which the missionary Johannes Warneck (not referred to by her) had made after experience among the Bataks of Sumatra, where ten to fifteen years typically elapsed before substantial response (for Māori, in this study, replicated between 1814 and 1829), and full Christianization followed after forty-five years; but very much sooner for Māori.[31] Binney discerned the importance of the "domestic natives" at Te Waimate,[32] who formed a Christian community, and such additional factors as Henry Williams's peacemaking in the context of a mood of "despair" (Wright's "apathy"), epidemics, the disruption of traditional Māori society, and the literacy factor where Māori set out "to master the secrets of the European world."[33] Here the link with Peel and Horton is marked; power and control were at issue and "the book" was seen as a key to

---

28. Maxwell, "Writing the History," p. 386; cf. D. L. Whiteman, *Missionaries and Melanesians* (Pasadena, Calif.: William Carey Library, 1983), pp. 188-89, 222.

29. H. M. Wright, *New Zealand, 1769-1840: Early Years of Western Contact* (Cambridge: Harvard University Press, 1959), pp. 141-57.

30. J. M. R. Owens, "Christianity and the Māoris to 1840," *NZJH* 2 (April 1968): 18-40; quotation from J. Binney, "Christianity and the Māoris to 1840: A Comment," *NZJH* 3 (1969): 143-65, at 143.

31. J. Warneck, *The Living Forces of the Gospel,* trans. N. Buchanan (Edinburgh: Oliphant, Anderson, Ferrier, 1909), p. 188.

32. Binney, "Christianity and the Māoris," pp. 147, 156.

33. Binney, "Christianity and the Māoris," pp. 149, 151-53, 154, 155.

both. Conversion for the historian has to be linked to the second of Newbigin's three pointers, membership of the visible community; and appendices of baptisms, communicants in numbers, allied to Clarke's estimated 64,000 worshipers, Binney regarded as a safer (and more accessible) guide than inner-personal conversions. On Owens's emphasis on choice she wrote: "the question remains: why does a new set of beliefs, of whatever form, become acceptable? Is it simply the stimulus of new concepts or is it that the need exists? If the latter, the need can only be expressed in terms of a newly created dissatisfaction with the older beliefs. This dissatisfaction would not have occurred without the impact of European culture. In this sense the Māori were not free to choose."[34] In a reference to Raymond Firth's work, she argued that "religious belief would only be introduced if it fulfils some definite need."[35] While agreeing with Owens that religion is a social phenomenon and that, in the end, its appeal has to be seen in spiritual terms, she argued that the social context of tribal disruption provided the real key to religious change.[36] K. R. Howe, reviewing this debate in his book *Where the Waves Fall*, wrote: "the search for a solution has proved futile and the debate has rather unsatisfactorily fizzled out,"[37] though we have seen that he himself has put questions against the Wright thesis in relation to the Thames-Waikato area, where disease was not present and other factors like war weariness were less prominent though, as Binney indicated, not entirely absent.[38]

James Belich published *Making Peoples* in 1996. In it, he too handled the subject of conversion. Although he agreed that literacy was an important factor in Māori conversion, he saw Māori interest in Christianity as deeper than interest in "the book." If there was a delay in assimilation, it lay primarily in the lack of opportunity, through scarcity of missionaries and their weak grasp of language in the early years; Henry Williams did not preach in Māori for the first five years of his missionary life. As to peacemaking, Belich discerned rightly that behind the interventions of the missionaries lay Māori initiatives in promoting peacemaking occasions.[39] European technological superiority

---

34. Binney, "Christianity and the Māoris," p. 164.
35. Binney, "Christianity and the Māoris," p. 164; R. Firth, *Economics of the New Zealand Māori* (Wellington: R. E. Owen, 1928; 2nd ed. 1959), p. 436.
36. Binney, "Christianity and the Māoris," p. 165.
37. K. R. Howe, *Where the Waves Fall* (Honolulu: University of Hawaii Press, 1984), p. 225.
38. Binney, "Christianity and the Māoris," p. 150; cf. Howe, "The Māori Response to Christianity in the Thames-Waikato Area 1833-40," *NZJH* 7 (1973): 28-46.
39. J. Belich, *Making Peoples: A History of the New Zealanders from Polynesian Settlement to the End of the Nineteenth Century* (Auckland: Allen Lane, 1996), pp. 164-66.

played a part in *change*, but not in *conversion*.[40] What did change was received Christianity; a vivid symbol of this was a Madonna and child image with Māori *moko*.[41] He concluded: "mercenary and superficial conversion did occur, especially in the 1830s but the balance of evidence suggests that, by the 1840s, Māori engagement with Christianity was real, deep and broad. By the 1850s, over 60% of Māori considered themselves as Christians and I do not dispute their claim. Whether their Christianity was what the European missionaries hoped for is another matter. A Māori conversion of Christianity was apparent from the first. Not only was it used as a means of obtaining literacy and mana, but it was also adjusted by its Māori missionaries."[42] After reviewing the Māori prophetic movements like Papahurihia and others, he asked "whether there was much difference between Māori Christianity, as practised out of sight of European missionaries, and the prophetic movements."[43] Here was a "new Māori religion . . . which converted European Christianity as much as it was converted by it . . . the conversion of conversion," a syncretistic blending of the old and the new. In this judgment, Belich recalled to the writer the judgment of one student (of mainly African responses) who used an analogy from chemistry to describe religious encounter: "a solution" resulted, whereby the receptor religion and the Christian input formed a third compound.[44] So, "Christianity made by Māori into Māori religion was changed in the process,"[45] and Māori missionaries were not wholly unlike the Māori prophets.[46]

In a stimulating essay published since Belich's book came out, Lyndsay Head has strengthened the case for indigenous Māori initiatives against a picture of either passivity or victimhood[47] in postcolonial, historical narratives. Such factors as the agreement to petition the British Crown for protection in 1831, a first step toward the Treaty of Waitangi, may have been missionary initiated but, in the context of cultural change in the 1830s, were voluntarily engaged in by the chiefs. This became part of a general grappling with change,

---

40. Belich, *Making Peoples*, p. 213, emphasis added.
41. Belich, *Making Peoples*, p. 218.
42. Belich, *Making Peoples*, p. 219.
43. Belich, *Making Peoples*, p. 222.
44. Belich, *Making Peoples*, p. 223. I owe the analogy from chemistry to Dr. Andrew Ross at a North Atlantic Missiology Project symposium in Cambridge (23-26 September 1996); cf. C. Orange, *The Treaty of Waitangi* (Wellington: Allen and Unwin, 1987), p. 7.
45. Belich, *Making Peoples*, p. 218.
46. Belich, *Making Peoples*, p. 223.
47. Lyndsay Head, "The Pursuit of Modernity in Māori Society: The Conceptual Bases of Citizenship in the Early Colonial Period," in *Histories, Power, and Loss,* ed. A. Sharp and P. McHugh (Wellington: Bridget Williams Books, 2001), pp. 97-121.

which included a search for a value system judged adequate to the challenges. From this Māori openness arose the intense interaction between traditional understandings and Christian faith; the "northern chiefs felt that a choice of futures had to be made."[48] Head does not accept the idea of a kind of benevolent deceit in Henry Williams's use of Māori terminology at the Treaty of Waitangi, which she found "implausible," though she recognized that the missionary was a "conscious agent of change"; in her view, Māori understood the language used and what Henry Williams meant to convey through it, and they "moved voluntarily" in the direction of the British.[49] Māori were actors in their own history, and the treaty was agreed to with moral seriousness. Head's account underscored that, as in the religious realm, so here in the political realm, the mistake is to posit passivity; and the key to understanding in both cases is indigenous agency.

Support for most of these positions can be found in the present study. Context cannot be overlooked, and Owens, who canvassed the importance of ideas toward change, wrote later that the alignment of social and cultural dislocation with movement into Christianity is "probably not coincidental."[50] European technological skills and economic benefits played their part. Here, however, the importance of Christian input in terms of both ideas and a pattern of living, as discerned by Firth in the Tikopia and by Owens and Howe among the Māori, is a reminder of their importance in an underlying *religious* change, so that an alternative cosmology and the steady appropriation of the Bible, measured against the pattern of living discerned in the households of the missionaries, proved attractive to Māori. As well as the significance of the returned prisoners of war and slaves, the importance of the so-called domestic natives (the two categories sometimes overlapped), noticed by Lila Hamilton and, less emphatically, by Judith Binney, should not be overlooked. Here were Māori who had daily contact with the missionaries and saw at first hand embryonic Christian communities in their households, whether that of Richard Davis, the Kemps, or the Williamses among the CMS families, where Christian life and practice caused some to seek to emulate what they observed. For such Māori, there was a religious attraction in what was experienced on the mission compounds, leading some into Christian prayer and observation of Christian *tapu,* such as the strict Sabbath observance as practiced in the CMS and WMMS stations. It was from these indi-

---

48. Head, "The Pursuit of Modernity," p. 103.
49. Head, "The Pursuit of Modernity," p. 105; cf. Belich, *Making Peoples,* pp. 193-97.
50. Owens, in W. H. Oliver and B. R. Williams, eds., *Oxford History of New Zealand,* pp. 37-38.

viduals that a minor Christian contagion originated. Allied with this, as the 1830s progressed, was the enthusiasm for "the book," by which Māori became not only readers but soon masters of such material, turning them frequently into competent debaters on Christian subjects. Later this mastery led some to risk their lives in evangelistic forays to often hostile tribes, whether in the case of Tamihana and Matene by perilous canoe journeys to the South Island (however ambiguous their mission may have seemed to South Island Methodists) or in the kinds of martyrdoms that lie strictly outside the scope of this study, when Nereopa and Te Manihera Poutama lost their lives at Taupo in 1847, bent on evangelizing a tribe known to be hostile to them.

Nevertheless, there was inevitably both loss and gain. Social dislocation, not least by loss of chiefly status, has been identified by various writers. In the old order, the status of chiefs was enhanced by their possession of up to four wives,[51] not to mention numbers of slaves. Te Heuheu told Jerningham Wakefield that there had been a "levelling"; for Bronwyn Elsmore the whole fabric of Māori society was thereby destroyed.[52] Ranginui Walker has described an attack on Māori culture by the missions, typified for him by the missionary objections to Māori carving, which included phallic representations offensive to Victorian sensibility.[53] Raymond Firth also noticed the undermining of chiefly authority through the abolition of slavery and polygamy and judged that economic disadvantage resulted from the undermining also of the *tohungas*. Although A. R. Tippett argued that Māori society rapidly regrouped around Christian practice and so avoided dislocation, in Firth's view "it has taken the best part of a century for a communal spirit of cooperation to be built again."[54] The *mana* of chiefs was subverted by young men who became literate and therefore influential.[55] Against this picture of breakdown,

---

51. J. Metge, *The Māori of New Zealand* (London: Routledge and Kegan Paul, 1967; rev. ed. 1976), pp. 21, 230.

52. E. J. Wakefield, *Adventures in New Zealand from 1839 to 1844* (Christchurch, NZ: Whitcombe and Tombs, 1908), pp. 430, 516-17; B. Elsmore, *Mana from Heaven: A Century of Māori Prophets in New Zealand* (Tauranga: Moana Press, 1989), pp. 33-35; cf. W. Williams, *Christianity among the New Zealanders*, p. 289 ("whole fabric").

53. R. Walker, *Ka Whawhei Tonu Matou — Struggle without End*, rev. ed. (Auckland: Penguin, 2004); William Williams Journal, 23-24 August 1849 (against Māori carving in church), C N/O 95/220.

54. Firth, *Economics of the New Zealand Māori*, p. 488; Firth, *Primitive Polynesian Economy* (London: Routledge and Kegan Paul, 1939), p. 183; cf. Metge, *Māori of New Zealand*, p. 31.

55. C. Orange, in K. Sinclair, ed., *The Oxford Illustrated History of New Zealand* (Auckland: Oxford University Press, 1990), p. 33; cf. W. Brown, *New Zealand and Its Aborigines* (London: Smith and Elder, 1845), p. 88.

those who chronicled developments on the east coast held that, because of the intensely communal nature of the response to Christianity, this "did (not) lead to a disturbance of the traditional social structures."[56] Once more there is danger in generalizing from the Bay of Islands and the Ngapuhi on Christian response, and room needs to be made for diversity.

What of the gains? Intertribal war, in the view of Peter Buck, was ended: "the conversion of the tribes to the gospel of peace ended the inter-tribal wars."[57] Cannibalism, stripping *(muru)*, slavery and slave killings, and polygamy were all largely eradicated.[58] More borderline practices than these such as tattooing (which was to revive as a cultural symbol); slashing *(haehae)*, which waned as Christian burial practices increased; dancing and games were all affected in the view of Dieffenbach, who was a contemporary.[59] Suicides, which Polack had recorded as an everyday occurrence, were reduced,[60] as were infanticides, which both Robert Maunsell and Richard Taylor held to have been common.[61] With the decay of the *tohunga* went an equivalent decay of *makutu* (sorcery), although there were signs that the influence of *tohunga* lasted well into the twentieth century, outside as well as within the Christian framework.[62]

Conversion itself is always difficult to analyze. A writer like William Ellis, as Bruce Hindmarsh has shown, in accounting for Christian mission in the Pacific from a background of the evangelical revival in England, was baffled by the lack of classic conversions; to him and others from this context, it was puzzling that converts from a background of cannibalism, infanticide, and human sacrifice did not show the kind of emotional revolution that such observers expected.[63] William Williams provided a contrast, as Frances Porter

---

56. W. H. Oliver and J. M. Thomson, *Challenge and Response: A Study of Development of the East Coast Region* (Gisborne, NZ: East Coast Development Research Association, 1971), p. 33.

57. P. Buck, *The Coming of the Māori*, 2nd ed. (Wellington: Whitcombe and Tombs, 1950), pp. 281-82.

58. K. Shawcross, "Māori in the Bay of Islands 1709-1840: A Study of Changing Māori Responses to European Contact" (M.A. thesis, University of Auckland, 1966), p. 361.

59. E. Dieffenbach, *Travels in New Zealand*, 2 vols. (London: John Murray, 1843), p. 19.

60. J. S. Polack, *New Zealand: Being a Narrative of Travels and Adventures during a Residence in That Country between the Years 1831 and 1837*, 2 vols. (London: R. Bentley, 1838), 2:361-62.

61. Maunsell to Coates, 5 November 1838, C N/O 64/9; R. Taylor, *Te Ika a Maui or New Zealand and Its Inhabitants* (London: Wertheim and Macintosh, 1855), pp. 165-69.

62. F. M. Keesing, *The Changing Māori* (New Plymouth, NZ: T. Avery and Sons, 1928), p. 91.

63. W. Ellis, *Polynesian Researches* (London: Fisher, Sow and Jackson, 1829), 2:317; B. Hindmarsh, in *Christian Mission and the Enlightenment*, ed. B. Stanley (Richmond: Curzon Press; Grand Rapids: Eerdmans, 2001), pp. 81-89.

has shown in her preface to the *Turanga Journals:* conversion for him was "never an emotional response" and he was deliberately against "excitement," although she still saw him as holding conversion as "paramount," an individual affair, not just to the Māori church nor even to wider Māori society but to Christ and the reign of God.[64] Both Methodist and Anglican missions did recount individual conversions in some detail, stories that certainly made good copy for the home supporters. Some do, however, retain a sense of authenticity, as that of Marianne Williams's accounts of her Māori girl and her husband, Poto, the girl after a long struggle, which Allier would have recognized, and Edward Markham's account from outside the missionary enclave of the chief, Matangi, in 1834. Matangi was a man of fifty-four with a long record of cannibalism, theft, and fighting, who convinced Markham of a changed life, "a thoroughly changed man and like Saul baptized," whose "conversion is well attested."[65] A chief like Noble (Nopera Pana-kareo), whose gold sovereign for a New Testament was the first one Colenso saw in New Zealand and who gave up polygamous marriages, converted, and became a preacher and evangelist to the tribes of the north of the North Island, provided another example of authentic conversion.[66] Gunson's study drew attention to the two forms of conversion, "heart acceptance of the faith," which involved change of religion, and the wider "displays" for the benefit of the missionaries, who were all too aware of the formalism of some of the claims.[67] Here tribal loyalty and corporate pressures played a part; "missionaries had difficulty in coping with mass conversions" owing to strong "tribal and sub-tribal loyalties," and Hadfield, for one, was wary of a rush to baptism for such collective "conversions" while Hamlin judged that the commitment was to observances rather than anything deeper.[68]

This narrative has described the general context of conversion after 1840, and it can occasion no surprise that writers like Polack, Wade, and Jerning-

---

64. F. Porter, ed., *The Turanga Journals: Letters and Journals of William and Jane Williams, Missionaries to Poverty Bay* (Wellington: Victoria University Press, 1974), p. 38.

65. E. Markham, *New Zealand or Recollections of It*, ed. E. H. McCormick (Wellington: Alexander Turnbull Library, 1963), p. 95 n. 79; C. Fitzgerald, ed., *Letters from the Bay of Islands: The Story of Marianne Williams* (London: Sutton Publishing, 2004), pp. 176-77.

66. *DNZB*, 1:327-28 (Angela Ballara); W. Colenso, *Fifty Years Ago in New Zealand* (Wellington: George Didsbury, 1888), pp. 20-21; W. Puckey to CMS, 21 September 1839 (wives), C N/O 72/14.

67. N. Gunson, *Messengers of Grace: Evangelical Missionaries in the South Seas, 1797-1860* (Melbourne: Oxford University Press, 1978), p. 220.

68. C. Lethbridge, *The Wounded Lion: Octavius Hadfield, 1814-1904* (Christchurch, NZ: Caxton Press, 1993), p. 82; H. J. Ryburn, *Te Hamara: James Hamlin, 1803-1865* (Dunedin: Privately published, 1979), p. 112.

ham Wakefield cast doubts on the reality of the conversions.[69] The mass movements of the post-1835 period contained the mixture of "soul" and "cultural" conversions. But if, with Judith Binney, we make numbers recorded a surer test than inner analysis, the *Missionary Register* of 1844 showed a figure of 2,000 attenders in 1840 becoming 35,000 in 1844, while one year later George Clarke gave his estimate of 64,000 adherents to the three denominations out of an estimated Māori population of 110,000. For the most numerous group, the Anglicans, an average figure of 2,000 church attendances in the 1837-39 period became 8,760 in 1840, and then 29,320 and 35,000 in 1841 and 1842.[70] By then, with the help of the BFBS, it was estimated that the missionaries had made New Testaments available for one in every two Māori, meeting an unsatisfied demand for "the book."[71] These were the factors that caused Selwyn to make the judgment that "we see here a whole nation of pagans converted to the faith."[72]

Apart from the factors already noticed, two others stand out as of very great significance. The first is the issue of power or control. In the words of one historian, "Māori had to discern the sources of secular power of the Europeans."[73] The erosion of the traditional power base led to conversion as an attempt to reclaim power.[74] Second, and as part of the first, is the Māoris' own capacity to accept and initiate change. K. R. Howe made the same judgment of the Māori as Darrell Whiteman made of Melanesians: "for too long the Māori have been considered the passive agents" in relation to Western contact, matched in Melanesia: "too much of anthropological research has portrayed indigenes as passive recipients and ignored their dynamic and innovative activity in the change process," and "the Melanesians, not the missionaries, were the innovators."[75] The Māori were a spiritual people in whose precontact life

---

69. Wakefield, *Adventure*, p. 354; W. R. Wade, *Journey in the North Island of New Zealand* (Christchurch, NZ: Capper Press, 1977), p. 185; Polack, *New Zealand*, 2:161; cf. Ann Parsonson, in Oliver and Williams, *Oxford History of New Zealand*, pp. 169-71.

70. *MR* (1844), p. 229; G. Clarke, in A. K. Davidson and P. J. Lineham, eds., *Transplanted Christianity: Documents Illustrating Aspects of New Zealand Church History*, 3rd ed. (Palmerston North: Massey University, 1995), p. 46.

71. Wright, *New Zealand, 1769-1840*, p. 53.

72. A. H. McLintock, *Crown Colony Government in New Zealand* (Wellington: R. E. Owen, 1958), p. 119 n. 2.

73. M. P. K. Sorenson, in Oliver and Williams, *Oxford History of New Zealand*, p. 293; cf. Buck, *Coming of the Māori*, p. 521.

74. K. P. Sinclair, "Maramatanga: Ideology and Social Process among the Māori of New Zealand" (D.Phil. thesis, Department of Anthropology, Brown University, June 1976), p. 293; cf. Peel, *Yoruba*, pp. 216-17, among Yoruba.

75. Howe, "The Māori Response," p. 46; Whiteman, *Missionaries and Melanesians*, p. 5.

religion entered at every point, so that Peter Buck held that Māori society could not function without the activities of the *tohunga*.[76] This spiritual people reinterpreted Christianity in their own cultural setting, creating a symbiosis or "Māorified Christianity."[77] Signs of this were observed by Shortland, the Cambridge-educated physician, who wrote of a Christian teacher who made *noa* through Christian prayer at *kumara* ceremonies in a *pa* "wisely . . . adapting so much of old ceremonial" and allaying dangers from *atua* by Christian *karakia*; or by the *tohunga* who added the Lord's Prayer to traditional *karakia*,[78] while Wade found that grace after meals could remove *tapu*.[79] Such symbiosis was present and is evidence that a colonizing of consciousness by the missionaries, if allied to an apparent passivity on the part of the missioned, does not do justice to the historical process. In the words of one recent overview, "the greatest difficulty faced by those who have tried to argue that Christian missions were a form of cultural imperialism has been the overwhelming evidence that the agents of conversion were local people, not foreign missionaries."[80] The missionaries should be given their due as religious and social catalysts, whose self-denying labors made an undoubted impression on the Māori, leading to trust and a guaranteed living space.[81] But the conclusion of this study must be that the agents of conversion were the Māori themselves, to whom Christianity proved attractive for a wide variety of reasons, and who, once they had embraced it in their own way and forms, proved adept at propagating it and securing the response of a whole people.

---

76. Buck, *Coming of the Māori*, p. 476.

77. Metge, *Māori of New Zealand*, pp. 49, 54, 319-20; Orange, *The Treaty of Waitangi*, p. 7; Belich, *Making Peoples*, pp. 217-23.

78. E. Shortland, *Māori Religion and Mythology* (London: Longman, 1882).

79. Wade Journal, 14 March 1837, DUHO Misc. MS 324.

80. N. Etherington, ed., *Missions and Empire* (Oxford: Oxford University Press, 2005), p. 7, from the editorial introduction to this companion volume to the *Oxford History of the British Empire*.

81. Orange, *The Treaty of Waitangi*, p. 90; Owens, in Oliver and Williams, *Oxford History of New Zealand*, p. 39: "they (missionaries) were indeed most influential when they could exert least control, through the printed word or Māori evangelists."

APPENDIX

Richard Quinn and A. T. Yarwood

Richard Quinn's book on Samuel Marsden, *Altar Ego* (2008), is both counsel for the prosecution and, as part of that, a substantial assault on A. T. Yarwood's life of 1977. In Quinn's account, Yarwood "excused almost anything SM did" (Quinn, p. 9), a "clothing of SM in robes of great piety" (p. 10). This is unlikely to be the view of unbiased readers of Yarwood's book, in which (whatever else more meritorious is written about him) Marsden's use of punishments as a magistrate revealed "an element in his character that later evolved in the minds of his contemporaries nagging doubts as to his fitness for the profession of a Christian minister" (Yarwood, p. 80) and whose correspondence in later life Yarwood described as "odious," in respect of a letter in which Yarwood accused him of lying and misrepresenting facts to Governor Darling "at every stage of his recital" (p. 254).

Quinn is on more solid ground in accusing Marsden of anti–Roman Catholic bias, which came into play in an early case of a drunken convict, Simon Burn (Quinn, p. 20). Yarwood described Marsden's letter to Governor Hunter on the case as "clearly biased" (Yarwood, p. 45), but he saw Burn's violent end as the result of yet another drunken brawl, whereas Quinn gave a better gloss to the incident by showing Burn to have been stabbed in attempting to intervene between a violent husband and the wife he was beating (Quinn, pp. 19-20). This leads to the Paddy Galvin case, where anti-Catholic bias had the addition of an Irish dimension, for Marsden a toxic mix. Yarwood makes no bones of the colony's barbarity in its reaction to Irish convicts suspected (but not convicted) of insurrection: Judge Advocate Dore and his committee punished them with 100-500 lashes of the ghastly cat-o'-nine-tails, which Marsden and Richard Atkins followed by an "unstated number of lashes" on Galvin between 28 and 30 September 1800, to which Yarwood appends Marsden's "shocking" account to Governor King (Yarwood, p. 79) before adding (which to Quinn is an attempt to ameliorate), "Marsden had been deeply corrupted by the values and practices of the penal colony," and "in ordering the use of torture to extract a confession from Galvin" he raised doubts about his fitness for Christian ministry (Yarwood, p. 80 and supra). Yarwood does not balk at the "flogging parson" charges: Quinn rightly showed Commissioner Bigge writing of Marsden's punishments as being "more severe than those of the other magistrates" and that "the general opinion of this colony is, that his character, as displayed in the administration of the penal law, is marked with severity." It was a "severity" and "lack of gentleness" that Yarwood reported was the judgment of the missionary Richard Taylor as common among the old settlers in regard to the convicts "following Commissioner Bigge's comments on Marsden" (Yarwood, p. 272). Taylor saw it in the chaplain, as also in many others.

The magistracy and all that went with it can be held to have occasioned Marsden with genuine doubts; had there not been, it is surely unlikely that he would have gone to the trouble of consulting his friend and mentor Miles Atkinson of Leeds in the letter Yarwood reproduced (pp. 50-51). It is, however, also undeniable that, having been appointed by Hunter (1795-1807), he was reappointed by Macquarie in 1812, dismissed in March 1818, reappointed in March 1822, and dismissed again in August 1822. Where Quinn accused him of "much illegal punishment" between 1815 and 1822, Yarwood wrote (p. 248) that "the chaplain . . . was unable to challenge the fact of his use of illegal sentences in 1815, 1820 and 1822"; and his use of "indefinite sentences" to extract information had been legally disallowed by a New South Wales act. Yarwood judged that this practice served to emphasize "the party spirit and vindictiveness with which the grand jury had been motivated" and that "Hannibal Macarthur and Marsden had led the way in this malpractice" (p. 248). This is hardly exoneration.

Probably the outstanding case of malpractice in magistracy was that of the convict girl Ann Rumsby. Quinn may be right that Yarwood could have given more space to this complex affair, which involved H. G. Douglass and Marsden's attempt to destabilize a rival for the governor's favor. Nevertheless, Yarwood recorded faithfully enough the adverse reaction of Lord Bathurst at the Colonial Office, as of James Stephen and Chief Justice Forbes, with, most telling of all, the loss of confidence in Marsden by his long-term supporter William Wilberforce as his doubts grew about Marsden's testimony in this affair (Quinn, pp. 47-50; Yarwood, pp. 232-33, 249). Quinn's bias against Wilberforce, whose political record he termed "piebald" and whom he described as an "arch reactionary politician" (Quinn, p. 46), might have been mitigated if he had recalled that Wilberforce, unlike many Tories, supported Roman Catholic emancipation in 1829. Less defensible was Wilberforce's encouragement to one whom he regarded as an embattled chaplain to communicate to him anonymous information for use in Parliament. Yarwood recorded the use of this "surreptitious path" in this case by Marsden (p. 246), who had not used this path to make complaints against the powers that be. Yarwood judged that in this case Marsden had not juggled the truth but told a "deliberate and demonstrable lie" (p. 254) in the account to Governor Darling. Quinn gave Yarwood credit — "even Yarwood finally calls him a liar" (Quinn, p. 49) — but added, very much less than justly, that Yarwood had tried to "sanitise Marsden's life" prior to the Rumsby case (p. 50). Evenhandedness is here treated as bias.

One of the charges against Marsden was avarice. Quinn showed himself most reluctant to accept Yarwood's rebuttal of this in relation to the orphanage of which Marsden was treasurer. The governor had encouraged him to take his percentage (2½ percent) of the income as remuneration for the work involved, but Marsden acted gratuitously. This was in contrast to the businessman Robert Campbell, who became treasurer in Marsden's absence. Yarwood wrote of "returning to the fund a sizeable sum due to him as treasurer's commission" (p. 74; cf. p. 111) (it amounted to some £250, a large sum at the time, whatever Marsden's income). Quinn posed the question, "if it was done gratuitously, why was there a need to return the money?" (p. 53), a strange way to discredit either Marsden or Yarwood. If the money was returned, he acted gratuitously. Yarwood is less congratulatory later, when he recorded Marsden's attempts to evade regulation against trade by the military and civil officers of the colony by acting through agents for his wool and textile dealings: "Marsden's behaviour reveals again the degree to which he had been corrupted by the values of his society. It was the more discreditable for having been carried on after he received the handsome increases in salaries and allowances which were designed to free the clergy from the temptations of the market place" (p. 260).

On the question of Marsden's attitude toward the Australian aborigines, a frequent source of criticism by contrast to his efforts for the Māori and Polynesians, Yarwood is equally open. Like Quinn, he quoted the damning judgment of the Quaker missionaries that "his influence for harm in Aboriginal policy was almost without parallel" (Quinn, p. 60; Yarwood [here quoted], p. 261). But Yarwood also recorded Marsden's willingness, against his own better judgment and experience of failure with aborigines, to help with the founding of an institution for their education (pp. 160, 238-41).

APPENDIX

Finally there is the accusation of gunrunning both to the LMS missions and to the mission to the Māori. It seems that Marsden gave his Māori friend Ruatara a gun, and that, to dissuade Hongi Hika from visiting England, he offered him a sporting gun that had been in the care of William Hall, the early missionary. Opinion will vary, however, on whether after he disowned the practice to CMS secretary Josiah Pratt and forbade it to the New Zealand missionaries, he had himself used muskets as trade counters with the Māori. Much hinged on an occasion when a consignment of what purported to be leather goods for Thomas Kendall was revealed on the deck of the *Dromedary* to contain guns. For Yarwood such importing of guns was done by Marsden "unwittingly"; Quinn, who had noted that Marsden opened certain cases before transmission from Sydney, made this the basis for a charge of complicity. Apart from the element of supposition involved over the opening of this case, it seems unlikely that Marsden would have risked his reputation against stated policy both to the CMS in London and to the missionaries *in situ* after 1816. Quinn prints the accusation of the missionary John Butler about the *Dromedary* incident in full in an appendix with Marsden's reply (Quinn, pp. 190-96) written in 1822, accusations that Yarwood regarded as "substantially untrue" (p. 244) because he believed that Marsden had been "made the unwitting tool of Kendall's gun running" (p. 220). Here, and in another case in relation to a Captain Hansen trading cannon for pork in the Society Islands on a voyage to the LMS missions, Yarwood conceded that gun trading went on in areas for which Marsden had formal responsibility (p. 194), Kendall in New Zealand being a known trader in guns, but without (in the Hansen case) Marsden's knowledge and in the New Zealand cases without his approval (Yarwood, pp. 193-94).

One thread that runs through the different accounts is that between Macquarie as governor and Marsden. Both men achieved a great deal in the colony. Subsequent historiography has sometimes resulted in advocacy for "Australia's first great democrat" (Macquarie), who could also be described as autocratic and allergic to opposition or criticism, though charitable to emancipist convicts; and the "Apostle of New Zealand," who was also described as vindictive and malevolent by Macquarie himself, the same governor who thanked Marsden for his "unwearied exertions as a Magistrate" (Yarwood, p. 143) and equally dismissed him from the office. Yarwood is surely right when he warns of the danger of "simplistic traditions" and then attempts to replace them with "the flawed but satisfying reality of what I take to be the true Samuel Marsden" (Yarwood, p. xii). Similarly, Marsden's contemporaries, aware of his public disgrace and official censure in the past, at the time of his death put aside his "human failings" in the acknowledgment of his "immense achievements" (p. xii). The great procession of carriages at his funeral, one of the largest ever seen in the colony, indicated the truth of this. In the words of Stephen Neill, "his faults, which were many, are outweighed by his merits, which were great."

Sources

University of Birmingham

The CMS archive is kept in the Special Collections Department of the university library (Heslop Room). Letters and journals of CMS missionaries and others were consulted there, as listed. The reference for New Zealand is C N:

Ashwell, B. Y.; Baker, C.; Bedgood, J.; Bobart, H.; Brown, A. N.; Burrows, R.; Campbell, R.; Carlisle, W.; Chapman, T.; Clarke, G.; Cowell, J.; Davies, C. P.; Davis, C.; Davis, R.; Dudley, W. C.; Edwards, J.; Fairburn, W.; Flatt, J.; Ford, S.; Gordon, C.; Hadfield, O.; Hall, F.; Hamlin, J.; King, J.; Kissling, G. A.; Knight, S.; Mason, J.; Matthews, J.; Matthews, R.; Maunsell, R.; Morgan, J.; Norman, J.; Pilley, H. M.; Preece, J.; Puckey, W. G.; Reay, C. L.; Shepherd, J.; Spencer, S.; Stack, J.; Telford, J.; Wade, W. R.; Williams, H. W.; Williams, W.; Wilson, J. A.; Yate, W.

New Zealand

Auckland
Auckland Institute and Museum
Richard Taylor; Marianne Williams
St. John's College, Auckland
John Hobbs; William White

Dunedin
Hocken Library, University of Otago
Dr. Hocken obtained some of the most significant missionary holdings from the CMS. The reference is DUHO.

Sources

Samuel Marsden; George Clarke Sr. and George Clarke Jr.; William Colenso; Richard
    Davis; James Hamlin; James Kemp; John King; W. R. Wade
John Butler; William Hall; Thomas Kendall
Public Library, Dunedin
J. W. Stack (autobiographical MS)

Wellington
Alexander Turnbull Library
Papers and journals relating to: George Clarke Jr., Octavius Hadfield, Kate Hadfield,
    John Hobbs, G. A. Selwyn, Sarah Selwyn, Philip Tapsell, William Wakefield,
    Marianne Williams, J. A. Wilson, Anne Wilson, William White, William Woon.

Rome
Marist Generalat, via Poerio
Propaganda Fide, Piazza di Spagna

United States

Salem Whaling Museum, Salem, Mass. (Peabody Museum); J. B. Knights; J. B. Williams
Yale Divinity School, New Haven, Connecticut
Methodist Holdings on Microfilm
Methodist records of WMMS are also available on microfiche from IDC Publishers, P.O.
    Box 11205, 2301 EE Leiden, the originals being held at SOAS in London.

Bibliography

Adams, P. *Fatal Necessity: British Intervention in New Zealand, 1830-47.* Auckland: Oxford University Press, 1977.
Allier, R. *La Psychologie de la conversion chez les peuples uncivilisées.* Paris: Payot, 1925.
Anderson, G. H., ed. *Biographical Dictionary of Christian Missions.* New York: Simon and Schuster, Macmillan, 1998.
Ballara, A. *Iwi: The Dynamics of Māori Tribal Organisation, c. 1769 to c. 1945.* Wellington: Victoria University Press, 1998.
Barton, R. J., ed. *Earliest New Zealand: Journals and Correspondence of the Late Rev. John Butler.* Masterton, NZ: Palamontain and Petherick (Printers), 1927.
Bawden, P. *The Years before Waitangi: A Study of Māori European Contact in New Zealand.* Auckland: Privately published, 1987.
Beaglehole, J. C. *The Exploration of the Pacific.* London: A. & C. Black, 1934; 3rd ed. 1966.
———, ed. *Journals of Captain James Cook on His Voyages of Discovery.* Cambridge: Hakluyt Society, 1955-67.
Begg, A. "The Conversion of the South Island Māoris in the 1840's and 1850's." *Historical and Political Studies* 3 (1972): 11-17.
Belich, J. *Making Peoples: A History of the New Zealanders from Polynesian Settlement to the End of the Nineteenth Century.* Auckland: Allen Lane, 1996.

Best, E. *Some Aspects of Māori Myth and Religion*. Wellington: Dominion Museum, 1922.
———. *The Māori*. 2 vols. Wellington: H. H. Tombs, 1924.
Binney, J. *The Legacy of Guilt: A Life of Thomas Kendall*. Auckland: Oxford University Press, 1968.
———. "Christianity and the Māoris to 1840: A Comment." *NZJH* 3 (1969): 143-65.
———. *Redemption Songs*. Auckland: Oxford University Press, 1995.
Binney, J., J. Basset, and E. Olsen, eds. *An Illustrated History of New Zealand, 1820-1920*. London: Allen and Unwin, 1990.
Breward, I. *A History of the Churches of Australasia*. Oxford: Oxford University Press, 2001.
Brock, P., ed. *Indigenous Peoples and Religious Change*. Leiden: Brill, 2005.
Brown, W. *New Zealand and Its Aborigines*. London: Smith and Elder, 1845.
Buck, P. *Anthropology and Religion*. New Haven: Yale University Press, 1939.
———. *The Coming of the Māori*. 2nd ed. Wellington: Whitcombe and Tombs, 1950.
———. *The Vikings of the Sunrise*. Christchurch, NZ: Whitcombe and Tombs, 1954.
Buick, T. L. *The Treaty of Waitangi*. Christchurch, NZ: Capper Press, 1976.
Burns, P. *Fatal Success: A History of the New Zealand Company*. Auckland: Heinemann Reed, 1989.
Burridge, K. *In the Way: A Study of Christian Missionary Endeavours*. Vancouver: University of British Columbia Press, 1991.
Butler, P., ed. *The Life and Times of Te Rauparaha by His Son*. Martinborough, NZ: Alister Taylor, 1980.
Byrnes, G., ed. *The New Oxford History of New Zealand*. Oxford: Oxford University Press, 2009.
Campbell, J. *Poenamo: Sketches of Early Days in New Zealand*. London: Williams and Norgate, 1881.
Carey, H. M. *God's Empire: Religion and Colonialism, c. 1801-1908*. Cambridge: Cambridge University Press, 2011.
Carleton, H. *The Life of Henry Williams, Archdeacon of Waimate*. 2 vols. Auckland: Upton, 1877.
Chambers, W. A. *Samuel Ironside in New Zealand, 1839-1858*. Auckland: Ray Richards and Wesleyan Historical Society, 1982.
Clarke, G. *Notes on Early Life in New Zealand*. Hobart: J. Walch, 1903.
Coates, D., J. Beecham, W. Ellis. *Christianity the Means of Civilisation*. London: R. B. Seeley and Burnside, 1837.
Colenso, W. "On the Māori Races of New Zealand." *TPNZI* 1 (1868): 339-424.
———. *Fifty Years Ago in New Zealand*. Wellington: George Didsbury, 1888.
———. *The Authentic and Genuine History of the Signing of the Treaty of Waitangi, New Zealand, February 5 and 6, 1840*. Wellington: R. C. Harding, 1890.
Comaroff, John L., and Jean Comaroff. *Of Revelation and Revolution: Christianity, Colonialism, and Consciousness in South Africa*. 2 vols. Chicago: University of Chicago Press, 1991, 1999.
Corbalis, J. *Tapu: A Novel*. London: Sinclair and Stevenson, 1996.
Cruise, R. A. *Journal of Ten Months Residence in New Zealand*. London: Hurst, Rees, Orme, Brown, 1823.

Darch, J. *Missionary Imperialists? Missionaries, Governments, and the Growth of Empire in the Tropics, 1860-1885*. Milton Keynes: Paternoster, 2009.

Davidson, A. K. *Christianity in Aotearoa: A History of Church and Society in New Zealand*. Wellington: New Zealand Education for Ministry Board, 1991.

Davidson, A. K., and P. J. Lineham, eds. *Transplanted Christianity: Documents Illustrating Aspects of New Zealand Church History*. 3rd ed. Palmerston North: Massey University, 1995.

Davis, C., and P. J. Lineham. *The Future of the Past: Themes in New Zealand History*. Wellington: Massey University, 1991.

Dictionary of New Zealand Biography, 1769-1869. Vol. 1. Wellington: Allen and Unwin and Department of Internal Affairs, 1990.

Dieffenbach, E. *Travels in New Zealand*. 2 vols. London: John Murray, 1843.

Dillon, P. *Narrative and Successful Result of a Voyage in the South Seas*. London: Hurst, Chance, 1829.

Earle, A. *Narrative of a Residence in New Zealand*. Edited by E. H. McCormick. Oxford: Oxford University Press, 1966.

Easdaile, N. *Missionary and Māori: Kerikeri, 1819-1860*. Lincoln, NZ: Te Waihora Press, 1991.

Elder, J. R., ed. *Marsden's Lieutenants*. Dunedin: A. H. Reed, 1934.

Ellis, W. *Polynesian Researches*. London: Fisher, Sow and Jackson, 1829.

Elsmore, B. *Like Them That Dream: The Māori and the Old Testament*. Tauranga: Moana Press, 1985.

———. *Mana from Heaven: A Century of Māori Prophets in New Zealand*. Tauranga: Moana Press, 1989.

Etherington, N., ed. *Oxford History of the British Empire: Missions and Empire*. Oxford: Oxford University Press, 2005.

Findlay, G. G., and H. W. Holdsworth. *The History of the Wesleyan Methodist Missionary Society*. 5 vols. London: Epworth Press, 1921-24.

Firth, R. *Economics of the New Zealand Māori*. Wellington: R. E. Owen, 1928; 2nd ed. 1959.

———. *Primitive Polynesian Economy*. London: Routledge and Kegan Paul, 1939.

———. *Rank and Religion in Tikopia: A Study in Polynesian Paganism and Conversion to Christianity*. London: Allen and Unwin, 1970.

Fisher, R. "Henry Williams' Leadership of the CMS Mission in New Zealand." *NZJH* 9, no. 2 (October 1975): 142-53.

Fitzgerald, C., ed. *Letters from the Bay of Islands: The Story of Marianne Williams*. London: Sutton Publishing, 2004.

Fitzroy, R. *Remarks on New Zealand as a Colony in 1846*. London: W. and H. White, 1846.

Forman, C. W. *Island Churches of the Pacific*. New York: Orbis, 1982.

Garnett, H. *Te Manihera: The Life and Times of the Pioneer Missionary Robert Maunsell (1810-94)*. Auckland: Reed Books, 1991.

Garrett, J. *To Live among the Stars: Christian Origins in Oceania*. Suva and Geneva: WCC and Institute of Pacific Studies, University of the South Pacific, 1982, 1985.

Girard, C. *Lettres reçues d'Oceanie par l'adminstration générale des pères maristes pendant le généralat de Jean-Claude Colin*. 3 vols. Rome: Centre d'études maristes, 1999.

SOURCES

Gittos, M. B. *Mana at Mangungu: A Biography of William White, 1794-1875.* Auckland: St. Alban's Print, 1982.

———. *Give Us a Pakeha.* Auckland: Privately published, 1997.

Glen, R., ed. *Mission and Moko: Aspects of the Work of the Church Missionary Society in New Zealand, 1814-1882.* Christchurch, NZ: Latimer Fellowship (NZ), 1992.

Goldman, I. *Ancient Polynesian Society.* Chicago: University of Chicago Press, 1970.

Gorst, I. *The Māori King.* London: Macmillan, 1864.

———. *New Zealand Revisited.* London: Isaac Pitman, 1908.

Gunson, N. *Messengers of Grace: Evangelical Missionaries in the South Seas, 1797-1860.* Melbourne: Oxford University Press, 1978.

Hall, N. *"I Have Planted" . . . a Biography of Alfred Nesbitt Brown.* Palmerston North: Dunmore Press, 1981.

Hammond, T. G. *"In the Beginning": The History of a Mission.* Auckland: Methodist Literature and Colporteur Society, 1915; 2nd ed. 1940.

Havard-Williams, P., ed. *Marsden and the New Zealand Mission: Sixteen Letters.* Dunedin: University of Otago Press and A. H. and A. W. Reed, 1961.

Head, L. "The Pursuit of Modernity in Māori Society: The Conceptual Bases of Citizenship in the Early Colonial Period." In *Histories, Power, and Loss,* edited by A. Sharp and P. McHugh. Wellington: Bridget Williams Books, 2001.

Hefner, R. W., ed. *Conversion to Christianity: Historical and Anthropological Perspectives on a Great Transformation.* Berkeley: University of California Press, 1998.

Higgins, T. *Soles and Souls: A Life of John King of Swerford, 1781-1854.* Swerford: Privately published, 2001.

Hilliard, D. *God's Gentlemen: A History of the Melanesian Mission, 1849-1942.* St. Lucia: University of Queensland Press, 1978.

Howe, K. R. "The Māori Response to Christianity in the Thames-Waikato Area 1833-40." *NZJH* 7 (1973): 28-46.

———. *Where the Waves Fall.* Honolulu: University of Hawaii Press, 1984.

Hyam, R. *Britain's Imperial Century, 1815-1914.* Basingstoke: Palgrave Macmillan, 1976.

Hyam, R., et al., eds. *A History of Magdalene College Cambridge, 1428-1988.* Cambridge: Magdalene College Publications, 1994.

Irwin, J. *An Introduction to Māori Religion.* Adelaide: Australian Association for the Study of Religions, 1984.

Jagose, A. *Slow Water.* Wellington: Victoria University Press, 2003.

Keegan, T. *Colonial South Africa and the Origins of Racial Order.* Leicester: Leicester University Press, 1996.

Keesing, F. M. *The Changing Māori.* New Plymouth, NZ: T. Avery and Sons, 1928.

Keys, L. *The Life and Times of Bishop Pompallier.* Christchurch, NZ: Pegasus Press, 1957.

King, M. *The Penguin History of New Zealand.* Auckland: Penguin Books, 2003.

Kock, L. de. *Civilising Barbarians: Missionary Narrative and African Textual Response in Nineteenth Century South Africa.* Johannesburg: Witwatersrand University Press and Lovedale Press, 1996.

Landau, P. *The Realm of the Word: Language, Gender, and Christianity in a Southern African Kingdom.* London: Heinemann, 1995.

Lang, J. D. *New Zealand in 1839.* London: Smith and Elder, 1839.

Lange, R. "Indigenous Agents of Religious Change in New Zealand 1830-1860." *JRH* 24, no. 3 (October 2000): 279-95.

———. *Island Ministers: Indigenous Leadership in Nineteenth Century Pacific Island Christianity.* Canterbury, NZ: MacMillan Brown Centre for Pacific Studies, 2005.

Larsen, T., ed. *Biographical Dictionary of Evangelicals.* Leicester: Inter-Varsity Press, 2003.

Lessard, G., ed. *"Colin Sup.": documents par l'étude du généralat de J-C. Colin 1836-1854.* Rome: Centre d'études maristes, 2007.

Lethbridge, C. *The Wounded Lion: Octavius Hadfield, 1814-1904.* Christchurch, NZ: Caxton Press, 1993.

Lineham, P. J. *Bible and Society: A Sesquicentennial History of the Bible Society in New Zealand.* Wellington: Daphne Brasell Associates Press and the Bible Society, 1996.

Macintosh, N. K. *Richard Johnson, Chaplain to the Colony of New South Wales: His Life and Times, 1755-1827.* Sydney: Library of Australian History, 1978.

Macmorran, B. *Octavius Hadfield.* Wellington: Privately published, 1971.

Maning, F. E. *Old New Zealand.* Auckland: Creighton and Scales, 1863; new ed. (ed. A. Calder) Leicester: Leicestershire University Press, 2001.

Markham, E. *New Zealand or Recollections of It.* Edited by E. H. McCormick. Wellington: Alexander Turnbull Library, 1963.

Marsden, S. *The Letters and Journals of Samuel Marsden, 1765-1838.* Edited by J. R. Elder. Dunedin: Coulls, Somerville, Wilkie, 1932.

Marshall, W. B. *A Personal Narrative of Two Visits to New Zealand.* London: J. Nisbet, 1836.

Martin, M. *Our Māoris.* London: SPCK, 1888.

Mathew, F., and S. Mathew. *The Founding of New Zealand.* Edited by J. Rutherford. Dunedin and Wellington: A. H. and A. W. Reed, 1940.

Matthews, S. C., and L. J. Matthews. *Matthews of Kaitaia.* Dunedin: Reed, 1940.

Maxwell, D. "Writing the History of African Christianity: Reflections of an Editor." *Journal of Religion in Africa* 36, nos. 3-4 (2006).

McLintock, A. H. *Crown Colony Government in New Zealand.* Wellington: R. E. Owen, 1958.

McNab, R. *Old Whaling Days: A History of Southern New Zealand, 1830-40.* Christchurch, NZ: Whitcombe and Tombs, 1913.

Metge, J. *The Māori of New Zealand.* London: Routledge and Kegan Paul, 1967; rev. ed. 1976.

Miller, C., ed. *Mission and Missionaries in the Pacific.* New York: Edwin Mellen Press, 1985.

Moon, P. *This Horrid Practice: The Myth and Reality of Traditional Māori Cannibalism.* Auckland: Penguin, NZ, 2008.

Neill, S. C., et al., eds. *A Concise Dictionary of the Christian World Mission.* London: Lutterworth Press, 1971.

Nicholas, J. L. *Narrative of a Voyage to New Zealand, 1814 and 1815.* London: James Black, 1817.

Oliver, W. H. *The Story of New Zealand.* London: Faber and Faber, 1960.

Oliver, W. H., and B. R. Williams, eds. *The Oxford History of New Zealand*. Wellington and Oxford: Oxford University Press, 1981.

Oliver, W. H., and J. M. Thomson. *Challenge and Response: A Study of Development of the East Coast Region*. Gisborne, NZ: East Coast Development Research Association, 1971.

Orange, C. *The Treaty of Waitangi*. Wellington: Allen and Unwin, 1987.

———. *The Illustrated History of the Treaty of Waitangi*. Wellington: Bridget Williams Books, 2004.

Orbell, M. *Hawaiki: A New Approach to Māori Tradition*. Christchurch, NZ: University of Canterbury Press, 1985.

Owens, J. M. R. "Christianity and the Māoris to 1840." *NZJH* 2 (April 1968): 18-40.

———. *Prophets in the Wilderness: The Wesleyan Mission in New Zealand, 1819-1827*. Auckland: Oxford University Press, 1974.

———. *The Mediator: A Life of Richard Taylor, 1805-73*. Wellington: Victoria University Press, 2004.

Parsonson, A. "Experience of a Competitive Society: A Study of Social History." *NZJH* 14, no. 18 (1980): 45-60.

Parsonson, G. S. "Marsden, Samuel." In *DNZB*, 1:271-73.

Pattinson, J. *Exploring Māori Values*. Palmerston North: Dunmore Press, 1991.

Peel, J. D. Y. *Aladura: A Religious Movement among the Yoruba*. London: Oxford University Press for International African Institute, 1968.

———. *Religious Encounter and the Making of the Yoruba*. Bloomington: Indiana University Press, 2000.

Percy, M., ed. *Previous Convictions: Conversion in the Present Day*. London: SPCK, 2000.

Piggin, S. *Making Evangelical Missionaries, 1789-1856*. Appleford: Sutton Courtenay Press, 1981.

Polack, J. S. *New Zealand: Being a Narrative of Travels and Adventures during a Residence in That Country between the Years 1831 and 1837*. 2 vols. London: R. Bentley, 1838.

———. *Manners and Customs of the New Zealanders*. 2 vols. London: James Madden, 1840.

Pompallier, J. B. F. *The Early History of the Catholic Church in Oceania*. Auckland: H. Brett, 1888.

Pool, D. I. *The Māori Population of New Zealand, 1769-1971*. Auckland: Oxford University Press, 1977.

Porter, A. *Religion versus Empire? British Protestant Missionaries and Overseas Expansion, 1700-1814*. Manchester: Manchester University Press, 2004.

———, ed. *The Oxford History of the British Empire: The Nineteenth Century*. Vol. 3. Oxford: Oxford University Press, 1999.

Porter, F., ed. *The Turanga Journals: Letters and Journals of William and Jane Williams, Missionaries to Poverty Bay*. Wellington: Victoria University Press, 1974.

Price, M. T. *Christian Missions and Oriental Civilisations: A Study in Culture Contact*. Shanghai, 1924.

Prytz-Johansen, J. *The Māori and His Religion*. Copenhagen: Munksgaard, 1954.

Pybus, T. A. *Māori and Missionary: Early Christian Missionaries in the South Island of New Zealand*. Wellington: A. H. and A. W. Reed, 1954.

Sources

Quinn, R. *Samuel Marsden: Altar Ego*. Wellington: Dunmore Publishing, 2008.
Reeves, W. P. *The Long White Cloud: Ao Tea Roa*. 4th ed. London: Allen and Unwin, 1950.
Roach, K. J. "J-C Colin and the Foundation of the New Zealand Catholic Mission." *NZJH* 3, no. 1 (April 1969): 74-83.
Rogers, L. M. *Te Wiremu: A Biography of Henry Williams*. Christchurch, NZ: Pegasus Press, 1973.
———, ed. *Early Journals of Henry Williams*. Christchurch, NZ: Pegasus Press, 1962.
Ross, C. R. *Women with a Mission*. Auckland: Penguin, 2006.
Ryburn, H. J. *Te Hamara: James Hamlin, 1803-1865*. Dunedin: Privately published, 1979.
Sahlins, M. *Islands of History*. Chicago: University of Chicago Press, 1985.
Salmond, A. *Two Worlds: First Meetings between Māori and Europeans, 1642-1771*. Auckland: Viking, 1991.
———. *Between Worlds: Early Exchanges between Māori and Europeans, 1772-1815*. Honolulu: University of Hawaii Press, 1997.
Savage, J. *Some Accounts of New Zealand, Particularly the Bay of Islands*. London: John Murray, 1807.
Scholefield, G. H., ed. *A Dictionary of New Zealand Biography*. 2 vols. Wellington: Department of Internal Affairs, 1940.
Selwyn, G. A. *Letters from the Bishop of New Zealand to the Society for the Propagation of the Gospel*. London: SPCK, 1843.
———. *Letters to the SPG and Extracts from Journals from July 1842 to July 1843*. London: SPG, 1844.
Servant, L. C. *Customs and Habits of the New Zealanders, 1838-42*. Translated by J. Glasgow. Edited by E. R. Simmons. Wellington: Reed, 1973.
Sharp, A., ed. *Duperrey's Visit to New Zealand in 1824*. Wellington: Alexander Turnbull Library, 1971.
Sharp, A., and P. McHugh, eds. *Histories, Power, and Loss: Uses of the Past — a New Zealand Commentary*. Wellington: Bridget Williams Books, 2001.
Shirres, M. P. *An Introduction to Karakia*. Auckland: University of Auckland Press, 1986.
———. *Te Tangata: The Human Person*. Auckland: Accent Publications, 1997.
Shortland, E. *Traditions and Superstitions of the New Zealanders*. London: Longman, 1854.
———. *Māori Religion and Mythology*. London: Longman, 1882.
Simmons, E. R. *Pompallier, Prince of Bishops*. Auckland: CPC Publishing, 1984.
Sinclair, K., ed. *A History of New Zealand*. London: Penguin, 1959.
———. *The Oxford Illustrated History of New Zealand*. Auckland: Oxford University Press, 1990.
Smith, B. *European Vision and the South Pacific, 1768-1850*. Oxford: Oxford University Press, 1960.
Smith, S. P. *Hawaiki: The Original Home of the Māori with a Sketch of Polynesian History*. Auckland: Whitcombe and Tombs, 1921.
Sorenson, M. P. K. "'How to Civilise Savages': Nineteenth Century New Zealand." *NZJH* 9 (1975): 97-110.
Stack, J. W. *Early Māoriland Adventures of J. W. Stack*. Dunedin and Wellington: A. H. Reed, 1933.

Stanley, B. "Conversion to Christianity: The Colonisation of the Mind?" *IRM* 92, no. 366 (July 2003): 315-31.

———, ed. *Christian Missions and the Enlightenment*. Richmond: Curzon Press; Grand Rapids: Eerdmans, 2001.

Stock, E. *The History of the Church Missionary Society: Its Environment, Its Men, and Its Work*. 4 vols. London: CMS, 1899, 1916.

Taylor, R. *Te Ika a Maui or New Zealand and Its Inhabitants*. London: Wertheim and Macintosh, 1855.

———. *The Past and Present of New Zealand*. London: William Macintosh, 1868.

Temple, P. *A Sort of Conscience: The Wakefields*. Auckland: University Press, 2002.

Thomson, J. "Some Reasons for the Failure of the Roman Catholic Mission to the Māoris 1838-60." *NZJH* 3, no. 2 (October 1969): 166-75.

Tippett, A. R. *People Movements in South Polynesia: A Study in Church Growth*. Chicago: Moody Press, 1971.

Underwood, A. C. *Conversion: Christian and Non-Christian; A Comparative and Psychological Study*. London: Allen and Unwin, 1925.

Wade, W. R. *Journey in the North Island of New Zealand*. Christchurch, NZ: Capper Press, 1977.

Wakefield, E. J. *Adventures in New Zealand from 1839 to 1844*. Christchurch, NZ: Whitcombe and Tombs, 1908.

Walker, R. *Ka Whawhei Tonu Matou — Struggle without End*. Rev. ed. Auckland: Penguin, 2004.

Wannan, B. *Very Strange Tales: The Turbulent Times of Samuel Marsden*. London: Angus and Robertson, 1963.

Ward, K., and B. Stanley, eds. *The Church Mission Society and World Christianity, 1799-1999*. Richmond: Curzon Press; Grand Rapids: Eerdmans, 2000.

Wards, I. *The Shadow of the Land: A Study of British Policy and Racial Conflict in New Zealand, 1832-1852*. Wellington: A. R. Shearer for Historical Publications, Department of Internal Affairs, 1968.

Warneck, J. *The Living Forces of the Gospel*. Translated by N. Buchanan. Edinburgh: Oliphant, Anderson, Ferrier, 1909.

White, J. *Te Rou: The Māori at Home*. London: Low, Marston, Searle, 1874.

———. *The Ancient History of the Māori, His Mythology and Traditions*. 4 vols. Wellington: G. Didsbury, Govt. printer, 1887-90.

Whiteman, D. L. *Missionaries and Melanesians*. Pasadena, Calif.: William Carey Library, 1983.

Williams, H. W. "The Reaction of the Māori to the Impact of Civilization." *JPS* 44 (1935): 216-43.

Williams, W. *Christianity among the New Zealanders*. London: Seeley, Jackson, and Halliday, 1867.

Williment, T. M. I. *John Hobbs, 1800-1883: Wesleyan Missionary to the Ngapuhi Tribes of Northern New Zealand*. Wellington: Government Printer, 1985.

Wiltgen, R. M. *The Founding of the Roman Catholic Church in Oceania, 1825-50*. Canberra: ANU Press, 1979.

Sources

Winks, R., ed. *Oxford History of the British Empire.* Vol. 5, *Historiography.* Oxford: Oxford University Press, 1999.
Wright, H. M. *New Zealand, 1769-1840: Early Years of Western Contact.* Cambridge: Harvard University Press, 1959.
Yarwood, A. T. *Samuel Marsden: The Great Survivor.* 2nd ed. Melbourne: Melbourne University Press, 1996.
Yate, W. *Letters to the Revd. William Yate from Natives of New Zealand Converted to Christianity.* London: J. Nisbet, 1836.
———. *An Account of New Zealand and the CMS Mission in the North Island.* Introduction by J. Binney. Dublin: Irish University Press, 1970.

Contemporary Periodicals

Church Missionary Record
Missionary Register

Unpublished Theses

Argurin, J. "Marie, l'Église et la Mission des prêtres Marists selon Jean-Claude Colin." Ph.D. diss., University of Laval, Canada, 1999.
Davidson, J. W. "European Penetration of the Pacific 1779-1842." Ph.D. diss., University of Cambridge, 1942.
Fitzgerald, T. "'In a Different Voice': A Case Study of Marianne and Jane Williams' Missionary Education in North New Zealand 1823-35." Ph.D. diss., University of Auckland, 1995.
Hamilton, L. "Christianity among the Māoris: The Māoris and the Church Missionary Society's Mission, 1814-1868." Ph.D. diss., University of Otago, 1970.
Parkinson, P. "Our Infant State: The Māori Language, the Mission Press, the British Crown and the Māori 1814-1838." Ph.D. diss., Victoria University, Wellington, 2003.
Roach, K. J. "Venerable Jean-Claude Colin and the Mission in New Zealand 1838-1848." Louvain diss., Pontifical Gregorian University, Rome, 1963.
Ross, C. R. "More Than Wives? A Study of Four Church Missionary Society Wives in Nineteenth Century New Zealand." Ph.D. diss., University of Auckland, 2003.
Shawcross, K. "Māori in the Bay of Islands 1709-1840: A Study of Changing Māori Responses to European Contact." M.A. thesis, University of Auckland, 1966.
Shirres, M. P. "Tapu: Being with Potentiality for Power." M.A. thesis, University of Auckland, 1979.
Sinclair, K. P. "Maramatanga: Ideology and Social Process among the Māori of New Zealand." D.Phil. thesis, Department of Anthropology, Brown University, June 1976.

Index

Active, 16, 23
Africa(n), 6-7, 18, 20, 33, 59, 117
Agriculture, 12, 15, 20-21, 45, 57
Akaroa, 85, 87, 113
Allen, Roland, 100, 126
Allier, Raoul, 117-18
American, 41
Amos, 70
Ancestors, 6
Annales, 85
ariki, 3, 6, 20, 117, 118
Ashwell, Benjamin, 74-75, 104
atamira, 82
atua, 5, 6, 23-24, 33, 45, 76, 117, 118, 120, 128
Auckland, 88, 110
Austen, Jane, 37
Australia, 12, 16, 49
Australian aborigines, 12, 67, 131

Baker, Charles, 65-66, 67, 73-74, 103
Banks, Joseph, 10
Baptism, 46, 61, 63, 66, 68, 70, 76-77, 83, 87, 101-2, 104-5, 110, 114, 121, 126
Barton, William, 111
Bataillon, Pierre-Maria, 82, 89
Bataks, 120
Baty, Claude-André, 82-87
Bay of Islands, 15-17, 33-38, 50, 65-66, 76-79, 88, 91, 100-109, 125
Bay of Plenty, 99-100
Beagle, 50

Beecham, James, 90
Belich, James, 116, 121
Bible, 69-70, 105, 123
Binney, Judith, 26, 39, 74, 116, 120-23, 127
Blankets, 38, 72, 76, 111
Bligh, Governor William, 14
Book of Common Prayer, 47, 101
Botany Bay, 10
Bounty, 14
Boyd, 15-16, 36, 38
Brampton, 31
Bridgnorth, 72
British and Foreign Bible Society (BFBS), 114, 127
Broggref, Jane, 57
Broughton, Bp. William Grant, 67, 73-74, 100
Broughton, William (Māori chief), 105
Brown, Alfred, 65-67, 77-78, 93-99, 102-4
Brown, David, 11
Buck, Sir Peter (Te Rangi Hiroa), 1, 6, 125, 128
Bumby, John, 111
Busby, James, 64-65, 93-95, 97
Butler, John, 23, 27, 29, 30-32, 35, 40-42

Calcutta, 15
Calverley, 11
Calvinism, 18, 57
Cambridge, 11

144

Index

Cannibalism, 4, 9, 15, 18-20, 29, 33-34, 44, 62, 66-69, 82, 113, 125
Catechists, 81, 109-10
Cavalli Islands, 17
Chanel, Pierre, 82-89
Chapman, Thomas, 67-68, 96, 106
Chiefs, Māori, 45, 58, 61-69, 72, 75-77, 82-93, 96, 102-6, 109, 110-12, 117, 122-24, 126-28
Church Missionary Society (CMS), 14, 20-21, 27-28, 33-39, 40-55, 57-70, 73, 80, 90, 97-111, 123
Church of England, 11, 95
Church of Rome, 95
Civilization and mission, 20-22, 118-19, 121-23
Clarke, George (Sr.), 45-46, 52, 65, 71-77, 94, 97, 99, 103, 127
Clarke, George (Jr.), 49-50
Clendon, James, 93
Cloudy Bay, 113-14
Coates, Dandeson, 42, 71-76, 90-92
Coke, Thomas, 20
Coldham, Marianne, 41. *See also* Williams, Marianne
Colenso, William, 65-69, 75, 93-95, 126
Colin, Jean-Claude, 80-81, 83-86, 110
Colonial Office, 90-91
Comaroff, Jean, 118-19, 120
Comaroff, John, 118-19, 120
Comte, Jean-Baptiste, 85-87, 97
Conversion, 91, 97, 100-101, 116-28
Convicts, 10, 16, 19, 64, 92
Cook, James, 2, 4, 8, 10
Cookeys, 30
Cook Islands, 1
Cook Strait, 64
Coromandel, 103
Creed, Charles, 113
Crowther, John, 11
Cruise, Richard, 23

Darch, John, 92
Darling, Governor Ralph, 129
Darwin, Charles, 50
Davis, Charles, 46
Davis, Richard, 45-48, 53-54, 65, 71-76, 92-94, 101, 123
Delaware, 102
Denison, Edmund, 73

Dieffenbach, Ernst, 8, 91, 125
"Domestic Natives," 53, 70, 78, 120, 123
Dominicans, 81
Duff, 13
Duke, Captain, 50
Dumont d'Urville, Jules Sebastian César, 26
Durham County, 37
D'Urville, Islands, 114

Earle, Augustus, 50-51, 77, 90
East Cape, 67, 96, 99, 100-105, 110
East India Company, 11
Elland Society, 11
Ellis, William, 125
Elsmore, Bronwyn, 124
Endeavour, 10
Endymion, 41
England, 27-28, 34, 38, 45, 74
English, 30, 50, 86, 92-93
Épalle, Jean-Baptiste, 82, 85, 88
Europe, 87-88, 109
Europeans, 2, 8, 10, 26-30, 36, 45, 51, 58, 64-65, 67, 76-78, 81-86, 88, 91-92, 97, 103, 105-6, 108-11, 112, 123
Evangelical(-ism), 11-12, 33, 44, 125

Fairburn, William, 47, 65-66, 69-70, 77, 102-3
Farish, William, 11
Farsley, 11
Fiji, 108
Firth, Sir Raymond, 2, 8, 116-18, 121-24
Fitzroy, Governor Robert, 98
Ford, Samuel, 76
Forest, Jean, 86, 116
Foulah, 20
France, 83, 85
Franciscans, 81
French, 19, 40, 64-65, 78, 81, 85-86, 92, 97
Friendly Islands, 34-35
Fristan, Elizabeth, 12
Futuna Island, 80, 82, 86

Garin, Antoine, 84
Genealogy *(whakapapa)*, 2
George III, King, 15
George IV, King, 15
Gittos, M. B., 60
Gods, 23-24

145

INDEX

Gordon, Charles, 21-22
Grey, Governor George, 8, 116
Gunson, Niel, 126

Hadfield, Octavius, 3, 100-101, 106, 113, 126
hae-hae, 61, 125
hahunga, 6, 56-57, 82, 85, 104
Hall, Francis, 23, 27-30, 40
Hall, Walter, 16
Hall, William, 15-19, 23-25, 36, 60-61, 64, 80
Hamilton, Lila, 53, 123
Hamlin, James, 43, 54, 104-5
Hammond, T. G., 111
hapu, 2, 3
Hassell, Thomas, 12, 26
Hatton Gardens, 34-35, 59, 80
hau, 4
Hawaiki, 1
Hawkes Bay, 99
Hebrew, 70
Herald, 48, 53
Hertford College, Oxford, 41
Hicks Bay, 67, 99, 100, 103
Hika, 39, 58
Hindmarsh, Bruce, 125
Hobart, 42
Hobbs, John, 36-39, 50-59, 61-66, 94-95, 111
Hobson, Governor William, 85-86, 91-98, 116
Hohana, 111
Hohepa Maru, 113
Hone Heke, 95-96
hongi, 8
Hongi Hika, 3, 16-19, 21-30, 35, 38-39, 43-58, 105
Horea, 114
Horton, Robin, 119-20
House of Commons, 73, 91
Howe, K. R., 105, 116, 121, 123, 127
Howley, Abp. William, 50
Hull Grammar School, 11
Hull Holy Trinity Church, 11
Huru, 13
Hyam, Ronald, 11

Idols, 7
Ina, 43-44
Infanticide, 37, 71, 125
Influenza, 76
Io, 4

Ironside, Samuel, 113
Islam, 119
Island Ministers, 108
Islington Institution, 72
iwi, 2-3

James, William, 117
Jesuits, 81
Jesus Christ, 47, 65, 72
Jews, 5, 76
Johnson, Richard, 11, 12

kainga, 7
Kaipara, 85
Kaitoke, 110
Kanaka, 117
Kapiti, 64, 96, 100-101
karakia, 3, 62, 66, 128
Kawakaura, 101
Kawhia, 59-60, 111, 128
Kemp, James, 22, 29-30, 44-48, 53, 65-66, 75-77, 123
Kendall, Jane, 27-29
Kendall, Thomas, 16-17, 23, 25-29, 31-35, 40-45, 75
Kent, Captain, 56
Kent, County of, 37-38
Kereopa, 106
Kevi-Kevi, 36, 40, 43, 49, 75
King, John, 15-16, 23-25, 33, 44-46, 53, 65-66, 92
King, Michael, 95
King, Governor Philip, 8-9, 13
kiore, 1
Kissling, George Adam, 103
kiwi, 1
Korako, 113
Korareka (Russell), 64, 82, 87, 109
Koro-koro, 16
Koukourarata, 113
kumara, 1, 3, 6, 24, 33, 43, 128
Kupe, 2

Lambton, 29
Lambton, John George, 49, 90
Lancashire, 34
Lange, Raymond, 108-10
Laplace, Captain, 13
Las Casas, Bartholomé de, 13
Lavaud, Captain, 85, 113

Index

Lawlessness, 64, 92
Lee, Samuel, 27, 48
Le Havre, 82
Leigh, Samuel, 11, 33
Lesotho, 117
Livingstone, David, 117
London, 38-39, 42-43, 53, 59, 67, 78, 86, 91, 97
London Missionary Society (LMS), 12-14, 20, 34, 108, 118
Luke, Saint, 17, 69
Luther, Martin, 101
Lyons, 80-81, 87, 89

McCormick, E. H., 51
McDonnell, Thomas, 60
Macquarrie (brig), 56
Macquarrie, Governor Lachlan, 16
Magdalene College, Cambridge, 7, 11
Mahia, 101
Maitrepierre, 86, 88
makutu, 6-7, 83, 116, 125
mana, 3, 22, 49, 96, 109, 122, 124
Manawetu, 96
Mangapouri, 102, 104
Mangungu, 39, 56-69, 60-61, 111
Maning, Frederick, 6, 52
Māori. *See* Chiefs, Māori
Māori Christian teachers, 102-7, 108-9, 110-13, 128
Māori departed souls, 1, 66
Māori language, 37-38, 42-43, 48, 50-53, 70, 75, 85, 121
Māori martyrs, 63, 106, 110-11, 124
Māori oratory, 25, 62, 84, 94-95
Māori preaching, 25, 65, 68, 77, 108-15
Māori religion and custom, 4-6, 18-19, 23-24, 43-44, 66, 70, 82-84, 109, 114
Māori society, 1-10
marae, 7, 113
Maraetai, 76, 104
Marion du Fresne, Marc-Joseph, 10, 51, 64
Marists, 79, 80-89, 110
Mark, Saint, 75
Markham, Edward, 126
Marlborough, 114
Marsden, Samuel, 7-8, 11-40, 42, 51, 54, 68, 74, 83, 128-33
Marsh, E. G., 40-41
Martin, William, 98

Matamata, 69, 78, 102, 104-6
Matangi, 126
Matene Te Whiwhi, 100, 107, 113, 124
Mathew, Felton, 94
Matiu, 110
Matthew, Saint, 72
Matthews, Joseph, 67-68, 97, 106, 112
Maui, 44, 66
Maunsell, Robert, 67-70, 74, 96-97, 103-4, 128
Maxwell, David, 119
Melanesians, 108
Melbourne, Lord, 90
Meri, 54
Methodists, 7, 20, 33-40, 56-64, 66, 70, 94, 108-13, 124-25
mihinare, 53, 85, 105-6
Milner, Joseph, 11
Milvian Bridge, 103
Missionaries: and "civilization," 14; defined by Marsden, 14; isolation of, 31, 69; physical demands on, 65-68; wives of, 41, 69
Missionary Register, 41
moa, 1
Moffatt, Robert, 117
moko, 8, 122
Moon, Paul, 8-9
Moravians, 54, 117
Morgan, John, 67-68, 76, 96, 102-4, 110
Moshesh, 117
Murderers' (Mordenaars) Bay, 10
muru, 7, 28, 38, 49-50, 63, 125
Murupaenga, 46
Muskets, 28-29, 57, 72, 105

Nakahi, 76
Naohu, 114
Napier, 96
Napoleon Bonaparte, 78, 85
Naylor, William (Te Awa-i-taia; Wiremu Nera), 59, 62
Neill, Bp. Stephen, 13, 133
Nelson, 58, 106, 114
Nelson, Jane, 41. *See also* Williams, Jane
Nereopa, 124
Newbigin, Bp. Lesslie, 116
New South Wales, 10-14, 27, 31-33, 51, 56-57, 64, 67, 78, 91
Newton, John, 12

INDEX

New Zealand: North Island, 1, 3, 28, 35, 52, 66-68, 71-73, 77, 91, 99, 106-8, 112; South Island, 1, 85, 97, 106-7, 111-13, 124
New Zealand Association, 90-91, 92-93
New Zealand Company, 90-91, 94, 114
Ngai Tahu, 107, 113
Ngapuhi, 15, 36, 39, 46, 77, 91, 100, 105, 109, 125
Ngatiruani, 106
Ngatiteata, 104
Ngati Toa, 113
Nigeria, 118
noa, 4, 104, 128
Noble (Nopera Pana-kareao), 96, 106, 126
Norfolk Island, 8
Normanby, Lord, 91, 93, 97-98
North Cape, 24, 71
Nottingham (shire), 40-41, 59

Oceania, 80, 82, 86, 89
Orange, Claudia, 96
Orton, J., 61, 63
Otago, 111, 113
Otaki, 96, 100, 106
Otaku, 112
Otawhao, 102, 105
Owai, 104
Owens, J. M. R., 53, 116, 120-23
Oxford (shire), 15; St. Edmund's Hall, 15

pa, 7, 84, 103, 128
Pacific Ocean, 1, 12, 15, 75-76, 81, 120, 125
Paihia, 42, 48-50, 62, 65-66, 74, 76, 101
pakeha, 9
Pane, 67
Papa, 4
Papahurihia, 76
Paris Evangelical Mission, 117
Parkinson, Philip, 74
Parramatta, 12-13, 23, 51
Patuone, 19, 39, 56-59, 65, 94-96
Peacemaking, 52, 66, 77, 83, 107, 120-21
Peel, J. D. Y., 118, 120
Petit, Louis-Maxime, 82, 85
Petit-Jean, Jean-Baptiste, 85, 88
Pézant, Jean, 110
Picpus Fathers, 80
Pikope, 85, 88, 95
Pita, 54
Pitt, William, 11

po, 6, 43, 71, 82
Pohio, 113
Pokau, 110
Polack, Joel, 5, 9-10, 125-26
Polygamy, 67, 124-25
Polynesians, 108-9, 117, 126
Pomare, 53
Pompallier, Bp. Jean-Baptiste, 79, 80-89, 93-95, 110
Porter, Frances, 125-26
Port Nicholson (Wellington), 88, 91, 97, 104, 111, 113
Poto, 34, 126
Poupinel, 88
Poverty Bay, 107
Power, 118, 120, 127
Pratt, Josiah, 20-21, 25-26
Preaching, 25, 58, 62, 72, 77
Preece, James, 65
Printing Press, 48, 85, 86
Protector of Aborigines, 45, 97, 103
Puckey, William (Sr.), 29, 31, 45, 65, 71
Puckey, William (Jr.), 43-47, 67, 70-72, 106
Punkura, 113
Puriri, 66, 67, 69, 73, 78, 99, 102
Pybus, T. A., 112-13

Queen Charlotte Sound, 91
Quinn, Richard, 129-33

Rakiura (Stewart Island), 112
rangatira, 3, 81
Rangi, 5, 39, 46, 54, 58, 71
Rangiawhia, 110
Rangihoua, 17, 22-23, 33
Rangitakia, 101
Rangitoto, 113
Rawire Te Maire, 113
Reading, 75, 78-79, 86, 100, 120, 124
Reay, C. L., 106
Reihana, 111
Rewa, 28, 47, 52, 61, 66, 94-95, 102
Rewataki, 104
Rihimona, 111
Rio de Janeiro, 68
Ripahau, 101
Ripi, 77
Roman Catholic, 95, 108-9, 114, 129
Roman Empire, 103
Romano, 109

148

Index

Rome, 101
Rongo, 4
Rotorua, 67, 77-78, 99, 103-6, 110
Rousseau, Jean-Jacques, 19
Roux, Jean, 10
Ruapuke Island, 112-13
Ruatara, 7, 13-17, 22-23, 83

Sabbath, 12, 72, 76, 100, 123
Salem, 47
Salisbury Square, 80
Salmond, Anne, 10
Samoa, 108
Schools, 23, 65, 74, 88
Scott, Thomas, 12
Selwyn, Bp. G. A., 65, 70, 81, 106, 109, 113, 116, 127
Servant, Louis Catherin, 82-83, 85-88, 93
Shepherd, James, 21, 36, 42-44, 53, 65, 70, 77
Shortland, Edward, 6, 128
Shropshire, 72
Sickness, 7, 30, 45, 59, 66, 69, 75-76, 82-83, 105, 120
Sierra Leone, 103
Simeon, Charles, 11-12
Simmons, E. R., 109-10
Skevington, John, 111
Slaves, 45, 66, 68, 84, 104, 111, 123-24
Society Islands, 1
Society of Mary, 80-89
Solomon, 105
South Australia, 90
Southwell, 37, 41, 49
Sovereignty, 93-94, 97, 122-23
Spain, William, 98
Stack, James, 23-38, 56-59, 67, 76, 96, 105, 112
Stephens, James, 90
Stewart, Captain, 64
Stewart Island, 97, 112-13
Stockwell, Richard, 16, 27
Suicide, 57, 67, 125
Sumatra, 120
Surville, Jean-Françoise-Marie de, 10
Sydney (Port Jackson), 14-17, 26, 36-38, 40, 48, 51, 64, 67, 72-73, 88, 100, 111

Table Cape, 102
Tafia, 118

Tahama Hone, 106
Tahama Te Rauparaha, 100, 107, 112-13, 124
Tahiti, 92, 108
Taiwhanga, 53-54
Tana, 7
Tane, 4
tangi, 6, 24
Taniwa, 45
Taonui, Abraham, 111
tapu, 3, 10, 22-23, 28, 43, 51-53, 66, 116, 128
Taranaki, 57, 91, 106, 110-11
Tarua, 110
Tasman, Abel, 10
Tasman Sea, 51
Tattooing, 8, 125
Taumata-a-kuri, 100
Taupo, 105-6, 124
Tauranga, 67-68, 78, 85, 96, 99, 102, 105, 110
Tawaihai, William, 104
Tawney, R. H., 2, 8
Taylor, Richard, 5, 7, 65-67, 73, 93, 125
Te Ara, 36, 38, 51, 58
Te Auroa, 87
Te Awa-i-tara (William Naylor), 59
Te Kemara, 94-95
Te Koki, 42
Te Manihera Poutama, 124
Te Morenga, 19, 75
Te Pahi, 14-15, 36-39
Te Papa, 78
Te Puhi, 58
Tepuna, 69, 76, 78
Te Rangihaeata, 96, 113-14
Te Rauparaha, 3, 64, 96, 100, 106, 113
Te Reinga, 6, 24, 47, 71, 83
Terraillon, Étienne, 84
Te Wherowhero, 96
Thames, 67, 78, 95, 102
Thierry, Charles de, 65, 92
Thomason, Thomas, 11
Tikopia, 117-18, 123
Tioka, 47, 56
Tippett, A. R., 124
Tiramorehu Matiaha, 112
Tobacco, 83
tohunga, 3-4, 6, 19, 28, 54, 76, 82, 100, 104, 106, 109, 112-13, 116, 124-25, 128
Tonga, 37-38, 58-59, 61-63, 72, 80, 108
Tory, 91, 113
Towhe, 28

INDEX

Trade, 37-39, 58, 60
Treaty of Waitangi, 85-86, 90-98, 103, 123
Trinity College, Dublin, 67
Tripe, Jean-André, 87
Tswana, 118
Tu, 5, 70
Tuberculosis, 76
Tuhimete, Mohi, 110
Tuki, 13
Tungaroa, 28
Tupana, 110
Turanga, 100-103, 126
Turikatuku, 46, 51, 54
Turner, Nathaniel, 36-39, 56, 60-63, 70
Tute, 72
Tutu, John Lee, 110
tutua, 3

Uawa, 101
utu, 3-4, 38, 63

Valparaiso, 32, 82
Venn, Henry (Sr.), 11
Venn, Henry (Jr.), 100
Viard, Philippe, 85, 88
Victoria, Queen, 96
Vulgate, 70

Wade, Luke, 36, 39
Wade, William, 73, 126
Waharoa, 77
Waiapu, 78, 96, 99, 101, 103, 116
Waiharakeke, 63
Waikanae, 10
Waikato, 27, 35, 52, 59, 67
Waikonaiti, 111
Waimate, 23, 45, 70, 72-78, 95
Wairau, 114
wairua, 6
Waitangi, 56, 65, 70, 84-85, 95-96
waka, 2, 111
Waka Nene, 56, 61-62, 65, 94-95, 111
Wakefield, Arthur, 90, 114
Wakefield, Edward Gibbon, 90
Wakefield, Edward Jerningham, 91, 124, 126
Wakefield, William, 91
Walker, Ranginui, 124
Wallis, James, 59, 63
Wallis Island, 80, 82, 86

Wanganui, 7, 96
Warepoaka, 76
Warneck, Johannes, 120
War-weariness, 77, 120
Waterloo, 78, 96
Watkin, James, 111, 113
Wellington, 88, 104, 111. *See also* Port Nicholson
Werahiko, 109
Wesley, John, 57
Wesleydale, 36-38, 47
whakapapa, 6
whanau, 2, 7
Whangaroa, 15, 20, 36, 38-40, 50, 57, 85
White, Eliza, 58, 61
White, William, 35, 36-38, 58-63
Whiteley, John, 59, 60-63, 96, 111-12
Whiteman, Darrell, 127
Wilberforce, William, 10, 12, 130-31
William IV, King, 64, 67
Williams, Henry, 3, 21, 29, 31, 40-48, 51-52, 59-66, 73-77, 86, 92-97, 100-106, 121-23
Williams, Jane, 48, 101. *See also* Nelson, Jane
Williams, John (LMS), 108
Williams, Lydia, 40
Williams, Marianne, 29, 31, 37, 42, 48-49, 51, 54, 59, 101, 126. *See also* Coldham, Marianne
Williams, Bp. William, 40, 48-49, 64-67, 70-79, 96, 99-106, 110, 116, 123, 125
Williment, T. M. I., 57
Wilson, Anne, 69
Wilson, Bp. Daniel, 15
Wilson, John, 67, 69, 77, 96
Wiro (Whiro), 5, 66, 70, 83
WMMS, 60-61, 80, 95-96, 108-11, 123
Wood, Lady, 69
Woon, William, 59-62, 94
Wright, Harrison, 12, 25, 42, 47, 105, 116, 120-21
Wright's Bank, 86

Yarwood, A. T., 32, 129-33
Yate, William, 52, 65-67, 71-74, 83, 99
Yorkshire, 11, 34, 41
Yoruba, 18, 118-19

Zambesi, 117